State Building and Late Development

State Building and Late Development

David Waldner

Cornell University Press

ITHACA AND LONDON

First published 1999 by Cornell University Press.
First printing, Cornell Paperbacks, 1999.

Printed in the United States of America

Cornell University Press strives to use environmentally responsible suppliers and materials to the fullest extent possible in the publishing of its books. Such materials include vegetable-based, low-VOC inks and acid-free papers that are recycled, totally chlorine-free, or partly composed of nonwood fibers.

Library of Congress Cataloging-in-Publication Data

Waldner, David.
        State building and late development / David Waldner.
            p.   cm.
        Includes bibliographical references and index.
        ISBN 0-8014-3554-4 (cloth : alk. paper). — ISBN 0-8014-8575-4
    (pbk. :k alk. paper)
        1. State, The.   2. Syria—Politics and government.   3. Turkey—
    Politics and government.   4. Korea—Politics and government.
    5. Taiwan—Politics and government.   I. Title
    JC131.W36   1998
    321'.09172'40904—dc21   98-30402

Cloth printing   10   9   8   7   6   5   4   3   2   1
Paperback printing 10   9   8   7   6   5   4   3   2   1

Contents

Abbreviations

ANAP	=	Motherland Party (Turkey)
DNP	=	Democratic Nationalist Party (Korea)
DP	=	Democratic Party (Turkey)
ELG	=	export-led growth
FDI	=	foreign direct investment
GDP	=	gross domestic product
GNP	=	gross national product
ISI	=	import-substituting industrialization
JP	=	Justice Party (Turkey)
KMT	=	Kuomintang (Taiwan)
LS	=	Syrian lira or pound
NSP	=	National Salvation Party (Turkey)
RPP	=	Republican People's Party (Turkey)
SEE	=	State Economic Enterprise (Turkey)
SPO	=	State Planning Office (Turkey)
TFF	=	Turkish Federation of Farmers
TL	=	Turkish lira
TOB	=	Turkish Chambers of Commerce (Turkiye Odalar Birligi)
TUCA	=	Turkish Union of Chambers of Agriculture
UAR	=	United Arab Republic

Acknowledgments

I first began thinking about the political requirements of economic development as an undergraduate in Yahya Sadowski's introduction to comparative politics at the University of California, Berkeley, in 1984. I thank him for introducing me to a topic that has engaged me so thoroughly for so long. I have had the good fortune to spend the intervening years in the company of friendly scholars and scholarly friends. At Berkeley, Ken Jowitt, Robert Price, Kiren Chaudhry, and Ira Lapidus were a wonderful source of intellectual inspiration and support. I thank Ilkay Sunar for introducing me to Turkish politics, arguing with me about my initial formulation of this study, and assisting me with my research in Turkey. Many of the ideas presented in this book were first sharpened in debate with the members of the seminar on state formation at the New School for Social Research, especially Charles Tilly, Carmenza Gallo, and Ariel Salzman. I also benefited from many stimulating conversations with colleagues at the Middle East Institute at Columbia University, especially Lisa Anderson, Greg Gause, Richard Bulliet, Henri Barkey, and Marty Malin.

My thinking about social science, and thus about all the arguments contained in this book, was indelibly influenced by years of intellectual exchanges with my Berkeley friends and cohorts—Bob Bullock, Russ Faeges, John Gerring, Steve Hanson, Peter Kingstone, Glenn Robinson, and Arun Swamy. More directly, I benefited from the advice of Gerard Alexander, Bob Bullock, and Herman Schwartz, who read and commented generously on successive drafts of this book. I am particularly indebted to Sayres Rudy for so often lending me his amazing analytic and editorial skills. I also thank Henri Barkey, Dale Copeland, Joshua Dienstag, John Echeverri-Gent, Robert Fatton, Steve Heydemann, John McLaren, Carol Mershon, Debra Morris, Soli Ozel, William Quandt, Len

Schoppa, and Brantly Womack for reading drafts of chapters and responding to my questions. Roger Haydon of Cornell University Press has provided invaluable support and editorial assistance. Finally, I'm grateful to all of the Syrian and Turkish academics and civil servants, too numerous to mention, who helped me with my field research, and to all of my friends in Syria and Turkey who made my research seem less like work.

Books are not written on collegiality alone. Field research was funded by a Fulbright Institute for International Education fellowship for study in Syria and a Fulbright-Hays Doctoral Dissertation Research Abroad fellowship for study in Turkey. The Institute for International Studies at Berkeley provided funding for writing. Language study was funded by Foreign Language Area Studies fellowships, as well as a Carnegie grant administered by the Center for Middle East Studies at Berkeley. The Shannon Center for Advanced Studies at the University of Virginia granted me leave to write the final version of the manuscript.

My wife, Elizabeth Thompson, has been writing about the modern history of Lebanon and Syria for as long as I have been studying the political economy of Syria and Turkey. We have shared not only the often difficult and humbling experiences of learning new languages, navigating foreign cultures, and translating our research and experiences into books, but also the joys of making new friends, exploring new places, and sharing our lives. I dedicate this book to her with love and gratitude.

A Note on Transliteration

The conventions of transliteration are not needed by specialists and are of little use to nonspecialists. I have thus omitted all Arabic and Turkish diacritic marks except the medial and final Arabic `ayn. This simple presentation of Arabic and Turkish names will give readers access to all bibliographic material.

D. W.

Charlottesville, Virginia

CHAPTER ONE

Institutional Origins and Economic Outcomes

In Syria today, the old Arab saying "the lion built a cage but placed himself in it" resonates poignantly. The Arabic word for lion, *al-asad,* is also the name of the president of Syria, Hafiz al-Asad. A commentary on the inevitable limits of power, the proverb suggests that institutions constructed to serve a particular function often produce unintended and undesirable outcomes that constrain their builders. My position in this book is that Syrian and Turkish elites devised new state institutions that promised both political stability and economic development. Because those institutions performed their political functions well, however, the political leadership retained them even after recognizing their deleterious economic consequences. Seemingly powerful leaders were trapped by the institutional cages they had built. State building did not promote economic development.

But not all cages are similarly constraining. Korean and Taiwanese elites also crafted new state institutions that secured regime incumbency—but simultaneously fostered spectacular economic growth and industrial transformation. Numerous studies argue that properties unique to the Korean and Taiwanese states enabled officials to formulate and implement developmental policies that guided economic activity into higher value-added products while attaining and retaining competitiveness in international markets. Different paths of state building, then, yield different economic outcomes.

Why does state building sometimes promote economic development, but at other times impede or even derail it? This book answers that question by offering propositions related to two general themes. First, it provides a framework that explains the origins of particular state institutions. State institutions are the intervening variable of this book. Second, it offers a framework systematically linking state institutions and atten-

1

dant policies to economic outcomes. Economic outcomes, as defined below, are the dependent variable of this book. The resulting argument explains the relatively poor economic performance of Syria from 1963 to 1980 and Turkey from 1950 to 1980, as well as the spectacular economic performance of Korea and Taiwan from the mid-1960s to 1980. These periods were critical junctures whose influence extended into the 1980s and 1990s.

Divergent institutional profiles are accounted for through analysis of the transition from mediated states, in which state elites rule through an alliance with local notables, to unmediated states, in which institutions replace notables to link state, economy, and society. With the passage from indirect rule through local mediators to direct rule, old institutions are redefined, new institutions are established, and the state expands its provision of public goods; the creation of unmediated states, in other words, entails the elaboration of new institutional profiles. Four institutionalized arrangements define the developmental capacity of the state: state-society relations, the nature of the bureaucracy, state fiscal practices, and patterns of state economic intervention. By analyzing paths of macrostructural political change, I identify the origins of specific expressions of each of these institutions and their combination into distinct institutional profiles.

More specifically, I analyze two paths of state transformation. In Syria and Turkey, state transformation occurred simultaneously with the incorporation of lower classes into cross-class coalitions. In Chapter 2, I demonstrate how the conjunction of state transformation and coalition building determines the attributes of resulting political-economic institutions. In contrast, in Korea and Taiwan, state building preceded popular incorporation; because Korean and Taiwanese elites were not indebted to the support of popular classes at the time of institutional transformation, they were able to shape new institutions that proved to be more conducive to economic development. As a result, whereas state building in Syria and Turkey produced what I will call *precocious Keynesian states,* state building in Korea and Taiwan produced developmental states. To be sure, Korean and Taiwanese elites eventually incorporated popular-sector support, but they did so only after ten years of rapid growth and industrial transformation. In short, the timing of popular-sector incorporation relative to state transformation and substantial industrial development best explains the results of sustained efforts to achieve economic development.

But what explains different patterns of state building? I explain how macrostructural change produces institutional outcomes by exploring the micro-level choices made by political elites as they navigate between the demands of political incumbency and the dictates of economic devel-

opment. The cases of Syria and Turkey support the proposition that institutions, which Riker powerfully describes as "congealed tastes," embody
the efforts of domestic actors to inscribe their preferences in the rou-
tinized practices of quotidian politics.[1] But the context in which political
actors advance or defend their preferences must also be analyzed, because even the most powerful political forces in a society are often constrained in the formation of institutions, as the comparisons in this book
demonstrate. The basic preferences of Syrian and Turkish political elites
for political stability, security of incumbency, and rapid economic development did not fundamentally differ from those of their Korean and Taiwanese counterparts: what distinguishes the two classes of cases is the
context in which elites pursued their basic preferences and built the institutions designed to meet these goals. Varied contexts induced actors with
the same basic preferences to generate different institutional outcomes.

More specifically, I focus on the constraints and opportunities created
by the structural context in which choices were made. Structure and
agency, however, combine differently across the cases. Syrian and Turkish
elites confronted structural conditions that highly constrained them, so
that, in effect, they had no choice. In contrast, Korean and Taiwanese
elites enjoyed greater latitude in choosing from a menu of institutional
options. This difference creates a causally asymmetric argument: although I identify conditions that were necessary and sufficient for the
Middle Eastern cases, producing highly determined outcomes, I identify
necessary but not sufficient outcomes for the East Asian cases, in which
outcomes were less determined by structural factors. In my analysis, in
other words, structure and agency are true variables, not parametric constants.

My hypothesis is that levels of elite conflict determine whether state
transformation occurred simultaneously with or before popular incorporation. Levels of elite conflict varied across the two sets of cases, creating
incentive structures for Syrian and Turkish elites different from those
confronted by Korean and Taiwanese elites. Syrian and Turkish elites initiated new rounds of state building under conditions of intense conflict
that divided the elite and militated against compromise. This conflict re-
volved around competing visions of the proper relationship of the state to
the economy. Elite conflict was resolved only when sectors of the elite in
each country mobilized popular-sector support as a means of providing a
social base for vanquishing their opponents and consolidating their rule.
Popular-sector incorporation, in other words, was a function of the level

---

[1] William Riker, "Implications from the Disequilibrium of Majority Rule for the Study of
Institutions," *American Political Science Review* 74 (June 1980): 432–46.

of elite conflict: intense elite conflict lowered elite resistance to popular incorporation, making it a more preferable strategy than it would have been under conditions of elite unity.

In Korea and Taiwan, elites were relatively cohesive and thus able to forge compromises among themselves. Consequently, the incentives they faced dictated continued popular-sector exclusion. In Taiwan, elite-level conflict was extremely manageable, and at no time did any segment of the elite consider a strategy of popular-sector mobilization. The Korean case falls between the two extremes, and, as Chapter 6 shows, there are some indications that in the early 1960s Korea was on the verge of taking the Syrian path. But Korean elites ultimately rallied around General Park Chung Hee, eliminating incentives for popular-sector mobilization. State building therefore spoke less to the immediate needs of political consolidation and more to the longer-term needs of economic development that would itself help to stabilize rule. Thus, by shaping incentive structures, the dynamics of elite conflict influence the extent to which state building is associated with the incorporation of lower classes into alliances supporting the state.

Coalition arguments are often criticized for reducing politics to the play of powerful social forces and ignoring the autonomous role of the state. In the four cases surveyed here, however, state elites and not social groups took the initiative in constructing coalitions. They did so by concluding bargains with societal constituents. Turkish and Syrian elites did not forge broad cross-class coalitions because they confronted more pressing demands from social groups; they did so because, in these cases, intense conflict dividing the elite prompted powerful political forces to place a premium on incorporating mass support.[2] Of course, the claim that dynamics of elite conflict explain state types answers one question only at the expense of raising an equally pressing question: What explains the different dynamics of elite conflict? Hypotheses related to this question are presented in Chapter 6.

In sum, state building through popular-sector incorporation addressed the immediate needs of newly incumbent elites. Under these circumstances, Syrian and Turkish elites shaped state finances, development strategy, and key institutions to secure their rule. The political arrangements they crafted promised economic bounty but could not deliver on this promise. In Korea and Taiwan, on the other hand, elites who were relatively secure in their incumbency had the luxury of creating state institutions and policies that were more conducive to long-term economic development.

---

[2] Contrast Samuel P. Huntington and Joan Nelson, *No Easy Choice: Political Participation in Developing Countries* (Cambridge: Harvard University Press, 1976).

My argument draws inspiration from the burgeoning literature on the institutional foundations of economic outcomes in both developed and developing countries. Although the arguments constituting this literature take many forms, they share an analytic focus on how cross-national variations in institutional configurations shape distinctive patterns of economic change. Institutions influence economic outcomes in these studies by defining the autonomy of elites to formulate policy reflecting their preferences, the instruments by which elites implement policy, and the capacity of interest groups and social classes to contest policy. Institutions also determine the relative ease with which factors of production can be reallocated in response to changing economic conditions. This book makes two contributions to that literature through its focus on the origins of institutions and on the specific mechanisms translating institutional constraints, capacities, and opportunities into different economic outcomes.

Although since the early 1980s political scientists and economists have devoted a great deal of attention to researching the causal significance of political and economic institutions, they have paid little attention to the origins of institutions.[3] Peter Evans, for example, echoes the dominant research tradition when he writes, "My aim is *not* to explain the origins of predatory, developmental, and intermediate states, a task for historical scholarship that goes well beyond the ambitions of this study. Instead, the idea is to take existing structural types as starting points. . . ."[4] Evans and his collaborators are certainly justified in restricting their analytic focus. Institutionalist scholars have identified neoliberal economists, who ignore the role of institutions, as their primary theoretical rivals; thus, their most pressing goal has been to demonstrate that institutions matter, a task that obviously precedes exploring the etiology of institutional formation. But this task has been accomplished. General scholarly consensus that institutions matter now exists, so it seems appropriate to enlarge the domain of our theoretical and empirical inquiries. As Robert Bates suggests, "Those studying developing areas face a subject that stands at the very frontier of the field of political economy: the problem of institutional origins. . . . [B]y working on this problem, they can generate results that will themselves feed back into the study of development."[5]

[3] Kathleen Thelen and Sven Steinmo, "Institutionalism in Comparative Politics," in *Structuring Politics: Historical Institutionalism in Comparative Analysis,* ed. Sven Steinmo, Kathleen Thelen, and Frank Longstreth (Cambridge: Cambridge University Press, 1992), 14.

[4] Peter Evans, *Embedded Autonomy: States and Industrial Transformation* (Princeton: Princeton University Press, 1995), 45, emphasis added.

[5] Robert H. Bates, "Macropolitical Economy in the Field of Development," in *Perspectives on Positive Political Economy,* ed. James E. Alt and Kenneth A. Shepsle (New York: Cambridge University Press, 1990), 48.

This book addresses both of these analytic tasks. The focus on coalition formation provides the fundaments for a theory of state building and state structures in late developers. But a theory of development cannot conclude here, because accounting for specific institutions while arguing that institutions matter is not equivalent to demonstrating and theorizing about *how* institutions matter. Robert Wade, who has played a prominent role in articulating an institutional framework for analyzing development, remarks that although scholarship on the developmental state in East Asia has established plausible correlations between state types and economic outcomes, it has not advanced a coherent theory explaining these correlations.[6] The theory we work toward must be capable of explaining not only the successful outcomes achieved by East Asian states but also the less successful outcomes of Middle Eastern and other states.

One false step in developing that theory would be to assume that Syrian and Turkish leaders made unintelligent and uninformed choices, deliberately sacrificed developmental potential to their short-term political imperatives, or were corrupt leaders who exploited the economy for personal gain. On the contrary, the political-economic arrangements they put into place were, in principle, consistent with and supportive of long-term development. Payments to class constituencies not only purchased political stability, they also expanded the size of the domestic market. Protectionist policies then guaranteed that domestic industries would face no competition in the expanding market. Every Syrian pound or Turkish lira paid to peasants or workers created demand that increasing industrial output satisfied. The exchange of material benefits for political loyalty, in other words, acted as a rudimentary form of demand stimulus; this strategy of state building was thus roughly analogous to the Keynesian welfare policies of advanced industrial states in the postwar period.

Because Syria and Turkey implemented their policies in basically preindustrial economies, I refer to these arrangements as *precocious Keynesianism*. In some respects, precocious Keynesianism promoted industrialization in Syria and Turkey. By 1980, both countries were substantially more industrialized than they had been three decades earlier, in terms of both the share of manufacturing in gross domestic product and the range of manufacturing activities they engaged in. But in both countries, further industrialization was tied to continued inflows of foreign capital; when these capital inflows dried up in the late 1970s, industrialization ground to a halt, and elites in both countries suddenly confronted the urgent task of altering their most fundamental political and economic arrangements.

---

[6] Robert Wade, "The Role of Government in Overcoming Market Failure: Taiwan, Republic of Korea, and Japan," in *Achieving Industrialization in East Asia,* ed. Helen Hughes (Cambridge: Cambridge University Press, 1988), 130–31.

In other important respects, however, precocious Keynesianism was a failure, even during its more prosperous times. In both countries, industrialization basically meant the expanded production of labor-intensive and low value-added goods. Even more important, those goods were overwhelmingly low-quality yet high-cost and thus not competitive in international markets. Furthermore, by 1980, Syria and Turkey were dependent on the international economy not only for capital inflows, but also for product and process technology. Neither Syria nor Turkey had forged an industrial order capable of self-sustaining growth or international competitiveness. While postwar Keynesian practices stabilized politics and facilitated economic growth in the advanced industrial countries, precocious Keynesianism, unfortunately, interfered with development.

Why was the record so mixed? Why were the Syrian and Turkish states capable of promoting investments in new industries but incapable of promoting industrial efficiency and transformation? Chapter 7 defines economic development semantically as changes in economic structures or processes that enhance the capacity to create value. An operational definition of development is proposed that incorporates four dimensions: new investments producing real increases in per capita national income; the creation of intersectoral and interindustry linkages; upgrading the productivity of the production process of any given industrial sector; and movement into the production of higher value-added goods. Finally, I argue that progress along each of these four constituent elements of development is predicated on resolving collective dilemmas. Collective dilemmas occur when private and collective rationalities diverge, so that the activity of rational, profit-maximizing individuals results in suboptimal collective outcomes.[7] The problem is one of reconciling individual and social rationality. Adam Smith argued that markets spontaneously achieve this reconciliation, but this process is actually fraught with difficulty.

Although Chapter 7 addresses a range of collective dilemmas, for simplicity I distinguish between those that impede capital accumulation and investment in new industrial plant and those that obstruct efforts to enhance the economic performance of existing industrial enterprises, including upgrading productivity, lowering costs, and improving the quality of goods. I call the former *Gerschenkronian collective dilemmas* and the latter *Kaldorian collective dilemmas*. The institutions and policies produced by their paths of state formation rendered the Syrian and Turkish states capable of resolving Gerschenkronian collective dilemmas but only at the expense of exacerbating Kaldorian collective dilemmas. The Syrian and Turkish states had the capacity to promote investment but not to make

[7] Collective dilemmas include collective action problems, coordination problems, and distributional conflicts. See Robert H. Bates, "Contra Contractarianism: Some Reflections on the New Institutionalism," *Politics & Society* 16 (1988): 387–401

the ensuing industries work well. Developmental states in East Asia, on the other hand, resolved both Gerschenkronian and Kaldorian collective dilemmas, producing a distinctive trajectory of economic development.

In summary, coalition analysis illuminates patterns of state building, expressed as properties of resulting institutions. Collective action theory specifies the capacities or incapacities of these institutions to promote economic transformation. The capacities of state institutions and policies that are artifacts of state building resolve different combinations of collective dilemmas. Depending on the attributes of their state institutions, national economies advance at different rates along these four axes, producing distinct developmental trajectories. Thus, superimposing institutional profiles over collective dilemmas accounts for a range of developmental outcomes.

The combination of coalition theory and collective action theory yields the following propositions, summarized in Figure 1. Intense inter-elite conflict (1) results in the construction of broad, cross-class coalitions; (2) these coalitions are a sufficient condition for the formation of precocious Keynesian states; and (3) this type of state can resolve Gerschenkronian collective dilemmas only at the expense of exacerbating Kaldorian collective dilemmas. This extended causal chain is sustained through an examination of the Syrian and Turkish cases. Conversely, examining the Korean and Taiwanese cases reveals that (1) the dynamics of inter-elite conflict differed markedly from those of the Syrian and Turkish cases; (2) Korean and Taiwanese elites chose different coalition strategies; (3) these different coalition strategies permitted the construction of developmental states; and (4) these states had starkly superior capacities to solve collective dilemmas, producing a different developmental trajectory. The Korean and Taiwanese cases provide substantial confirmation of these propositions, although more definitive conclusions must await further comparative research.

The proposed theory has implications for the central debate among scholars of development, which pits neoliberal economists against partisans of a state-centered approach. Neoliberal analysis discredits efforts to supplant market signals with state intervention. Neoliberals draw on their nineteenth-century heritage to argue that market-based development is a superior mode of allocating scarce economic resources, whereas state intervention inevitably produces welfare losses. In addition, neoliberals have fortified their critique by focusing on the dynamic aspects of trade policy. They argue that barriers to free trade induce unproductive rent-seeking behavior—the squandering of resources in a quest for the economic rents created by protection. Rent-seeking behavior, in these studies, explains why heavily protected economies characteristically lack the innovation and dynamism spurred by competition from abroad, resulting in stagnant and inefficient economies.

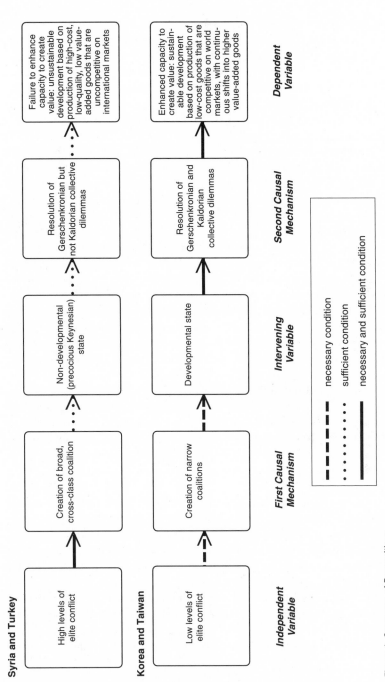

Figure 1. Summary of Propositions

9

This analysis does not refute the neoliberal claim, but it does restrict its empirical domain. Chapter 7 argues that inefficient rent-seeking behavior is a product of the type of state intervention associated with precocious Keynesian states. But not all rent-seeking behavior is inefficient. Indeed, in Korea and Taiwan, rent-seeking behavior is productive: entrepreneurs earn rents from state intervention, but only insofar as they engage in efforts to enhance productivity and international competitiveness that have positive externalities for overall economic performance. The type of rent-seeking behavior that results from state intervention and has extremely significant implications for development is a function of the institutional capacities of the state, which are in turn products of specific paths of state formation. Briefly, states that resolve Kaldorian collective dilemmas induce productive rent-seeking behavior; those that cannot do so encourage unproductive rent-seeking behavior.

Indeed, neoliberals have never convincingly accounted for the origins of rent-seeking behavior. Characteristically, they attribute it to the actions of venal, self-serving politicians and bureaucrats.[8] The problem with this approach is that it predicts uniform outcomes, even when we observe diversity. Robert Bates avoids this error by proposing that particular coalition strategies result in different dynamics of rent-seeking behavior.[9] This book builds on Bates's work by specifying the logic by which different coalition strategies are selected. In brief, different dynamics of inter-elite conflict pose incentives for different coalition strategies. These strategies are in turn realized through the elaboration of new institutions and policies—in short, by different patterns of state building. The institutions of transformed states possess divergent capacities to solve different combinations of collective dilemmas, resulting in distinctive developmental trajectories. This argument should not only allow us to distinguish between the developmental outcomes of, on one hand, precocious Keynesian states such as Syria and Turkey and, on the other hand, developmental states such as Korea and Taiwan, but should also be applicable to outcomes among states in other regions of the developing world.

The theoretical framework presented in this book provides important insights into the processes by which some peripheral states prosper while others remain trapped in unpromising economic conditions. It remains now to justify the choice of cases used to generate and test this theory; in other words, why Syria and Turkey? After all, basing a general inquiry into the sources of divergent developmental trajectories on these two cases

[8] For an overview of this approach, see the essays in Gerald M. Meier, ed., *Politics and Policy Making in Developing Countries: Perspectives on the New Political Economy* (San Francisco: International Center for Economic Growth, 1991).

[9] Robert H. Bates, *Markets and States in Tropical Africa* (Berkeley: University of California Press, 1981).

poses certain problems. Syria and Turkey are not well represented in the literature on development and are not widely known outside the community of Middle East specialists. Area specialists, conversely, might plausibly object to the comparison based on the manifest and manifold differences that distinguish the two countries. There is no denying that Syria and Turkey differ according to almost every category commonly used by social scientists. In some respects, Syria and Turkey traversed trajectories of political and economic change that were inverse images of each other. The following brief survey of these trajectories and other aspects of these two countries illustrates these differences as well as their key similarity, which is high levels of elite conflict. Indeed, it is because they are so different in a variety of ways but also similar in one crucial respect that they are of specific value for comparative analysis. Note, however, that this inductive, empiricist method first elaborated by John Stuart Mill is insufficient for generating or confirming causal claims. The logic underlying the following research design has been subject to compelling critiques, many of which I accept. I address them in Chapter 10 and propose an alternative methodological formulation that incorporates the spirit of Mill's methods while replacing their underlying empiricist logic with an emphasis on causal mechanisms. The following specification of the research design simply introduces the main cases and initiates a methodological dialogue that is concluded at the end of this book.

In February 1963, Syrian military officers attached to the Ba`th party staged a coup in Syria, bringing the party elders as well as younger cadres into power and abolishing a parliamentary regime through which the country had been governed, albeit with numerous periods of military rule, since 1946. The new governing elite created an authoritarian political system that denied significant sectors of the population low-cost and regularized access to the major decision-making institutions influencing national policy decisions.

Turkey followed a contrasting path of political change. In May 1950, the Democrat Party won national elections in Turkey, replacing the Republican People's Party, the political party founded by Mustafa Kemal Ataturk that had ruled the country through authoritarian means since the 1920s. Since that time, the political system of Turkey has been predominantly inclusionary, providing to nearly all adult citizens the right to participate in making decisions binding on the national political community, generally by selecting governing parties through open competition. Like the Syrian parliamentary system of the 1950s, military coups have regularly interrupted democratic governance.

In both countries, state economic intervention is extensive, encompassing not only a high level of regulation, if not determination, of prices in a broad series of markets but also state ownership of industrial plants. But important differences remain. In Turkey, the public industrial sector co-exists with a large private industrial sector that includes dozens of large-scale corporations. Although the two sectors compete in some products, such as textiles, they largely complement one another. The public sector is concentrated in upstream provision of industrial inputs that require greater capital investment and technological sophistication, and the private sector specializes in the production of finished consumer goods. The rapid expansion of the private industrial sector began in the mid-1950s and stands in sharp contrast to the previous two decades, during which the exigencies of development and resource mobilization during World War II led the Turkish state to establish a large public industrial sector and later nationalize several private firms.

Just as political transformation in Syria was the inverse image of the Turkish case, so too did the new Ba`th regime transform the Syrian property regime in ways that contrasted sharply with those of Turkey. Although the economic role of the Syrian state had expanded from 1946 to 1963, economic development was largely advanced by private entrepreneurs operating in an environment of relatively low state regulation compared to that of the post-1963 period. The new leadership that took command of the state in 1963 radically transformed this property regime, instituting large-scale land reform and nationalizing the largest industrial firms, banks, commercial houses, and insurance companies. From 1963 through the 1980s, Syrian industrial development was largely a product of state planning and investment, with private economic actors limited to small-scale industrial activity and the nontradables sector—for example, retail trade, construction, real estate, and tourism.

While differences in political and property regimes most clearly distinguish the two cases, Syria and Turkey represent different values of many other variables as well. In the period leading up to state transformation, Syrian workers and peasants agitated for political and economic change, whereas Turkish lower classes did not engage in collective action. In the posttransformation period, leaders in the two countries have professed contrasting ideologies, with Syrian leaders after 1963 making continuous, often uncompromising commitments to socialism, while most governing elites in Turkey have remained firmly wedded to capitalist development. Patterns of recruitment into the elite are quite different in the two countries. In pre-1963 Syria, agrarian oligarchs and professional politicians from Damascus and Aleppo dominated civilian politics. Since 1963, the vast majority of state officials have been members of the Ba`th party. An overwhelming percentage of these officials come from modest rural or provincial city backgrounds, and members of the minority Alawi sect are dramatically overrepresented within this elite. In addition, military officers are the largest group among the elite. In Turkey, the 1950 watershed also produced a major change in the social background of the political elite. Whereas in Kemalist Turkey the governing elite was mainly comprised of members of the military and state bureaucracy, after 1950 an alternative elite emerged, as professional politicians replaced state officials in legislative and executive positions. Lawyers and businessmen composed the bulk of this new elite, whose influence was often based on local connections and authority. There is no evidence of geographic or ethnoreligious concentration analogous to the Syrian case.

In addition, Turkish economic relations have been oriented primarily toward the West, and major economic projects have been undertaken with Western technological assistance and materials. But although much of Syrian trade is directed toward the West, and Western firms have participated in development projects, particularly in the petroleum sector, many industrial projects were implemented by Eastern bloc countries. This variable is potentially important, because the two countries had differential access to technology and technological assistance. Furthermore, while foreign direct investment (FDI) in Turkey amounted to only $228 million between 1954 and 1979, FDI did amount to a substantial share of total investment in several industrial sectors.[10] Syria, on the other hand, has not been the recipient of any FDI through the early 1990s. Finally, Syria earned substantial oil rents during the period of this study, but Turkey did not. The literature on the rentier state would thus predict that Syrian development would differ from its Turkish counterpart.[11]

The two countries also differ in terms of military alliances and expenditures and in their security context. Turkey has been a member of the North Atlantic Treaty Organization since 1952, and the bulk of military assistance has come from the United States. Syria, conversely, forged close ties to the Soviet bloc in the 1960s, and the Soviet Union was Syria's main source of military equipment and training into the 1980s. They also faced different levels of external threat. Syria exists in a tense security environment and engaged in large-scale conflict with Israel in 1948, 1967, 1973 and 1982. Although Turkey occupied a strategic position on the Soviet border, Turkish territorial integrity was never threatened and the Turkish army engaged in only one skirmish on the island of Cyprus in 1974. This variable is important, as several scholars have suggested that external threats stimulated the construction of a developmental state in Korea and Taiwan.[12] This difference in the security environment was reflected in the level of Syrian and Turkish military expenditures, a variable

---

[10] Organisation for Economic Cooperation and Development, *Foreign Investment in Turkey* (Paris: OECD, 1983).

[11] This literature is discussed further in Chapter 5.

[12] See for example, David C. Kang, "South Korean and Taiwanese Development and the New Institutional Economics," *International Organization* 49 (Summer 1995), 582–87.

that has been used to account for developmental outcomes.[13] Between 1966 and 1975, average annual military expenditures in Syria amounted to 13 percent of gross national product; the corresponding average for Turkey was only five percent.[14]

Finally, Syria and Turkey exhibit stark ethnic differences and the politicization of these differences. Both countries are heterogeneous societies, composed of a multitude of ethnolinguistic and religious groups. The major cleavage in Syria separates the majority Sunni Muslim community from numerous heterodox Shi`i sects. A second cleavage divides Arabs from the Kurdish minority located in the northeast of the country. In addition, there is a significant Christian minority, of which a subset is of Armenian origin. In Turkey, on the other hand, national consolidation was greatly advanced by the elimination of Armenians and the expulsion of Greeks early in the twentieth century. Still, although most citizens are ethnic Turks, a large Kurdish minority exists, as does a significant Arab community. In addition, the Turkish population is divided by religion, with the majority adhering to Sunni Islam but a significant minority professing Shi`i Islam.

Despite this similarity, the politicization of ethnic and religious differences has proceeded quite differently in the two countries. Following a series of Kurdish revolts in the 1920s and 1930s, ethnic cleavages did not play a major role in Turkish politics until after 1980, and the category of ethnicity has not been used by political scientists to analyze Turkish politics and economics during that period.[15] In Syria, on the other hand, ethnic antagonisms and conflicts have been more prominent, and ethnic and religious cleavages have been a mainstay in discussions of Syrian politics. Finally, Islamist movements that have challenged both states took different forms: Turkish Islamists formed parties to compete in elections, and Syrian Islamists engaged in violent uprisings.

[13] See Saadet Deger and Ron Smith, "Military Expenditures and Growth in Less Developed Countries," *Journal of Conflict Resolution* 27 (June 1983): 335–53.

[14] International Institute for Strategic Studies, *The Military Balance* (London: IISS, various years).

[15] In the 1960s and 1970s, Kurdish activists joined left-wing movements. Kurdish nationalism and political activity emerged in the 1980s. See Henri Barkey and Graham E. Fuller, "Turkey's Kurdish Question: Critical Turning Points and Missed Opportunities," *Middle East Journal* 51 (Winter 1997), 62–67. Anecdotal evidence suggests that the Turkish Shi`i minority has tended to support the left-of-center Republican People's party. Despite this, until the 1980s, the Sunni-Shi`i religious cleavage in Turkey was not manifestly an issue in Turkish politics; that is to say, political elites and groups did not openly stake positions around this cleavage, nor did the two groups engage in violent political confrontations. That situation has unfortunately been altered since the mid-1980s. For a sensitive discussion of ethnic identities and politics in Turkey, see Sengun Kilic, *Biz ve Onlar: Turkiye'de Etnik Ayrimcilik* (Istanbul: Metis Yayinlari, 1991).

Syria and Turkey represent different values of many variables that social scientists commonly employ. Do these differences preclude comparative analysis? Empirically, they would suggest concomitant differences in the constraints and opportunities facing political leaders, their methods of formulating public policy, and the capacity of social groups to express dissatisfaction with those policies and demand their modification. Methodologically, specialists place priority on comparability, rendering Syria and Turkey unlikely candidates for comparative analysis.[16]

These objections lose force under closer scrutiny, however. Scholars have regularly invoked every one of the variables for which Syria and Turkey represent different values to explain developmental outcomes. Consider, for example, the effect of democratic political institutions on economic outcomes. An extensive literature argues that because politicians running for office must exchange patronage for votes, democratic systems produce suboptimal economic outcomes. This literature is complemented by an equally extensive literature claiming that authoritarian regimes are better able to mobilize resources and implement unpopular policies needed to foster development. But if we explain Turkey's economic outcome with reference to democracy, we are unable to account for the similar Syrian outcome, which occurred in the absence of democracy. Similarly, if we explain Syria's economic outcome with reference to its overwhelmingly large state sector and the absence of a large-scale, private industrial sector, we are unable to account for the similar Turkish outcome, which occurred despite the presence of a large private industrial sector.

Thus, the differences between Syria and Turkey are not obstacles to comparison; they are the basis for comparison. Syria and Turkey represent the same value of the dependent variable, and therefore, according to the basic logical principle that a particular instance of a variable cannot be the cause of the outcome if it is absent when the outcome is present, we can eliminate these variables from further consideration.[17] Instead, our task is to find a shared independent variable. If Syria and Turkey share numerous independent variables, we will not be able to determine which of them is causally significant. The large number of vari-

[16] In an influential statement of this position, Arend Lijphart counsels comparative analysts to overcome the problem of having too few cases by focusing on "comparable" cases: "Similar in a large number of important characteristics (variables) which one wants to treat as constants, but dissimilar as far as those variables are concerned, which one wants to relate to each other." See his "Comparative Politics and the Comparative Method," *American Political Science Review* 65 (September 1971), 687.

[17] Morris Zelditch Jr., "Intelligible Comparisons," in *Comparative Methods in Sociology: Essays on Trends and Applications*, ed. Ivan Vallier (Berkeley: University of California Press, 1971), 267–307.

ables that they do *not* share thus greatly facilitates our task, for we can conclude with some confidence that these dissimilar variables are not causally significant.[18] But note that eliminating variables that Syria and Turkey do not share presupposes that their causal effect is deterministic, not probabilistic; that multiple causes do not exist; and that these variables do not combine in complex and contingent ways to cause similar outcomes. These assumptions are further examined in Chapter 10.

The comparison of Syria and Turkey affords primary causal significance to one theoretically relevant independent variable they share: high levels of elite conflict resolved by popular-sector incorporation.[19] My argument is not based simply on establishing a correlation between elite conflict, institutional profiles, and economic outcomes. Instead, I use deductive logic to supply causal mechanisms linking the independent, intervening, and dependent variables. Moreover, subsequent chapters provide evidence for these causal mechanisms.

Recent methodological writings, however, have cast doubt on the value of this research design. King, Keohane, and Verba claim, for example, that research designs based on particular values of the dependent variable cannot support causal claims, because we have no knowledge of the causal relations present when the dependent variable takes on other values.[20] Although this argument has merit, it is overstated. We can learn a great deal from this research design precisely because a large number of theoretically relevant variables have been eliminated. Moreover, as Douglas Dion argues, selecting on the dependent variable is warranted when testing necessary, as opposed to sufficient, conditions.[21]

Still, we do need to know what happens when the dependent variable takes on other values. Our confidence in the validity of the hypothesis that high levels of elite conflict led to the Syrian and Turkish outcomes is

---

[18] In rejecting those variables that Syria and Turkey do not share, I do not mean to suggest that they play absolutely no role in the idiographic narration of each case; of course it matters that Syria is authoritarian and Turkey is democratic. But these differences emerge as specific modes of expressing the more general processes highlighted in this book. Causal significance resides in the relations between the state and its class constituencies and the effects these relations have on fiscal practices, policies, and institutions. That these relations are organized differently in the two countries does not fundamentally alter the more basic causal mechanisms that produce similar outcomes.

[19] John Stuart Mill, who first elaborated the logic of this research design, called it the Method of Agreement in his *A System of Logic, Ratiocinative and Inductive*, 8th ed. (New York: Harper & Brothers, 1884), 611–12.

[20] Gary King, Robert O. Keohane, and Sidney Verba, *Designing Social Inquiry: Scientific Inference in Qualitative Research* (Princeton: Princeton University Press, 1994), 129. The technical term for inferential errors due to unvarying dependent variables is "selection bias."

[21] Douglas Dion, "Evidence and Inference in the Comparative Case Study," *Comparative Politics* 30 (January 1998): 127–45. Expressed as a necessary condition, my argument is that the absence of high levels of elite conflict is necessary for sustained economic development and industrial transformation.

greatly strengthened by evidence that low levels of elite conflict produced starkly different outcomes in other cases. More important, if low levels of elite conflict did not produce different outcomes in other cases, our confidence in the relationship of elite conflict to economic outcomes in the Syrian and Turkish cases would be seriously weakened. Thus, the incorporation of material from the cases of Korea and Taiwan is necessary to establish valid causal inferences. Based on the Syrian and Turkish cases, we would expect that in Korea and Taiwan, which arrived at markedly different economic outcomes, elite conflict should have been low. The discussion of Korean and Taiwanese state building confirms this proposition.

Furthermore, many other theoretically relevant variables are held constant across the four cases, supporting the decision to eliminate these variables from consideration. Consider the hypothesized beneficial developmental consequences of authoritarian political systems. Comparing Korea, Taiwan, and Turkey might prompt us to support this finding; the first two cases have authoritarian systems and rapid development, whereas democratic Turkey did not achieve rapid development. But authoritarianism in Syria did not produce an outcome similar to those in Korea and Taiwan. Because this value of an independent variable is present when the outcome is absent, we eliminate it from further consideration. Each variable discussed above is similarly controlled by comparing all four cases. The most significant theoretically relevant variable that systematically covaries with the dependent variable across all of the four cases is the level of elite conflict.[22] Furthermore, empirical material drawn from the Korean and Taiwanese cases supports the proposition that levels of elite conflict and their mode of resolution significantly determine policies and institutions that in turn yield divergent outcomes and supports the validity of the causal mechanisms I specify.

Of course, other variables also vary systematically with the dependent variable, including religion and trade regime. This problem is addressed extensively in the case studies and in Chapter 10. This research design simply furnishes initial plausibility to the hypothesis that levels of elite conflict and the causes of variance in that conflict are the starting points of extended causal chains that best explain distinctive institutional profiles and different economic outcomes.

The organization of this book is as follows: Chapter 2 explores the dynamics of state building in postcolonial societies and traces the process by which political arrangements, institutions, and public policies are created or redefined. Chapter 3 looks at state transformation and the construc-

---

[22] Mill called this research design the Method of Indirect Difference, which compares "two *classes* of instances respectively agreeing in nothing but the presence of a circumstance on the one side and its absence on the other." *A System of Logic*, 611.

tion of cross-class coalitions in Turkey, and Chapter 4 does the same for Syria. Chapter 5 investigates the four institutions that make up the Syrian and Turkish political economies. Chapter 6 examines the cases of Korea and Taiwan, exploring the coalitional consequences and institutional concomitants of low levels of elite conflict, and presents hypotheses explaining different levels of elite conflict.

Chapters 2 through 6 present the independent and intervening variables of the book. Chapter 7 marks a shift from explaining the origins of state institutions to exploring how state institutions shape economic outcomes. Chapter 7 presents analytic and empirical critiques of neoliberal growth theory, drawing on evidence from East Asia. The chapter then offers a semantic and operational definition of development and argues that development is predicated on overcoming a series of collective dilemmas. Chapter 8 treats developmental outcomes in Syria, Turkey, Korea, and Taiwan. The evidence supplied here supports the claim that while developmental states resolved both Gerschenkronian and Kaldorian collective dilemmas, precocious Keynesian states resolved Gerschenkronian collective dilemmas but only at the expense of exacerbating Kaldorian collective dilemmas. Chapter 8 argues that institutional profiles best account for these outcomes and presents a simple bargaining model explaining the causal link between institutions and economic development. Chapter 9 explores the responses of Syria and Turkey to the economic crisis of the early 1980s. Chapter 10 concludes the book with a methodological appraisal of the argument.

CHAPTER TWO

State Building and the Origins of Institutional Profiles

Since the mid-1980s, scholars have rediscovered and made analytically central the role of institutions in constraining behavior; shaping preferences, goals, and strategies; and even constituting identities. But nagging questions about the origins of institutions still accompany the growing consensus about the explanatory value of institutional analysis. Neoclassical economists present a strong case that entrepreneurs make incremental alterations of institutions in response to shifts in relative prices.[1] This chapter, in contrast, offers a "big bang" approach to the origins of institutions,[2] accounting for periods of rapid and comprehensive institutional elaboration by analyzing the transition from mediated states, in which states rule indirectly through alliances with local notables, to unmediated states based on direct rule, in which institutions supplant elites to forge links between state, economy, and society. As Weber describes this process, the prince "paves the way for the expropriation of the autonomous and 'private' bearers of executive power who stand beside him, of those who in their own right possess the means of administration, warfare, and financial organization, as well as politically usable goods of all sorts."[3] To be sure, states range along a continuum, and no states occupy the extremes of fully mediated or fully unmediated rule. Moreover, the shift to the unmediated side of the spectrum is reversible, as contemporary history attests. But over the past two centuries, the global shift toward unmediated rule is unmistakable.

[1] Douglass C. North, *Institutions, Institutional Change, and Economic Performance* (Cambridge: Cambridge University Press, 1990), 83.

[2] Stephen Krasner applies the geological notion of punctuated equilibrium to the study of rapid and comprehensive institutional change in his "Approaches to the State: Alternative Conceptions and Historical Dynamics," *Comparative Politics* 16 (January 1984): 223–46.

[3] "Politics as a Vocation," in *From Max Weber: Essays in Sociology,* ed. H. H. Gerth and C. Wright Mills (New York: Oxford University Press, 1946), 82.

The transformation in the political infrastructure of the state from indirect to direct rule—emblematic of modern political organization—decisively alters existing institutions while establishing new ones. Understood in this generic sense, the concepts of mediated and unmediated states provide minimal analytic purchase for explaining observed variations. But contemporary unmediated states evince institutional heterogeneity; the transition from ideal-typical mediated states to ideal-typical unmediated states produces institutional diversity, not uniformity.[4] The generic transition to unmediated states results in variant institutional outcomes because the transformation to direct rule has occurred along multiple paths. The specific attributes of resulting institutional portfolios are a function of the path from mediated to unmediated states followed in different historical contexts.

Many variables need to be incorporated into the analysis of large-scale political transformation. In the first section of this chapter, however, levels of elite conflict, the independent variable of my argument, are shown to best account for divergent paths from mediated to unmediated states.[5] Other variables, such as class conflict, position in the global economy, security threats, and colonial legacies are incorporated into the analysis of levels of elite conflict. More specifically, levels of elite conflict determine whether significant state transformation precedes the emergence of mass politics through the incorporation of lower classes into political coalitions or occurs simultaneously with popular incorporation. These two paths of state transformation produce different institutional profiles. The second section of this chapter analyzes the causal effect of these different routes to direct, unmediated rule and demonstrates how the simultaneous occurrence of state transformation and popular-sector incorporation creates a specific set of institutions different from the institutional outcomes of state transformation that precedes popular incorporation. These institutional formats are the intervening variable of my argument.

Although this analysis accounts for a great deal of institutional variation, to more fully specify economic outcomes, I introduce a third variable in the third section of this chapter: the onset of substantial industrial development. I introduce and discuss the concept of precocious Keynesian states, of which Syria and Turkey are examples. Taken as a whole, the

---

[4] Following Reinhard Bendix's recommendation, I understand political modernity as a nominal concept, not as an underlying teleological force driving history. For Bendix's critique of modernization theory and his substitution of a nominal for a reified conception of modernity, see *Nation-Building and Citizenship* (Berkeley: University of California Press, 1964), 361–434.

[5] For a related approach, see Richard Lachmann, "Elite Conflict and State Formation in 16th- and 17th-Century England and France," *American Sociological Review* 54 (April 1989): 141–62.

chapter focuses on cases where state transformation, popular-sector incorporation, and the onset of industrial development temporally converge, contrasting these cases to those in which the three processes occur sequentially. Through this analysis, I account for the origins of precocious Keynesian and developmental states.

The Transition from Mediated to Unmediated States

State building has multiple meanings, ranging from the initial differentiation of governmental functions from social institutions, to the centralization of power in absolutist states, to the proliferation and rationalization of state institutions.[6] For the purposes of this study, the meaning of *state building* is restricted to the transition from mediated to unmediated states, or from indirect to direct rule.[7] In mediated states, rulers rule indirectly, through the mediation of local elites.[8] Mediated state structures resulted from the incapacity of premodern states to overcome a basic structural dilemma inherent in the logistics of political power: pre-modern political units were created by concentrating military forces, but rule over conquered peoples required the dispersal of political power. Moreover, each conquest of territory pushed the frontiers of the state against territory controlled by potential rivals, forcing conquerors continuously to expand their domains. Consequently, rulers regularly conquered extensive territories too large to be administered effectively.[9] Direct rule by the army was possible only in core territorial regions. Bureaucrats could be dispersed, but this implied dispersing finite political resources as well. The limited power at the disposal of state agents restricted their capacity to force local compliance. Moreover, because logistical factors restricted the capacity of the state to monitor its dispersed agents, a constant danger

[6] For exemplars of each of these approaches to state building, see, respectively, Michael Mann, *The Sources of Social Power: A History of Power from the Beginning to a.d. 1760* (Cambridge: Cambridge University Press, 1986); Perry Anderson, *Lineages of the Absolutist State* (London: Verso, 1974); and Max Weber, *Economy and Society*, ed., Guenther Roth and Claus Wittich (Berkeley: University of California Press, 1978).

[7] These concepts have been used most recently by Charles Tilly, *Coercion, Capital, and European States, ad 990–1990* (Cambridge, Mass.: Basil Blackwell, 1990). In his discussion of patrimonial states, Weber writes of "mediatized" subjects, and of the desire of the prince to rule his subjects directly. *Economy and Society*, 1058.

[8] See Theda Skocpol's definition of agrarian bureaucracies, which "were not in a position to control directly, let alone basically reorganize, local agrarian socioeconomic relationships." *States and Social Revolutions: A Comparative Analysis of France, Russia, & China* (New York: Cambridge University Press, 1979), 48.

[9] As Genghis Khan is reported to have said, an empire cannot be ruled on horseback. See the excellent discussion in Mann, *Sources of Social Power*, 142–46.

existed of military and bureaucratic officials assimilating to local society, pursuing their own interests, and ceasing to be effective agents of rule.

This structural impediment to direct rule forced central state elites to collaborate with urban and rural elites—local aristocrats, large landlords, tribal heads, guild leaders, religious dignitaries—to secure political control and exercise authority.[10] Weber's important distinction between patrimonial and feudal modes of domination must not obscure this point. As Weber notes, "The patrimonial ruler cannot always dare to destroy these autonomous local patrimonial powers . . . if the ruler intends to eliminate the autonomous *honoratiores* [landowning notables], he must have an administrative organization of his own which can replace them with approximately the same authority over the local population."[11] But few rulers possessed an administrative apparatus that could more than temporarily supplant local allies. Consequently, as Weber continues, "as a rule the prince found himself compelled to compromise with the local patrimonial authorities or other *honoratiores*; he was restrained by the possibility of an often dangerous resistance, by the lack of a military and bureaucratic apparatus capable of taking over the administration, and, above all, by the power position of the local *honoratiores*."[12]

In mediated states, local elites performed many of the functions that we associate with sovereign states, ranging from tax collection to military recruitment, from coining money to adjudicating disputes. Local elites were able to discharge these functions because they enjoyed autonomous control over socioeconomic resources. But this control gave them power not only over local populations but also vis-à-vis the state, obliging state agents to bargain with local elites over the terms of collaboration, especially the distribution of surplus extracted from local producers.[13] State builders relentlessly worked to expand and institutionalize their authority, but until relatively recently, they could only temporarily dispense with local elites as their agents.

In contrast to modern, unmediated states where a diverse array of institutions connect centralized public authority to society and economy, the structural dependence of mediated states on local elites precluded the elaboration of these institutional networks. Moreover, politics in mediated states was generally restricted to "the governance of conflicts within

---

[10] Elites are those persons who control a disproportionately high level of politically relevant social and economic resources, giving them the capacity to make decisions binding on the larger community. State elites are members of the political elite whose influence stems primarily from their positions in the top ranks of the state apparatus.

[11] *Economy and Society,* 1055.

[12] Ibid., 1058.

[13] For a theoretical analysis of these bargains, see Margaret Levi, *Of Rule and Revenue* (Berkeley: University of California Press, 1988).

the dominant classes, and within the main urban centres," and mediated states provided correspondingly few public goods to their populations, the bulk of whom lived in the countryside.[14] Over time, as Tilly notes, state involvement in the adjudication of disputes, control over production, and distribution of economic goods grew from "trivial to tremendous," but for most of European state building, coercive activities of preparing for and waging war predominated.[15] War making became perceived as a public good only with the rise of nationalism.[16] Of course, military pacification made possible orderly economic activity, and states provided some protection to international traders. As Frederic Lane details, however, into the sixteenth century, merchants often provided their own protection for trade.[17] Only with the gradual elaboration of direct rule did European states assume the manifold responsibilities with which they are today so closely associated.[18] The proliferation of public goods was both cause and outcome of the transition to direct rule. On one hand, the gradual extension of state services to the population and the creation of institutions providing these services eroded the authority of local elites. On the other hand, as the state became more firmly implicated in the daily lives of its citizens, the demand for further public goods increased, linking state, society, and economy more tightly together.[19]

The transition from a mediated to an unmediated state, then, entails two generic developments: the construction of institutional networks supplanting notables and linking the state to social classes and groups and the expansion of the state's provision of public goods, particularly as the state assumes responsibility for establishing infrastructure, regulating the economy, and managing ties to the global economy. This transition is generic but contingent. It represents neither an inexorable process or master narrative culminating in a uniform state type, nor an irreversible stage of political evolution. On the contrary, tracing this process in specific historical contexts discloses the origins of institutions critical for de-

---

[14] Anthony Giddens, *The Nation State and Violence* (Cambridge: Cambridge University Press, 1985), 57–58. See also Mann, *Sources of Social Power,* 94–98 and 148–52.

[15] *Coercion, Capital, and European States,* 97.

[16] Bruce Porter, *War and the Rise of the State: The Military Foundations of Modern Politics* (New York: Free Press, 1994), 121–25.

[17] Frederic Lane, "Oceanic Expansion: Force and Enterprise in the Creation of Oceanic Commerce," in *Profits from Power: Readings in Protection Rent and Violence-Controlling Enterprises* (Albany: SUNY Press, 1979), 37–49.

[18] Two recent works conceptualize state building as increases in the scale and extent of public goods. See Hendrik Spruyt, *The Sovereign State and Its Competitors* (Princeton: Princeton University Press, 1994); and Philip G. Cerny, "Globalization and the Changing Logic of Collective Action," *International Organization* 49 (Autumn 1995): 595–626.

[19] As Levi *Of Rule and Revenue,* 1, writes, "As specialization and division of labor increase, there is a greater demand on the state to provide collective goods where once there were solely private goods or no goods at all."

termining state capacity to foster development.[20] We need, in other words, a more highly elaborated theoretical framework explaining the specific institutions and public policies that emerge with the transition from mediated to unmediated states.

The framework presented here pivots on a fundamental distinction: either state builders first bargained with elites and only later, following the institutionalization of direct rule, bargained with popular classes, or they bargained with popular classes at the same time they transformed the state to one based on direct rule. The institutions and policies associated with direct rule differ in the two sets of cases. Martin Shefter, for example, argues that a legal-rational administrative structure was possible only if the establishment of universalist principles within the national civil service preceded mass incorporation. If mass incorporation occurred before or simultaneously with the elaboration or extension of a national administrative system, that system would likely be based on patronage appointments.[21] Later in this chapter a further set of hypotheses is advanced about the effects on state institutions of popular incorporation that occurs early relative to state transformation.

The timing of popular incorporation relative to state transformation is important because modern states were not built in accordance with a master blueprint. Early state builders sought to extract greater quantities of fiscal and military resources, to check the power of competitors, and to quell dissent. The cluster of organizational characteristics of modern states were by-products of these more discrete efforts. Even rulers consciously emulating earlier state builders could not build political organizations that reflected solely their preferences, because all state builders seeking to enhance their capacity to generate and control power had to bargain with groups and classes from among their populations.[22] The institutions and public policies constituting unmediated states resulted from these bargains. To analyze particular outcomes, we must determine with whom state builders bargained as well as the terms of those bargains.

Consider first state building in the core countries of western Europe. In early modern Europe, state builders initially forged alliances only with social classes capable of countering the power of the estates by serving as an administrative elite. Over time, as state builders forged durable bar-

---

[20] Of course, state building in the sense of increasing state power by redefining existing institutions or establishing new institutions occurs after the transition to an unmediated state. For the purposes of the argument developed here, we can restrict our focus to the institutional outcomes that directly follow from the transition from mediated to unmediated states.

[21] "Party and Patronage: Germany, England, and Italy," *Politics & Society* 7 (1977): 403–51.

[22] See Weber, *Economy and Society*, 1064, on the elements of the tacit or explicit compromise struck by early modern patrimonial bureaucracies with local notables.

gains with groups of local power holders, societies dominated by large landowners produced different state structures than those dominated by capitalists, because rulers bargained with different classes; despite their institutional heterogeneity, however, both types of society slowly converged on direct rule. State organizational characteristics reflected these bargains and thus the class structure of society.[23]

Popular classes were certainly not passive spectators of state building. The historical record chronicles their efforts initially to resist state building, which entailed greater fiscal extractions and more onerous military burdens, and later to demand that state institutions and policies respond to their grievances and speak to their interests.[24] But into the second half of the nineteenth century, the impact on state structures of interactions with non-elite actors was of secondary importance.[25] Even as European polities witnessed the growth of unmediated states, most politics continued to be local.[26] Mass actors had their greatest impact on state formation only when the gradual erosion of political localism resulted in institutionalized political incorporation in the late nineteenth and early twentieth centuries.[27] By the time of durable and sustained popular incorporation in the late nineteenth century, however, European state formation had produced unmediated states that were highly institutionalized relative to most of the non-European world. As Bendix argues, "Both the growth of a market economy and the gradual extension of the franchise gave rise to interest groups and political parties which mobilized people for collective action. . . . On the other hand, in the sphere of public authority, access to official positions was gradually separated from kinship ties, property interests, and inherited privileges. As a result, decision-making at the legislative, judicial, and administrative levels became subject to impersonal

---

[23] Tilly, *Coercion, Capital, and European States,* Chap. 5.

[24] See Charles Tilly, *The Contentious French* (Cambridge: Harvard University Press, 1986), for case studies and theorizing about changing forms of popular collective action in response to the encroachment of the capitalist economy and early-modern states.

[25] Tilly, *Coercion, Capital, and European States,* 102.

[26] See Suzanne Berger's observations about the character of rural politics in France before the integration of the peasantry in her *Peasants against Politics: Rural Organization in Brittany, 1911–1967* (Cambridge: Harvard University Press, 1972), 33–34.

[27] Political incorporation entails the politicization of excluded social actors through the creation of perceptions that issues of critical importance to their daily lives are implicated in decisions made at the national level, the organization of political conflict around a common set of issues, and the integration of previously excluded social actors into the national political community through the resolution of those issues in a way that reflects the interests of a significant portion of the population. I adapt this definition from the usage of the essays in *The New Authoritarianism in Latin America,* ed. David Collier (Princeton: Princeton University Press, 1979). Note that by this definition, incorporation need not entail political inclusion —the expansion to non-elite actors of the right of institutionalized political participation. On inclusion, see Robert A. Dahl, *Polyarchy: Participation and Opposition* (New Haven: Yale University Press, 1971), 1–9.

rules and attained a certain degree of freedom vis-à-vis the constellations of interest arising in society."[28] Moreover, the institutions of unmediated states constrained popular incorporation and shaped the goals and strategies of mobilizing movements and parties, limiting, to the extent possible, the impact of incorporation on state structures.[29] Mass political incorporation in Europe certainly disrupted old patterns of politics, leaving its imprint on state institutions. By this time, however, European unmediated states had already acquired many of their characteristic features, such as legal-rational administrative structures, extensive administrative and surveillance capacity, and efficient mechanisms for domestic resource extraction, characteristics that persisted into the era of mass politics.[30]

The timing of popular incorporation relative to state building has varied widely across historical time and space, and most, but not all, non-European states had very different experiences.[31] In a handful of non-European cases, such as Japan after the Meiji Restoration, state building preceded popular incorporation. In these cases, the impact of popular classes on state building was even more diluted, as nineteenth-century state-building projects of "defensive modernization" typically entailed sustained efforts to curtail the expansion of mass political participation.[32] More typically, however, the most common non-European pattern was for state transformation to occur simultaneously with mass popular incorporation. State building produced different institutional outcomes in these

---

[28] *Nation-Building and Citizenship,* 28.

[29] Ira Katznelson, "Working-Class Formation and the State: Nineteenth-Century England in American Perspective" in *Bringing the State Back In,* ed. Peter B. Evans, Dietrich Rueschemeyer, and Theda Skocpol (Cambridge: Cambridge University Press, 1985), 257–84; Victoria C. Hattam, "Institutions and Political Change: Working-Class Formation in England and the United States, 1820–1886," in *Structuring Politics: Historical Institutionalism in Comparative Perspective,* ed. Sven Steinmo, Kathleen Thelen and Frank Longstreth (Cambridge: Cambridge University Press, 1992), 155–87.

[30] Dating mass incorporation in Europe is difficult, particularly due to episodic and nondurable instances of incorporation. Bendix traces the beginning of movements struggling for political inclusion to 1848 and describes the numerous strategies elites employed to delay mass incorporation. *Nation-Building and Citizenship,* 114–22. According to Gregory Luebbert, before World War I workers fully entered politics only in England, France, and Switzerland, and then only gradually and as groups, not as cohesive classes. For the rest of Europe, workers and peasants became politically active and were incorporated only in the interwar period. See his "Social Foundations of Political Order in Interwar Europe," *World Politics* 49 (July 1987), 452. For a slightly different chronological scheme that also supports the broad argument offered here, see Robert H. Dix, "History and Democracy Revisited," *Comparative Politics* 27 (October 1994), 94.

[31] Huntington proposes, for example, that for most of Western political development, "an inverse correlation may exist between the modernization of governmental institutions and the expansion of political participation." Samuel P. Huntington, *Political Order in Changing Societies* (New Haven: Yale University Press, 1968), 94.

[32] See Ellen Trimberger's discussion of the depoliticization of the masses in her *Revolution from Above: Military Bureaucrats and Development in Japan, Turkey, Egypt, and Peru* (New Brunswick: Transaction Books, 1978), 110–25.

cases, because the elaboration of state institutions was more directly implicated in the exigencies of popular-sector incorporation.[33] Indeed, the act of popular incorporation itself placed the state in direct contact with the vast majority of its population. Mediating notables were swiftly pushed aside, but the administrative institutions and public policies needed to replace them did not yet exist. Building these institutions, then, took place during a period of emergent mass politics. State builders had to confront two tasks simultaneously, not sequentially: building the administrative apparatus required for sustaining an unmediated state and managing large-scale national politics.

We can thus identify two broad paths of state building: (1) a path by which popular incorporation occurred after the transition from mediated to unmediated states, as in much of western Europe, Japan during the Meiji Restoration, and, as demonstrated in Chapter 6, Korea and Taiwan and (2) a path by which popular incorporation was roughly simultaneous with this transition, as in most of the postcolonial world. Why did the two paths diverge? Explaining why non-European state building followed trajectories diverging substantially from its predominantly European predecessor has been the central research domain of political development. Huntington's seminal and controversial analysis proposes that the inevitable gap between rising expectations and limited opportunities for social mobility in developing countries motivates lower classes to press demands for political inclusion. Autonomous mobilization by lower classes disrupts politics, subverts nascent institutions, and results in non-institutionalized, unstable polities.[34]

The cases explored in subsequent chapters force us to reconsider Huntington's analysis. First, to the extent autonomous mobilization from below existed, it was a response not to diffuse grievances, but to political-economic arrangements highly biased in favor of existing socioeconomic and political elites. It was not modernization that destabilized politics, but established patterns of exclusionary politics and exploitative economics. Second, whereas Huntington's theory treated autonomous mobilization from below as a disruptive influence whose effect was relatively uniform in all cases, the contrast between Syria and Turkey indicates a stark variance in the level of popular mobilization from below, forcing us to be more cautious in assigning causal primacy to autonomous collective action. Specifically, at the time of state transformation in Turkey, popular

---

[33] Within a large literature, this issue is explored with particular acuity by Huntington, *Political Order in Changing Societies.* See also Michael F. Lofchie, "Political Constraints on African Development," in *The State of the Nations: Constraints on Development in Independent Africa,* ed. Michael F. Lofchie (Berkeley: University of California Press, 1971), 9–17.

[34] *Political Order in Changing Societies,* Chap. 1.

classes had neither organized nor mobilized to demand political incorporation. In Syria, conversely, a relatively powerful labor movement emerged
and pressed demands for political inclusion in the 1950s, while peasants engaged in acts of local resistance and a national party claimed to represent
their interests. Despite the higher level of collective action in Syria, popular
incorporation was not a response to lower-class demands, but rather was an
elite project of state building from above. Autonomous mobilization from
below thus is neither necessary nor sufficient for popular incorporation.

Indeed, subsequent analyses have demonstrated that Huntington pre-
sumed the primacy of popular mobilization while remaining insufficiently attentive to the political context within which mobilization occurs.
Internally divided elites contending for political supremacy share the
stage with subalterns resisting imposed political-economic arrangements
in these analyses.[35] Sidney Tarrow's concept of political opportunity structures, for example, highlights the role of cleavages within and among
elites as one of a group of "consistent—but not necessarily formal, permanent, or national—signals to social or political actors that either encourage or discourage them to use their internal resources to form social
movements."[36] Further, elite conflict can often be the primary animator
of political change, even in the absence of popular mobilization from below. Our analysis of state building, in other words, needs a theoretical
statement about elite conflict.

In his classic study of coalition formation, William Riker proposes the
"size principle," an interesting application of the more general axiom
that actors minimize the costs incurred in achieving their goals. As he
puts it, "In social situations similar to n-person, zero-sum games with side-
payments, participants create coalitions just as large as they believe will
ensure winning and no larger."[37] The principle applies not only to electoral and legislative coalitions, where the size of winning coalitions is
fixed by established rules, but, somewhat more crudely, to state-building
coalitions as well. Popular incorporation empowers mass actors to make
binding claims for alteration of established political and economic
arrangements. Elites, therefore, prefer to monopolize political power and

[35] In a later volume, Huntington and Nelson write, "The attitude of the political elites toward political participation is, in any society, the single most decisive factor influencing the
nature of participation in that society." Samuel P. Huntington and Joan M. Nelson, *No Easy
Choice: Political Participation in Developing Countries* (Cambridge: Harvard University Press,
1976), 28.

[36] "States and Opportunities: The Political Restructuring of Social Movements," in *Comparative Perspectives on Social Movements: Political Opportunities, Mobilizing Structures, and Cultural Framings,* ed. Doug McAdam, John D. McCarthy, and Mayer N. Zald (Cambridge: Cambridge University Press, 1996), 54.

[37] William H. Riker, *The Theory of Political Coalitions* (New Haven: Yale University Press,
1962), 32–33.

the privileges it confers. When possible, they will forestall popular mobilization; the default minimum coalition embraces only elites and completely excludes lower classes. Elite discord, however, effectively raises political elites' discount rates, forcing them to give priority to the requisites of short-term political survival at the expense of their future uncontested control of valued resources. From Riker's principle, therefore, we can derive the proposition that intense elite conflict is a necessary condition for popular-sector incorporation.

Popular incorporation is a strategy some elites deploy for resolving inter-elite conflict. As Schattschneider posits, "At the nub of politics are, first, the way in which the public participates in the spread of conflict and, second, the processes by which the unstable relation of the public to the conflict is controlled. The second proposition is a consequence of the first. The more important strategy of politics is concerned with the scope of conflict."[38] In this vein, Skocpol persuasively argues that political crisis born of deep divisions within the political elite transformed latent popular discontent into insurrectionary movements.[39] When sufficiently intense, elite conflict raises the threshold of the minimum coalition, making popular incorporation an acceptable strategy. Elite unity, on the other hand, sustains efforts to prevent popular incorporation.

Elite conflict, however, is a permanent element of mediated states, as elites contend among themselves and with the state over the distribution of extracted surplus. What, then, constitutes intense elite conflict? Contending elite groups seek allies by building cross-class coalitions when conflict threatens not only their short-term material interests but also their long-term capacity to reproduce their elite status. Intense conflict entails an absolute loss of an elite's capacity to extract surplus, not just reduced claims on surplus, such that the threatened elite feels that it will be unable to compete for surplus in the future.[40] Conflict typically intensifies when states attempt to displace mediating notables or during a decisive shift from an agrarian-based to an industrial economy. In both these cases, the very existence of an elite is jeopardized. But note that the costs of incorporating mass allies are not the same for all elites. An agrarian oligarchy, for example, can make only limited overtures to peasants without undermining the sources of its elite status.

[38] E. E. Schattschneider, *The Semisovereign People: A Realist's View of Democracy in America* (New York: Holt, Rinehart, and Winston, 1960), 3.

[39] *States and Social Revolutions*, Chap. 2. Here, popular mobilization has the same effect on the size of minimum coalitions as does elite conflict. But, as argued above, lower classes mobilized in Syria but not in Turkey. Although Syrian popular mobilization was an important element in Syrian politics, it did not directly result in popular incorporation. See Chapter 4 for further discussion.

[40] Richard Lachmann, "Class Formation without Class Struggle: An Elite Conflict Theory of the Transition to Capitalism," *American Sociological Review* 55 (June 1990): 398–414.

From the late nineteenth century and into the post–World War II period, three sources of conflict undermined elite unity and frequently fueled deeply divisive elite conflicts.[41] First, the increasing orientation of economic activity toward national and international markets has spurred demands for increased state economic intervention. State elites have regularly responded to these demands, recognizing that the provision of public goods to facilitate economic growth generates increased revenue and enhanced national power. But increased state activity has typically required the construction of new state agencies and necessitated the levying of new taxes, leading to intense distributional conflicts.[42] The gradual extension of state authority, in turn, has triggered political conflict between state officials and local elites.[43] Second, conflict between the agrarian elite and nascent industrialists over state policy began to constitute a major plank in national politics, opening fissures over whether the economic future of the nation will be based on agriculture or on industry, on participation in global markets or on inward-looking strategies. More generally, elites have split over competing visions of economic modernization.[44] The perception that this conflict was zero-sum amplified the intensity of conflict, making popular mobilization more palatable and even preferable.[45] Finally, elites have divided over how to deal with increasingly assertive popular classes that can no longer be controlled through traditional patron-client relations disrupted by integration into the global economy, urbanization, shifts in production patterns, and widespread poverty.[46]

Conflicts over these issues disrupted nineteenth- and twentieth-century European politics as well, prompting changes in the scope and patterns

[41] In Chapter 6, I explore the sources of variance in the intensity of inter-elite conflict.

[42] Conflicts over fiscal matters are vividly illustrated in Vincent C. Peloso and Barbara A. Tenenbaum, eds., *Liberals, Politics & Power: State Formation in Nineteenth-Century Latin America* (Athens, Ga.: University of Georgia Press, 1996). For an important theoretical statement, see Carmenza Gallo, *Taxes and State Power: Political Instability in Bolivia, 1900–1950* (Philadelphia: Temple University Press, 1991).

[43] Joel S. Migdal, *Strong Societies and Weak States: State-Society Relations and State Capabilities in the Third World* (Princeton: Princeton University Press, 1988).

[44] For a general theoretic statement of conflict over trade policy, see Ronald Rogowski, *Commerce and Coalitions: How Trade Affects Domestic Political Alignments* (Princeton: Princeton University Press, 1989).

[45] Again, elite conflict varies in intensity across cases. Compare, for example, the intense intra-elite conflict precipitating the Mexican Revolution with the less acute struggles prompting the Brazilian Revolution of 1930, as discussed in Ruth Berins Collier, "Popular Sector Incorporation and Political Supremacy: Regime Evolution in Brazil and Mexico," in *Brazil and Mexico: Patterns in Late Development*, ed. Sylvia Ann Hewlett and Richard S. Weinert (Philadelphia: Institute for the Study of Human Issues, 1982), 61–65.

[46] Ruth Berins Collier and David Collier, *Shaping the Political Arena: Critical Junctures, the Labor Movement, and Regime Dynamics in Latin America* (Princeton: Princeton University Press, 1991), 40, argue that even conspicuously weak labor movements such as in Columbia introduced a "constantly unsettling" dynamic into elite-level politics.

of politics, and altering state institutional capacities and the degree of state activism.[47] But in Europe, these conflicts occurred more or less sequentially and were resolved over longer periods of time.[48] More important, European states had acquired many of their central organizational characteristics before the eruption of these conflicts, characteristics that persisted into the era of mass politics. By the mid-nineteenth century, Marx could already depict the French state as

> This executive power with its enormous bureaucratic power and military organisation, with its artificial state machinery embracing wide strata, with a host of officials numbering half a million, besides an army of another half million, this appalling parasitic growth, which enmeshes the body of French society like a net and chokes all its pores, sprang up in the days of the absolute monarchy. . . . the seigniorial privileges of the landowners and towns became transformed into so many attributes of the state power, the feudal dignitaries into paid officials and the motley pattern of conflicting mediaeval plenary powers into the regulated plan of a state authority, whose work is divided and centralised as in a factory.[49]

We might be inclined to discount some of Marx's description as rhetorical flourish, but he is merely echoing Alexis de Tocqueville's account of how the French Revolution retained and even strengthened the centralized and penetrating administrative apparatus built before the Revolution.[50]

Compare Marx's description of the French state to the late nineteenth-century Brazilian state, which, despite its elaborate bureaucratic apparatus, was unable to control or even reach the periphery. Brazilian statesman Viscount Uruguay vividly depicts indirect rule in his description of the mediated Brazilian state as "all head, with neither arms nor legs."[51] When states rested on mediated structures well into the twentieth century, ruling elites faced fundamental, simultaneous challenges: to build institutions of centralized authority, to develop functional economies and

---

[47] Peter Gourevitch, *Politics in Hard Times* (Ithaca: Cornell University Press, 1986), details the coalitional consequences of economic crisis.

[48] Furthermore, the higher incidence of war in Europe probably induced greater elite cohesion, as did periodic popular mobilization from below that threatened elite privileges. On the role of class conflict in unifying European elites behind state-building projects, see Michael Hechter and William Brustein, "Regional Modes of Production and Patterns of State Formation in Western Europe," *American Journal of Sociology* 85 (1980):1061–1093.

[49] "The Eighteenth Brumaire of Louis Bonaparte," in *The Marx-Engels Reader,* ed. Robert C. Tucker, 2d ed. (New York: W. W. Norton, 1978), 606.

[50] *The Old Régime and the French Revolution,* trans. Stuart Gilbert (Garden City, N. Y.: Doubleday Anchor Books, 1955), esp. Part 2, Chap. 2.

[51] Cited in J. G. Merquior, "Patterns of State-Building in Brazil and Argentina," in *States in History,* ed. John A. Hall (Oxford: Basil Blackwell, 1986), 273.

manage relations with the global economy, and to create a stable political order embracing both elites and non-elite actors. Conflicts over state building and the proper relationship of the state to the economy converged. Political conflict was thus particularly divisive, creating further incentives for popular incorporation. And because non-European states telescoped the history of state formation, elite conflict, and the emergence of mass politics into a compact period, popular incorporation typically occurred in less institutionalized and thus more plastic mediated states. In Europe, even when elite conflict was intense, popular classes were incorporated into states whose central organizational characteristics preceded incorporation and persisted after the emergence of mass politics. In short, what distinguished most of the developing world from early state builders in Europe was that elite conflict led to popular incorporation before the construction of unmediated states. Consequently, the effects of popular incorporation on institutional profiles were more profound.

Of course, elite conflicts have varied cross-nationally within the non-European world. Simply stated, intense elite conflict in the developing world produced popular incorporation simultaneously with state transformation. In chapters 3 and 4, Turkey and Syria are presented as cases of intense elite conflict. More muted conflict, in contrast, allowed unified elites to continue excluding popular classes until after substantial state transformation. In chapter 6, Korea and Taiwan are shown to be cases of muted elite conflict. Finally, note that here and in the following case studies, elite conflict is treated as dichotomous. Analysis of a greater number of cases would undoubtedly suggest that elite conflict is a continuous variable. But even this minimally disaggregated conceptualization permits exploration of the logic linking levels of conflict to patterns of state building and institutional outcomes.

The convergence of state transformation and popular-sector incorporation produced institutional outcomes that differed from those resulting when the two processes occurred sequentially. Moreover, as I argue beginning in Chapter 7, these divergent institutional outcomes produce distinct developmental trajectories. Assume that given the demands of national sovereignty in an anarchic world—demands that weigh heavily on states recently liberated from colonial rule—political elites value economic development and realize that development demands state autonomy, depoliticized decision making, the capacity to extract resources from the domestic economy, and the latitude to intervene in the economy in ways that will produce rapid industrial development. Why don't all political leaders institutionalize these features?

The demands of political incumbency pose a powerful constraint that limits the capacity to achieve this project of state building and economic development, forcing politicians to reconcile the often conflicting logics of politics and of economics.[52] Resource extraction, depoliticized decision making, and developmental intervention frequently clash with the interests of social classes; although pursuing these goals may be developmentally effective, they also threaten political incumbency. If the power of social classes to press demands for privilege that conflict with the requisites of development varies cross-nationally and correlates with successful political and economic development, then a parsimonious explanation of varying developmental outcomes exists. However, this class-power model of political economy, which follows closely Huntington's model of political development (critiqued above), achieves parsimony at the expense of predictive failures. As clearly seen in the cases of Syria and Turkey, subaltern classes such as small farmers received privileges despite their political weakness, while powerful agrarian classes lost their political and economic positions. As an alternative, I have argued that polarizing conflicts among the political elite triggered episodes of state transformation and popular incorporation. Intense conflict compelled contenders for power to seek allies from lower classes, extending privileges to workers and peasants who lacked the capacity to make binding claims on the state.

When conflict was sufficiently intense, elites created new political-economic institutions, but not under conditions of their own choosing. Rather, intense elite conflict constrained the choices made in altering existing institutions and constructing new ones; it is a necessary and sufficient condition for the formation of a particular state type.[53] Under the influence of intense conflict, elites were forced to choose certain institutional arrangements that reflected their urgent concern for attaining and retaining political power more than they reflected their absolute preferences for institutional formats most conducive to long-term economic development. In other cases, however, elite conflict was far less intense. Consequently, the political constraints on state builders were less pressing, providing more latitude to construct state institutions consistent with what they saw as the dictates of development. Relatively low levels of elite conflict were a necessary condition for elites to be able to construct the

---

[52] Robert Bates articulates well the tight link between politics and economics from the point of view of political leaders. He writes, "But to win and retain political power, political aspirants must attract followers, and to do so they must offer advantages, such as the opportunity to prosper." See his "The Centralization of African Society," in his *Essays on the Political Economy of Rural Africa* (Berkeley: University of California Press, 1983), 41. See also Barry Ames, *Political Survival: Politicians and Public Policy in Latin America* (Berkeley: University of California Press, 1987).

[53] More specifically, intense conflict is a necessary and sufficient condition for elites to *attempt* a new state-building project. Other factors, present in other cases but not in Syria or Turkey, might thwart that attempt. My research design thus supports only the claim that intense conflict is a necessary condition.

institutional formats of developmental states. It is not basic elite preferences but the context in which elites advance or defend their preferences
that distinguishes institutional outcomes.

High levels of elite conflict in mediated states, then, provoked the convergence of state transformation and popular-sector incorporation. How
did this convergence produce distinct institutional outcomes? Elites that
incorporate a mass base as a political strategy confront two imperatives.
First, they must establish new political arrangements to organize expanded political participation, entailing both some form of organization
of mass actors and structures linking those actors to the political system to
control the participation of newly incorporated groups. These new political arrangements can range from relatively uncontrolled political participation to corporatist organizations designed to strictly limit popular political participation. In addition, incorporating elites typically take
measures to create mutual interests that bind them to their mass base. Although this strategy may take the form of ideological appeals, it characteristically includes at least some elements of material exchange, particularly commitments to welfare-enhancing policies. Political stability is most
commonly achieved when one group of contenders has captured the
state and used its resources to offer a set of incentives and sanctions that
limit further political conflict. State elites construct political institutions,
distribute state resources, and manipulate economic outcomes in ways
that disproportionately benefit select groups and classes whose strength
and support the elite relies on to maintain its rule. In other words, they
build mass-based coalitions.

Because coalitions are composed of "a group of persons working together who have some but not all goals in common,"[54] they are typically
constructed by means of side-payments, or compensatory arrangements
that balance the inequities stemming from cooperation.[55] Side-payments
connect coalitional strategies to institutional and policy outcomes. Consider a ruling elite that elicits needed political or administrative support
from one class, for example, a landed elite. The terms of the bargain seal-
ing this alliance are a function of a set of variables confined to the relations between the state and its bargaining partner, such as the balance of
power, transaction costs, and rulers' discount rates.[56] A ruling elite might

[54] Robert Gilpin, *War & Change in World Politics* (Cambridge: Cambridge University
Press, 1991), 18, citing Anthony Downs, *Inside Bureaucracy* (Boston: Little, Brown, 1967).

[55] H. Richard Friman, "Side-Payments versus Security Cards: Domestic Bargaining Tac-
tics in International Economic Negotiations," *International Organization* 47 (Summer 1993),
390.

[56] Margaret Levi bases her analysis of tax structures on these variables in her *Of Rule and
Revenue*.

make parallel, but essentially unrelated, deals with two constituencies, such as a landed elite and religious notables. In this case, both parties to the bargain enjoy gains without necessarily imposing costs on the other, and no fundamental barriers to cooperation exist.[57] Therefore, no side-payments are involved.

Now consider a ruling elite that seeks to elicit cooperation from an industrial bourgeoisie and from an industrial proletariat. The determination of the deals made with each constituency is more complicated, because the two constituencies have competing interests. The state's deal with the bourgeoisie will depend not only on the relative power of business but also on the deal made with the proletariat. Similarly, the deal made with the proletariat will depend on the offer made to the bourgeoisie. Each group will now receive some benefit or concession that it would not have received were it the state's sole bargaining partner, because most benefits made to workers, to peasants, or to both impose costs on a bourgeoisie, costs for which the bourgeoisie must ultimately be compensated.

In principle a diverse array of benefits can act as side-payments, but in practice, a delimited set of payments is regularly employed. For agrarian lower classes, states can provide subsidized inputs—credit, farming implements, seed, water, and fertilizer—and above-market prices for output. For urban working classes, states can provide guaranteed employment, above-market wages, social security provisions, and subsidies for basic necessities. The industrial bourgeoisie can receive protection from global competition, subsidized credit and inputs, and preferential access to foreign exchange, and the commercial bourgeoisie can receive foreign exchange allocations and permission to import industrial products. These lists are not exclusive, but they give the general idea of the sorts of provisions states can offer constituencies. Note that although this list of side-payments is composed entirely of rents, or payments to parties greater than they would receive in competitive markets, rents and side-payments are analytically and substantively distinct. Analytically, *side-payments* refer to coalition-building strategies, whereas *rents* refer to one category of inducements paid to constituencies.[58]

Incorporating elites offer a set of incentives and constraints to potential popular-class allies. The incentives to cooperate and sanctions against non-cooperators comprise the bargain struck between incorporating

[57] Of course, tax exemptions for one party could impose costs on the other party, complicating these bargains.

[58] For discussion of other substantive categories of side-payments, including payments of emotional satisfaction, see Riker, *Theory of Political Coalitions*, 108–14.

elites and their new mass allies.[59] The term *bargain* in this instance means neither negotiated settlement, which entails the formal exchange of proposals, nor social contract, which implies the mediation of a superior third party, but simply strategic interaction between two or more collective actors who dispose of unequal levels of politically relevant resources.[60] As the elite makes public its policies, it must take into account how its potential constituencies will respond. Likewise, when deciding how to react to this offer, popular-sector organizations and even individuals must calculate the costs they might incur if they defect from the coalition they have been invited to join. They make that calculation with great certainty about how the state would react should they decide to defect. Furthermore, given their relatively weak organizational resources, workers and peasants have limited room to maneuver against the vastly superior position of the state elite. Leaders of the Syrian labor movement, for example, resisted state control over their organizations and attempted to alter the terms of the bargain offered by the state; in response, the state simply swept them aside. For the most part, however, popular classes have few incentives to defect, because participation in cross-class coalitions provides them with substantial benefits.

The hypothesis linking levels of elite conflict to patterns of state building can now be more specifically reformulated. State building that is accompanied by, and realized through, high levels of side-payments produces institutional outcomes different from those of state transformation in the absence of side-payments. Recall the earlier argument that bargaining dynamics—with which classes does the state bargain, and what are the terms of those bargains?—explain patterns of state formation. Intense elite conflict impels one of the competing elite factions to incorporate a mass base: the state bargains with popular classes, exchanging material benefits for political support. This produces convergence between state transformation to an unmediated state and popular incorporation. In this case, elites build cross-class coalitions by making high levels of side-payments. I consider the level of side-payments to be high when payments to peasants, to workers, or to both substantially raise the factor costs of industrialists. When elite conflict is low, on the other hand, relatively unified elites build narrow coalitions that exclude popular sectors; they do not bargain with lower classes and make few side-payments. Thus, they prevent popular incorporation until after substantial state transformation. This proposition invites further inquiry into the specific mecha-

---

[59] See Ruth Berins Collier and David Collier, "Inducements versus Constraints: Disaggregating Corporatism," *American Political Science Review* 73 (December 1979): 967–86.

[60] Thus Bendix, citing Eric Hobsbawm, refers to workers' movements in early nineteenth-century Europe as "collective bargaining by riot." *Nation-Building and Citizenship*, 77.

nisms linking high levels of side-payments to specific institutional and policy outcomes.

Coalitions, Side-Payments, and Institutional Change

State institutional characteristics are shaped by bargaining dynamics. In many European cases of the transition to direct rule, states made substantial and durable bargains with popular classes only after the core institutions of unmediated states had been established. In Korea and Taiwan, the absence of intense elite conflict allowed elites to forgo bargaining with popular classes until after they had built unmediated states. Institutions in Korea and Taiwan were different from those in Europe because they reflected the preferences of unified elites for institutions conducive to rapid economic development in late-developing nations.

In Syria and Turkey, on the other hand, intense elite conflict divided the elite, leading one contending faction to bargain with popular classes before the transition to direct rule. Popular incorporation coincided with state transformation. The institutions expressing direct rule therefore strongly reflected the construction of cross-class coalitions built through high levels of side-payments. In this section, I argue that high levels of side-payments are a sufficient condition for what I call *precocious Keynesian states*. Low levels of elite conflict, on the other hand, are a necessary but not sufficient condition for developmental states. Although in some cases the structural constraints imposed by a particular pattern of state transformation are so overwhelming that they determine the attributes of resulting institutional profiles, in other cases constraints are less binding and leave more room for actors to shape institutional outcomes. This causal asymmetry stems from the relationship of structural constraints to the preferences of intentional actors. When elite conflict is high, elites are forced to build cross-class coalitions based on high levels of side-payments with necessary consequences for institutions. When elite conflict is low, elites can build narrow coalitions, leaving more room for the construction of developmental states.

The following pages explore the institutional consequences of building cross-class coalitions. High levels of side-payments produce states with the following institutional attributes: (1) a political relationship linking state and society based on the principle of constituency clientelism; (2) a politicized and thus heteronomous bureaucracy; (3) a distributive fiscal policy; and (4) patterns of state economic intervention motivated by the need to maintain political loyalties by protecting constituencies from the vagaries of the market, rather than by the goal of maximizing economic development.

State Building and the Recasting of State-Society Relations:
Constituency Clientelism

The political structures of mediated states exclude subaltern classes
from regularized, low-cost access to major decision-making institutions.
Although the transition to an unmediated state redefines the relationship of state to social classes, it does not necessarily entail granting
lower classes full inclusion in the polity. Instead, the institutional for-
mat born of incorporation bears the imprint of the particular path of
state transformation, which is best analyzed through a bargaining
framework.[61]

Elites who undertake mobilization of popular forces to further their
own goals typically face a dilemma: uncontrolled popular mobilization
threatens their rule, dictating that management and control of participation take precedence over institutionalizing autonomous participation.
Even in revolutionary situations, elites seeking to expand political participation to effect decisive change in society's most basic institutions eventually place a premium on forging new political institutions that prevent
"'unreconstructed' social and cultural forces from exercising any uncontrolled and undesired influence over the development and definition of
the institutions, values, and practices favored by the Party."[62] When elites
incorporate popular classes for instrumental and non-revolutionary purposes, they give even greater priority to controlling recently expanded
participation. In the absence of powerful organizations representing
lower classes, ruling elites inaugurating new projects of economic development typically value and defend their newly won monopoly over major
political organizations.

To acquire and sustain the loyalty of lower classes, elites seek substitutes
for uncontrolled participation by balancing repression with the provision
of either ideal or material incentives to collaborate. In Leninist regimes,
ideological appeals predominated but were often supplemented by material inducements.[63] In less revolutionary societies, material incentives typically replace ideological appeals, but here too they must be accompanied
by efforts to control political participation. Given the commitment made
by incorporating elites to high levels of side-payments, political stability

[61] For examples of this type of analysis, see Luebbert, "Social Foundations of Political Order in Interwar Europe," and Collier and Collier, "Inducements versus Constraints," and
their *Shaping the Political Arena.*

[62] Ken Jowitt, *New World Disorder: The Leninist Extinction* (Berkeley: University of California Press, 1992), 89.

[63] Moshe Lewin, "The Social Background of Stalinism," in *Stalinism: Essays in Historical
Interpretation,* ed. Robert C. Tucker (New York: W. W. Norton, 1977), 121; Janine Ludlam,
"Reform and the Redefinition of the Social Contract under Gorbachev," *World Politics* 43
(January 1991), 285.

can be secured by establishing a system I call *constituency clientelism.* Constituency clientelism has three elements that distinguish it from variants of patron-client relations that are well-covered in the literature.[64] First, the patron is the state, not individual elites. Second, entire social classes, and not individual members of subaltern classes, are clients.[65] Finally, instead of the personal exchange of private goods and services for loyalty to individual elites, class-specific public goods such as subsidies, support prices, and protected markets are impersonally exchanged for loyalty to the state and acceptance of strict controls on political participation.[66] In short, whereas patron-client relations are informal, voluntary, and individualistic, relations of constituency clientelism are institutionalized through public policy and political organizations, are compulsory, and embrace entire classes.[67]

In contrast to relations between the state and lower classes, relations between the state and businessmen—both industrialists and merchants— are complex and tend to correspond to more conventional models of clientelism for two reasons. First, in late-industrializing countries, only a small number of businessmen have the requisite skills and resources to undertake large-scale business activities: these businessmen are correspondingly important enough to enter into personalistic ties with members of the state or political elite. Second, many of the services that the state can supply to these businessmen are of a private rather than public nature. Consider the distinction between a tariff and an import quota, for example. The tariff is a public good insofar as it raises the price of imported goods and thus creates a captured market for all domestic producers. A quota, on the other hand, is partially a private good: only the merchant who is permitted to import a limited quantity of goods or the industrialist who receives a license to import machinery benefits directly from a quota. Quotas, import licenses, access to foreign exchange, state

---

[64] For the classic definition of patron-client relations, see James Scott, "Patron-Client Politics and Political Change in Southeast Asia," *American Politics Science Review* 66 (1972), 92.

[65] Lisa Anderson uses the term "corporate clientelism" to refer to patronage relations binding local communities to political leaders or parties. See her *The State and Social Transformation in Tunisia and Libya, 1830–1980* (Princeton: Princeton University Press, 1986), 26.

[66] Public goods are characterized by noncompetitiveness and nonexclusivity. This means that if they are provided to one member of a group, they are provided to all members of that group. Strictly speaking, these are not pure public goods in the sense that not every member of the society benefits from high agricultural prices in the way that everyone benefits from national defense or clean air. As Mancur Olson points out, "The first point is that most collective goods can only be defined with respect to some specific group. One collective good goes to one group of people, and other collective good to another group; one may benefit the whole world, another only two specific people." *The Logic of Collective Action: Public Goods and the Theory of Groups* (Cambridge: Harvard University Press, 1965), 14.

[67] These generic characteristics of patron-client ties are drawn from S. N. Eisenstadt and Louis Roniger, "Patron-Client Relations as a Model of Structuring Social Exchange," *Comparative Study of Society and History* 22 (January 1980): 42–77.

contracts, and other private goods can thus be used to create personalistic ties of clientelism between members of the elite and large businessmen. Thus, state-business ties combine constituency clientelism and individualized clientelist ties.

Patron-client relations are characteristic of mediated states. In more highly elaborate systems of clientelism, extended chains of patron-client ties converge on the state, and state resources are deployed by political brokers. This system typically results from the gradual inclusion of masses into more centralized systems dominated by oligarchic elites within which conflict stems from factional struggles for power, not programmatic cleavages.[68] Clientelistic systems typically undermine horizontal organizations and solidarities and thus effectively protect elite privileges by controlling the extension of participation.[69] Constituency clientelism, in contrast, creates horizontal organizations, albeit under the control of the state. Because of the class-specific nature of the goods supplied, it may even elicit class consciousness, though not necessarily class-based collective action.

Constituency clientelism typically results from a rapid extension of political participation engendered by intense inter-elite conflict. When anti-oligarchic movements construct unmediated states, constituency clientelism is the only available means to institutionalize state-society relations, because mediators capable of performing brokerage functions are deliberately stripped of political and economic power. Property-owning elites might incorporate elements of a brokerage system, but they will also have incentives to institute constituency clientelism as a means of preempting future challenges to their rule from previously autonomous state elites. In short, when elites in mediated states effect popular incorporation and the transition to an unmediated state, they control political participation while cultivating a mass base through high levels of side-payments. Conversely, relatively cohesive elites who need not incorporate a mass base can rely more heavily on repression and manipulation of subaltern organizations without supplying material incentives.

In return for guarantees of material improvement, recipients are expected to remain politically acquiescent. Regardless of regime type, consequently, organized labor, agrarian classes, and even businessmen will suffer organizational weakness and marginalization from the policy-making process. Characteristically, voluntary, cooperative interest organizations are suppressed in favor of corporatist arrangements strictly controlled by the state. But corporatist organizations provide only marginal

---

[68] Alex Weingrod, "Patrons, Patronage, and Political Parties," *Comparative Studies in Society and History* 10 (1968), 381.

[69] Nicos Mouzelis, "On the Concept of Populism: Populist and Clientelist Modes of Incorporation in Semiperipheral Polities," *Politics & Society* 14 (1985), 332.

bargaining power for groups to better their position; state or political elites dominate these groups and provide material inducements directly to constituencies. This circumvention of organizations of interest representation is a deliberate effort to preempt those organizations from amassing autonomous power. Thus, although corporatist interest organizations exist, they play only marginal roles in determining policy.[70] Constituency clientelism thus represents both an institutional linkage between state and society and substantive policy outcomes.

State Building and Politicized Bureaucracies

While students of East Asian development have identified an autonomous bureaucratic apparatus as a key element in successful late development, other scholars have indicted heteronomous or penetrated and politicized bureaucracies as the primary culprits behind failed development. Because state-led industrial restructuring displaces market signals through mechanisms such as subsidies, the socialization of risk, and administered pricing, "the government must create a central guidance agency capable of supplementing market signals by its own signals as to which sectors will be most profitable."[71] Examples of these pilot agencies are the Ministry of International Trade and Industry in Japan,[72] the Council for Economic Planning and Development and the Industrial Development Bureau in Taiwan,[73] and the Economic Policy Board in

[70] This observation is consistent with other criticisms of the corporatist literature for its focus on formal arrangements to the exclusion of studying substantive outcomes. For example, Gourevitch, *Politics in Hard Times*, 243, n. 15, observes that "The literature on corporatism has increased the attention given to intermediate associations and thus stimulated valuable research on the structure of these associations. Less clear at times is [its] ability to demonstrate clear linkages between these structures and policy outcomes." See also Alfred Stepan's caveats about equating the entirety of the political system with the formal institutional arrangements used to control the working class. He notes that all major policy decisions taken by the Velasco regime of Peru, an archetypical corporatist system, were taken by executive institutions whose members were recruited from the military and the police, two institutions that were *outside* the new system of interest representation. Therefore, "methodological and theoretical approaches used in non-corporatist systems to study machine or bureaucratic politics, clientelistic networks, or the military as a special form of a complex organization can—with appropriate contextual caution and modification—be applied to those political systems that display prominent corporatist features in some sectors." *The State and Society: Peru in Comparative Perspective* (Princeton: Princeton University Press, 1978), 66–71, quotation from 71.

[71] See Chalmers Johnson, "Political Institutions and Economic Performance: The Government-Business Relationship in Japan, South Korea, and Taiwan," in *The Political Economy of the New Asian Industrialization,* ed. Frederic C. Deyo (Ithaca: Cornell University Press), 151–56.

[72] Chalmers Johnson, *MITI and the Japanese Miracle: The Growth of Industrial Policy, 1925–1975* (Stanford: Stanford University Press, 1982).

[73] Robert Wade, *Governing the Market: Economic Theory and the Role of Government in East Asian Industrialization* (Princeton: Princeton University Press, 1990), 195–227.

Korea.[74] Today, even opponents of comprehensive state economic intervention recognize the need for a competent technocrat agency to supervise economic liberalization and market-based growth.[75]

To be capable of formulating and implementing long-term development plans, a bureaucratic agency must be endowed with certain organizational resources, including meritocratic norms of recruitment and promotion to ensure that the agency is staffed with the requisite talent; corporate coherence and status to ensure that individuals identify their personal goals with the achievement of organizational goals; and insulation from pressure groups to ensure depoliticized decision making. Peter Evans adds that bureaucrats must be not only insulated from society but also embedded in social networks to ensure sufficient information flows and to build the trust necessary for bureaucrat-entrepreneur collaboration on joint projects.[76] This emphasis on the organizational basis of successful state intervention raises new questions: What explains the disparate provision of these resources across cases? What are the social and political conditions necessary for the emergence of autonomous bureaucratic agencies? Why do Korea and Taiwan, almost alone among states in the developing world today, enjoy this level of bureaucratic insulation?

Analysts have generally answered these questions through logical deduction or historical induction. Employing the former, one school of thought roots inefficient bureaucratic practices in the utility-maximizing behavior of bureaucrats.[77] The problem with this approach is that it leads us to predict pervasive rent-seeking behavior in all bureaucracies and thus cannot account for the East Asian developmental bureaucracies.[78]

[74] Youngil Lim, *Government Policy and Private Enterprise: Korean Enterprise in Industrialization*, Korean Research Monograph, No. 6. (Berkeley: Institute of East Asian Studies, 1981), 16–17.

[75] See the World Bank's 1997 World Development Report, *The State in a Changing World* (Oxford: Oxford University Press, 1997). For discussion of the link between state capacity and economic liberalization, see Thomas Callaghy, "Towards State Capability and Embedded Liberalism in the Third World," in *Fragile Coalitions: The Politics of Economic Adjustment*, ed., Joan M. Nelson. (New Brunswick: Transaction Books, 1989), 115–38.

[76] Peter Evans, *Embedded Autonomy: States and Industrial Transformation* (Princeton: Princeton University Press, 1995), 30. Chalmers Johnson had earlier noted that state planners in East Asia receive continuous information from the private sector about "profit-and-loss conditions, export prospects, raw materials costs, and tax receipts." See his "Political Institutions and Economic Performance," 142.

[77] This claim has recently been codified into a school of analysis that endogenizes the voracious appetites of political "Leviathans" into mathematical models of the economy. See, for example, Ronald Findlay and John D. Wilson, "The Political Economy of Leviathan," in *Economic Policy in Theory and Practice*, ed. Assaf Razin and Efraim Sadka (New York: Macmillan, 1987), 289–305; and the collection of essays edited by David C. Colander, *Neoclassical Political Economy: The Analysis of Rent-Seeking and DUP Activities* (Cambridge, Mass.: Ballinger, 1984).

[78] Furthermore, as Peter Evans insightfully notes, a state composed entirely of utility-maximizing individuals could never be restricted to the neoclassical "nightwatchman" state required by economic theory. *Embedded Autonomy*, 25.

Alternatively, scholars have located the roots of bureaucratic insulation in a history of meritocratic recruitment of the technically most qualified personnel, high status afforded to bureaucrats, and a tradition of public-minded bureaucrats. While noting the insufficiency of the argument, Evans points out, for example, that the tradition of institutionalized exam-based civil service recruitment and meritocratic civil service examinations has been the means for staffing the Korean bureaucracy for more than 1,000 years, whereas Mexico still has not instituted such procedures.[79] Similarly, Chalmers Johnson makes brief reference to the high status of Japanese bureaucrats stemming from the tradition of samurai becoming administrative officials rather than warriors and to the militarization of Korean society and the diffusion of military techniques of management into the bureaucracy.[80]

This search for historical prerequisites for bureaucratic autonomy receives empirical support and theoretical elaboration from Martin Shefter's study of European political development. He argues that bureaucracies organized according to impersonal rules and that seek to defend their autonomy from political intervention act as a "constituency for bureaucratic autonomy." If such a constituency exists before mass mobilization, parties channeling popular mobilization will be unable to offer political appointments and jobs as inducements to supporters, thereby preserving bureaucratic autonomy. Otherwise, parties can adopt patronage politics and thus subvert meritocratic recruitment and impersonal routines.[81]

Shefter's argument comports well with other cases in suggesting that the level of politicization of state administrative agencies is determined by, on one hand, relations between political leaders and civil servants and, on the other hand, relations between political leaders and political constituencies.[82] But historical legacies of administrative rationality are insufficient for securing future bureaucratic autonomy; present incen-

---

[79] "The State as Problem and Solution: Predation, Embedded Autonomy, and Structural Change," in *The Politics of Economic Adjustment,* ed. Stephan Haggard and Robert Kaufman (Princeton: Princeton University Press, 1992), 155.

[80] *MITI and the Japanese Miracle,* 36–37; "Political Institutions and Economic Performance," 153.

[81] See his "Party and Patronage." I am restating Shefter's schema, in which the dependent variable is not the level of bureaucratic insulation but the nature of party appeals for support, which hinges on the nature of the bureaucracy: autonomous bureaucracies resistant to political intervention lead parties to make programmatic appeals. My thinking about the effects of popular incorporation on institutions is deeply indebted to Shefter's claim that the period in which popular mobilization first occurs is a "critical experience" with "character-forming" consequences for the character of politics and the attributes of the bureaucratic apparatus.

[82] Barbara Geddes, "Building 'State' Autonomy in Brazil, 1930–1964," *Comparative Politics* 22 (January 1990): 217–35; Richard C. Crook, "State Capacity and Economic Development: The Case of Cote d'Ivoire," *IDS Bulletin* 19 (October 1988): 19–25.

tives for politicians to reproduce autonomy are also necessary. The Turkish bureaucracy, for example, drew on the legacy of the Ottoman bureaucracy, which evolved as a high-status group whose members were recruited by impersonal means and who received specialized education. Yet political conditions precluded the extension of this legacy beyond 1950.[83] Chalmers Johnson posits that all politicians frequently face incentives to politicize economic decision making.[84] Incentive structures are thus key, prompting us to ask: What conditions induce political elites either to politicize or to depoliticize economic decision making?

First and foremost, the answer is elite conflict. Intense conflict compels political leaders to politicize economic policy making, and high levels of side-payments preclude the development of an autonomous bureaucratic agency. First, political elites may attempt to woo urban middle classes by expanding employment opportunities in the civil service. This policy is often accompanied by a policy of creating or expanding the size of the educated middle class through free education.[85] State employment, then, is a potential public good that can be used to purchase stability by employing bureaucracies as arenas of patronage. By blocking the implementation of meritocratic forms of recruitment and promotion, this strategy undermines the autonomy of the civil service and impairs its capacity to act as an effective agent of development through the formulation and implementation of industrial policy.

If patronage-based recruitment and promotion are confined to the lower and middle echelons of the bureaucracy, creating insulated agencies of high-ranking civil servants acting as an economic general staff may still be possible. But high levels of side-payments to popular classes generally sabotage such efforts, because, as we shall see later, the logic of creating and maintaining cross-class coalitions conflicts sharply with the logic of long-term industrial transformation and the cultivation of international competitiveness. Coalition maintenance requires *protecting* constituencies from the vagaries of the market by providing above-market prices for agricultural products along with below-market prices for inputs, above-market wages, guaranteed employment, and so forth. The logic of industrial transformation, in contrast, would inevitably erode these privileges and undermine the coalition basis of political stability and regime incumbency. Consequently, politicians face incentives not only to refrain from building autonomous state agencies, as in Syria, but

---

[83] For evidence of the meritocratic operations of the Ottoman and early Republican bureaucracy, see Metin Heper, *The State Tradition in Turkey* (Northgate, England: The Eothen Press, 1985).

[84] "Political Institutions and Economic Performance," 152–53.

[85] In an extreme case, the Egyptian state under Nasir both made higher education free and guaranteed employment to all university graduates.

also to subvert existing autonomous state agencies, as in Turkey. Political elites seek to limit the autonomy of bureaucrats as a way of securing their own incumbency, which is based on a commitment to distribution. Thus, although entry into high bureaucratic positions may be based on specialized education and knowledge, bureaucrats are unable to use this training because their programs have unacceptable political implications. Bureaucracies may be staffed with technocrats, but they are not technocracies.

Conversely, low levels of side-payments reduce the powerful incentives for political leaders to politicize decision making and are thus a necessary but not sufficient condition for a developmental state. Bureaucratic autonomy results only when the political leadership needs the skills and resources of a meritocratic and technocratic administrative staff more than it needs to use the civil service as a source of patronage to win popular support, and only when politicians need not fear that development projects implemented by an autonomous bureaucracy will conflict with the logic of cultivating mass support through the provision of immediate material benefits. Generally, this means that a politician–civil servant coalition has to exist before popular mobilization and that the two groups must agree both on the need to mobilize popular support and on the conditions under which this popular mobilization will take place.

State Building and Distributive Fiscal Policies

In the 1950s, Nicholas Kaldor, a British Keynesian economist, studied the taxation systems of several underdeveloped countries. He concluded that there were no inherent obstacles to raising the rate of government financial extraction. Implementation of this proposal would furthermore clearly contribute to capital accumulation and thus to development. Kaldor's conclusions were widely discussed in Turkey, which was included in his study, and his proposals to increase taxation created a political uproar and were not adopted. Returning to the academic life, Kaldor wrote an article whose title reflected his frustration with the inability of governments to follow his prescriptions: "Will Underdeveloped Countries Learn to Tax?"[86]

Was Kaldor correct that there were no inherent obstacles to increasing taxation? Students of Gabriel Ardant might argue that preindustrial economies pose intractable structural obstacles to efficient resource extraction.[87] But this approach is unsatisfactory, for it does not address other

[86] *Foreign Affairs* 41 (January 1963): 410–19.
[87] Gabriel Ardant, "Financial Policy and Economic Infrastructure of Modern States and Nations," in *The Formation of National States in Western Europe*, ed. Charles Tilly (Princeton: Princeton University Press, 1975), 164–242.

significant characteristics of fiscal practices in Syria and Turkey, such as consistent budget deficits in large part resulting from welfare expenditures to coalition members. Moreover, as Turkish parliamentary debates in the 1950s and 1960s made clear, the problem was not that Turkey had to learn to tax, but that political constraints induced preferences for low levels of taxation, high levels of welfare payments, and reliance on either capital inflows or loose monetary policy to finance budget deficits. Kaldor likely underestimated the political impediments to sound fiscal policy.

As some scholars have argued, bargains between rulers and citizens explain divergent levels of resource extraction and patterns of state expenditures. These studies take into account existing economic structures and administrative capacities, but these variables are used to analyze the process of bargaining; they do not directly explain emergent fiscal structures.[88] Analyzing these bargains raises the following questions: Which groups are being taxed and which groups are exempt from taxation? What is the content of state welfare policies and to which groups are they delivered? To what extent is the system capable of self-financing?

High levels of side-payments are a sufficient condition for distributive fiscal practices; indeed, distributive fiscal practices are one of the key mechanisms for supplying side-payments. Securing incumbency through commitments to raise constituents' standards of living forces state elites to trim tax burdens and expand transfer payments, resulting in budgetary deficits covered by external transfers and inflationary monetary policy. States may attempt some measures of resource extraction, but these will be through invisible mechanisms: taxes on foreign trade, overvalued exchange rates that overburden exporters, and the inflation tax. Low levels of side-payments, by implication, are a necessary but not sufficient condition for more extensive domestic resource extraction and less-generous welfare policies.

State Building and Patterns of State Economic Intervention

In a path-breaking study of the political economy of development, Robert Bates provides a rigorous analysis of the political foundations of patterns of state economic intervention in Africa.[89] By altering prices, especially lowering prices paid to farmers, state intervention creates artificial scarcities, or rents, captured by the state. These rents are then consumed by the political elite, transferred to the treasury, or redistributed as

---

[88] Levi, *Of Rule and Revenue;* Tilly, *Capital, Coercion, and European States;* Gallo, *Taxes and State Power.* See also Robert H. Bates and Da-Hsiang Donald Lien, "A Note on Taxation, Development, and Representative Government," *Politics & Society* 14 (1985): 54–70.

[89] Robert H. Bates, *Markets and States in Tropical Africa* (Berkeley: University of California Press, 1981).

patronage to constituencies to cement their political support. In general, organized and powerful constituencies such as businessmen, urban workers, and wealthy farmers receive economic privileges, while poor and unorganized farmers bear the costs.

Although the Syrian and Turkish cases provide support for the political logic underpinning patterns of state intervention identified by Bates, they do not support his analysis of coalition formation: While coalitional politics may explain state policies, coalitional politics themselves require further elaboration. In Syria and Turkey, high levels of side-payments provided benefits in the form of rents to urban classes and to wealthy as well as poorer farmers. Indeed, rather than the urban bias characteristic of Africa, in Syria and Turkey we find rural bias—prices are manipulated to privilege wealthy and small farmers, and subsidies to urban classes provided compensation for this bias. The inclusion of relatively poor and unorganized farmers in governing coalitions indicates that the composition of state-supporting coalitions cannot be deduced directly from the capacity of groups to act collectively—or, in the case of the economic elite, individually—on behalf of their interests.

Levels of elite conflict provide an alternative explanation of coalition formation. When conflict is intense, elites build large, cross-class coalitions through high levels of side-payments provided to both powerful and to relatively weak constituencies. In later chapters we see that the Syrian and Turkish states intervened in multiple markets in ways that cemented social support by providing rents to constituencies while protecting them from market forces. Conversely, when conflict is less intense, and political incumbency is secured without incorporating popular classes into coalitions, as in Korea and Taiwan, both poorer farmers and urban workers are excluded from these coalitions.

Furthermore, high levels of side-payments—that is, payments made both to capitalists and to workers, to peasants, or to both classes, such that the payments made to lower classes substantially increase the factor costs of industrialists—strongly influence the selection of trade policy. Late-developing economies in the twentieth century initially industrialized by moving into consumer nondurable industries that frequently use domestically produced agrarian products as inputs. If states make side-payments to peasants, particularly in the form of support prices for outputs that are above world-market prices, the price of inputs for industry such as cotton for textile manufacturers will also rise. If the state simultaneously attempts to incorporate urban workers into their support coalition, wages are likely to rise above market levels. Industrialists are squeezed from both sides, paying higher prices for both raw materials and labor, precluding them from producing goods competitive on international markets. Furthermore, state subsidies to lower classes typically fuel inflation, which, if not countered by steady devaluations, will price goods out of international markets.

Consequently, the industrial bourgeoisie must be compensated for its inclusion in the coalition. The result is straightforward; cross-class coalitions result in protectionist policies, where guaranteed access to the domestic market is one of the side-payments made to the industrial bourgeoisie. The high levels of side-payments on which this coalition is built are a sufficient cause of import-substituting industrialization (ISI). Because high levels of side-payments are a sufficient but not necessary condition, other causes of ISI may exist, and thus ISI may predate the creation of cross-class coalitions. In Turkey, policy makers attempted at times to move toward outward-oriented trade policies between 1950 and 1980, but high levels of side-payments sabotaged these experiments: As we shall see in Chapter 5, the causal effects of side-payments are directly observable. In Syria, on the other hand, policy makers chose ISI for multiple reasons and before 1980, did not experiment with export-led growth (ELG). In this case, although we cannot directly observe the causal effect of side-payments, Chapter 5 supports the counterfactual that even if Syrian policy makers had favored ELG, they still would have been constrained to pursue ISI.

Low levels of side-payments, on the other hand, are a necessary but not sufficient cause of ELG. State elites not committed to making side-payments to lower classes may not, for other reasons, elect to follow ELG; but if they do make those side-payments, they cannot pursue ELG.[90] Although Korean and Taiwanese governments did pursue ISI in the 1950s—again, high side-payments are a sufficient, but not necessary, cause—the absence of side-payments to lower classes made it possible for governments to shift decisively, though not completely, to ELG in the 1960s.[91]

Of course, state elites could elect to subsidize industrialists for higher factor costs while maintaining relatively open markets. But this strategy is unlikely to be chosen for two reasons. First, protection is a relatively inexpensive way to compensate industrialists. Some level of direct subsidy may be necessary to overcome capital scarcity, but implementing protection facilitates private investment. Barring protection, even higher levels of

[90] For a related argument, see James E. Mahon Jr., "Was Latin America too Rich to Prosper? Structural and Political Obstacles to Export-led Industrial Growth," *Journal of Development Studies* 28 (1992): 246–63.

[91] Bruce Cumings, "The Origins and Development of the Northeast Asian Political Economy: Industrial Sectors, Product Cycles, and Political Consequences," in *Political Economy of the New Asian Industrialism*, 69–70, stresses the absence of populism in Korea and Taiwan in the 1950s.

subsidies would be required, which would constitute an additional burden on state budgets already strapped by the loss of tariff revenues. Second, a feasible economic logic underpins the strategy of compensating industrialists through protection. Payments made to lower classes expand the size of the domestic market, providing increasing demand for the products of protected industries. Side-payments that induce protection therefore act as a rudimentary form of demand-stimulus management. As Edward Asfour argued in his 1959 survey of the Syrian economy, the combination of low levels of income and uneven income distribution "reduces further the possible local demand for local products, since the richer minority has a preference for imported manufactured goods, while the poorer majority has not got the means to buy on a large scale the locally manufactured goods with which they are generally satisfied."[92] For this reason, I refer to the Syrian and Turkish states as precocious Keynesian states.

Precocious Keynesian States

The argument so far has focused on the timing of popular-sector incorporation relative to state transformation. To fully account for economic outcomes, a third variable must now be introduced: the timing of substantial industrial development. In much of western Europe and in the East Asian newly industrialized countries, popular-sector incorporation occurred not only after the transition to direct rule but also after substantial industrial development. Consequently, political-economic institutions conducive to rapid economic development and industrial transformation were established before the onset of side-payments to popular classes, which in turn constituted less of a burden on an enlarged and growing economy. The gradual incorporation of workers and peasants certainly influenced institutions, but its effect was less dramatic and fundamental than in cases such as Syria and Turkey, where state transformation and popular-sector incorporation into cross-class coalitions converged with the onset of industrial development. The argument linking side-payments to ISI, for example, applies most forcefully to economies at earlier stages of industrial development; in more advanced economies, payments to lower classes can be balanced through increased capital intensity and enhanced productivity, so that capitalists fund higher wages from their profits without disturbing their competitive position in international mar-

---

[92] See his *Syria: Development and Monetary Policy* (Cambridge: Harvard University Press, 1969), 27.

kets.[93] For this reason the term *precocious Keynesian states* refers to a particular pattern of state building: the construction of broad, cross-class coalitions that transform states from mediated to unmediated structures, occurring in societies at early stages of industrial development.

I use the concept of precocious Keynesian states in part as a descriptive term, to distinguish the institutional and policy outcomes of high levels of side-payments from outcomes in developmental states, but also to distinguish Syria and Turkey from the more generic concept of populism. In studies of Latin America, for example, populism typically refers to antioligarchical political movements that incorporate labor into an alliance with urban middle and nascent industrial classes.[94] Furthermore, although analyses of populism often include discussion of public policy and economic outcomes, the concept itself refers only to a political movement.[95] Precocious Keynesianism, on the other hand, specifically refers to regimes anchored in cross-class coalitions embracing both urban and rural lower classes as well as agrarian elites, as in the case of Turkey. Moreover, precocious Keynesianism explicitly incorporates variables related to public policies and economic outcomes.

In its narrowest sense, Keynesianism refers to the policy implications of John Maynard Keynes' demonstration that economies can settle into stable equilibrium at less than full employment levels. More broadly, Keynesianism refers to a set of practices and policies used to manage advanced industrial economies; the hallmark of these policies is the political and economic inclusion of an organized labor movement.[96] Keynesian policies thus express cross-class coalitions and side-payments, but these poli-

[93] Thomas Ferguson, "From Normalcy to New Deal: Industrial Structure, Party Competition, and American Public Policy in the Great Depression," *International Organization,* 38 (Winter 1984): 41–94; and Adam Przeworski,*Capitalism and Social Democracy* (Cambridge: Cambridge University Press, 1985), 171–204.

[94] Robert R. Kaufman, "Industrial Change and Authoritarian Rule in Latin America," in *New Authoritarianism in Latin America,* 199–202.

[95] Populism is "a political movement characterized by mass support from the urban working class and/or peasantry; a strong element of mobilization from above; a central role of leadership from the middle sector or elite, typically of a personalistic and/or charismatic character; and an anti–status-quo, nationalist ideology and program." Collier and Collier, *Shaping the Political Arena,* 788. But see the discussion of "economic populism," in Rudiger Dornbusch and Sebastian Edwards, "The Macroeconomics of Populism," in *The Macroeconomics of Populism in Latin America* (Chicago: University of Chicago Press, 1991), 3. Economic populism bears resemblance to precocious Keynesian macroeconomic policies but remains silent on other institutional features incorporated into the concept of precocious Keynesianism.

[96] This meaning of Keynesianism is the consensus definition of a recent collection of essays dedicated to cross-national analysis of the adoption of Keynesian politics. Peter A. Hall, "Introduction," in *The Political Power of Economic Ideas: Keynesianism across Nations,* ed. Hall (Princeton: Princeton University Press, 1989), 5.

cies and practices *follow* substantial industrial development and the construction of legal-rational administrative structures.[97]

Precocious Keynesianism, on the other hand, refers to the simultaneity of state transformation, cross-class coalition construction, and the onset of industrial development; the convergence of these three processes produces outcomes that are different from those observed among Keynesian states. This contrast between Keynesianism and precocious Keynesianism thus emphasizes an important causal variable: the timing of state building and popular-sector incorporation relative to substantial industrial development. In summary, in contrast to Keynesianism, precocious Keynesianism occurs as a product of inter-elite conflict, embraces overwhelmingly large sectors of the population, and constitutes a major transformation of state structures in societies at early stages of industrial development. If the key institutions of the political economy are established before the introduction of Keynesianism, it may be possible to limit the impact of inclusionary policies on fiscal structures, administrative procedures, and state autonomy. If a society has decisively entered the industrial age and has developed numerous sectors competitive in international markets before the introduction of Keynesianism, resources needed to finance welfare-enhancing policies may be more readily available, limiting the impact of Keynesianism on the overall political economy. If populist-style policies are extended to only a small sector of the population, it may still be possible to design institutions and formulate policies more conducive to long-term growth. But precocious Keynesianism violates all three of these conditions and therefore produces a distinctive developmental trajectory.

The next four chapters present empirical cases illustrating and testing the propositions advanced above. Chapter 3 explores the emergence of elite conflict in a mediated state, the construction of new mass coalitions, and the transition to direct rule in Turkey; Chapter 4 does the same for Syria. Chapter 5 provides details on the institutional consequences of state transformation and popular incorporation through a survey of state-society relations, the nature of the bureaucracy, state fiscal practices, and

---

[97] Note also that in forging the class compromise underpinning Keynesianism, coalition members make concessions to one another: workers cease efforts to socialize capital while capitalists maintain the highest wage level consistent with the social reproduction of capital at acceptable profit margins. For discussion, see Przeworski, *Capitalism and Social Democracy*, 171–203. Indeed, Przeworski's enumeration of the political referents of this class compromise bears similarities to my discussion of institutional profiles. He writes, 202, "Class compromise implies a particular organization of political relations, a particular relation between each class and the state, a particular set of institutions, and a particular set of policies."

patterns of state economic intervention in Syria and Turkey. One important focus of Chapter 5 is to demonstrate that high levels of elite conflict resolved through the construction of cross-class coalitions yielded similar institutional features in Syria and Turkey, despite the numerous contrasts that otherwise distinguish the two cases. Finally, Chapter 6 explores the origins and consequences of low levels of elite conflict in Korea and Taiwan. Here, the coalitional and institutional outcomes made possible by low levels of elite conflict are discussed and some propositions explaining variations in elite conflict are advanced.

CHAPTER THREE

Constructing Coalitions and Building States: Turkey

In 1923 the Turkish War of Independence concluded with the estab-lishment of the Turkish Republic. Between 1923 and 1950 civilian and military state elites ruled Turkey in alliance with social elites mediating between the state and lower classes, who were excluded from political participation. In 1950 the Democrat Party (DP), an opposition party formed by defecting members of Turkey's ruling elite alliance, won Turkey's first competitive elections and established a new government. The DP won the 1950 elections by constructing an alliance uniting large and medium-sized rural producers, workers, and the bourgeoisie into a cross-class coalition. The 1950 elections constituted more than just a change of regime and of government; they signified a transition from a mediated to an unmediated state that occurred simultaneously with pop-ular-sector incorporation.

In Chapter 2 I argued that popular-sector incorporation converges with state transformation when intense elite conflict emerges in mediated states. The first section of this chapter discusses the initial condition of my analysis, the political infrastructure of the Turkish mediated state. The second section traces the emergence of intense inter-elite conflict over the proper relationship of the state to the economy; this section thus de-tails the independent variable of my argument. I demonstrate that state policies in the 1930s and 1940s threatened not only the short-term mate-rial interests of the socioeconomic elite but also those elites' control over the economic basis of power. With their most basic interests and their ca-pacity to reproduce their privileged position under attack, the socioeco-nomic elite faced new incentives to seek allies from popular classes as a strategy for protecting their elite status and their economic activities from an increasingly predatory state. In the third section, I survey the side-payments deployed in the construction and reproduction of this cross-class coalition, which is the first causal mechanism of my argument. In Chapter 5, I show how these side-payments determined the institutional character of Turkey's political economy.

The Mediated State in Turkey, 1923–1950

The Turkish Republic inherited a political infrastructure of indirect rule from the Ottoman Empire. Numerous modernizing reforms implemented between 1923 and 1950 retained intact the structure of a mediated states.[1] Local notables were valuable allies of the central state because only they could directly control the vast majority of the population which remained outside the reach of the state.[2] Indeed, the leader of the Turkish War of Independence, Mustafa Kemal, successfully prosecuted the war by forging an alliance between civilian bureaucrats, military officers, and the only social groups capable of mobilizing local support: tribal shaykhs, local notables, and religious leaders. Important allies were the merchants of Istanbul and the nascent Muslim bourgeoisie, who funded the independence army. This alliance of forces was reflected in the composition of delegates to the Erzurum Conference, which established the organizational basis for the independence struggle: of the 54 delegates to the conference, 17 were local notables (landlords and merchants), six were religious leaders, and the remainder were members of the bureaucratic elite.[3]

With the conclusion of the war, the state elite consolidated its rule by reforging an alliance with the socioeconomic elite, thereby reproducing a mediated state. As Yerasimos describes the political division of labor, "If the role of the Anatolian notables had, since 1919, been that of an indispensable intermediary between the state and the peasantry, the urban bourgeoisie took upon itself, starting in 1923, an analogous role with respect to the working class. The civilian and military bureaucracy, taking into its hands the reins of the state, granted the urban bourgeoisie and the rural notables representation of the vital forces of the nation, thus

[1] Ilkay Sunar and Sabri Sayari, "Democracy in Turkey: Problems and Prospects," in *Transitions from Authoritarian Rule: Southern Europe*, ed. Guillermo O'Donnell, Philippe C. Schmitter, and Laurence Whitehead (Baltimore: Johns Hopkins University Press, 1986), 169.

[2] Serif Mardin, "Center-Periphery Relations: A Key to Turkish Politics?" in *Post-Traditional Societies*, ed. S. N. Eisenstadt (New York: W. W. Norton, Inc., 1972), 183.

[3] Ergun Ozbudun, "The Nature of the Kemalist Political Regime," in *Ataturk: Founder of a Modern State*, ed. Ali Kazancigil and Ergun Ozbudun (London: C. Hurst, 1981), 82–83.

turning over to their discretion workers and peasants."[4] Consequently, even with the establishment of the Kemalist single party, the Republican People's Party (RPP), in 1923, political power in Turkey rested on this alliance of the military-bureaucratic elite at the national level and of small town and rural notables at the local level, while excluding popular classes. As Ilkay Sunar writes, "the Party leadership did not wish a head-on clash with the social notables. But rather it chose to renew the tacit elite partnership which had been forged in the early days of the Republic."[5] Between 1920 and 1946, state officials made up the plurality of Assembly members, while deputies from the free professions and "economic occupations," consisting of agriculture, trade, and banking, gradually increased their representation at the expense of religious figures whose numbers dropped from 20 to 4 percent.[6]

The alliance joining central state elites and dominant classes was based on a tacit compromise: social elites would support the continued hegemony of the bureaucratic elite and its modernizing reforms of state and cultural institutions as long as these reforms did not threaten the existing social and economic structure. "Thus, in such a situation, it was possible for the government to introduce a constitution and a modern legal code but not for it to pass and implement a land reform law."[7] This political pact was inherently unstable, however; as the state embarked on new projects of economic modernization in response to changing external conditions, it violated the terms of the bargain and threatened the most fundamental interests of its elite allies. The resolution of the intense elite conflict that resulted forced a major transformation of Turkish politics.

The Emergence of Inter-Elite Conflict in Turkey

The central issue provoking elite opposition to the Kemalist regime was one that had vexed Turkish politics since the nineteenth century: competing visions over the shape of the national market, its relationship to

---

[4] Stephane Yerasimos, "The Monoparty Period," in *Turkey in Transition: New Perspectives,* ed. Irvin C. Schick and Ertugrul Ahmet Tonak (New York: Oxford University Press, 1987), 76. The alliance of state and socioeconomic elites was explicitly hammered out at the 1923 Economic Congress of Izmir, "where the workers were represented by the Istanbul Workers' Union, founded by the Turkish National Commercial Union, an employers' association, and the peasants by a Farmers' Union whose most important action had been to reject the distribution of vacant land among the small peasantry."

[5] See his *State and Society in the Politics of Turkey's Development* (Ankara: Ankara University Faculty of Political Science, 1974), 74–75.

[6] Ozbudun, "Nature of the Kemalist Political Regime," 85.

[7] Feroz Ahmad, *The Turkish Experiment in Democracy* (London: C. Hurst, 1977), 3.

the world market, and the extent of state regulation over economic activity. State officials of the Ottoman Empire were concerned with the in-
trusion of the world market, identifying it with the rise of a powerful
merchant class allied to foreign capital, which would displace the bureaucratic elite from their premier surplus-extracting position.[8] Moreover, because many Ottoman merchants belonged to ethnic and religious minori-
ties, the state feared that their growing power would result in the breakup
of the Empire. The state sought to check these threats by inserting itself
between the local and international economies. Early in the twentieth
century, the state began to nurture a Muslim bourgeoisie that would be
more dependent on the state and loyal to the Empire.[9]

In the 1920s, elite opponents of Kemal's growing political power and
the passage from a constitutional monarchy to an absolutist republic
formed a self-proclaimed "liberal" opposition, organized as the Progressive Republican Party.[10] Alongside its defense of liberalism and democracy, the party called for reducing state economic intervention to a minimum by liberalizing domestic and foreign trade and welcoming foreign
capital. Turkish liberals, however, were not advocates of laissez-faire economic policies and called on the state to protect local industries and to
complement, not replace, private initiative.[11] Moreover, elite conflict was
relatively moderate in the 1920s, because the terms of the Treaty of Lausanne compelled the state to pursue a largely laissez-faire policy.[12] Indeed, public economic policy during the 1920s was limited to measures
restoring Turkey's devastated economy to its prewar level, and the decade
was a period of economic reconstruction and enrichment for the commercial bourgeoisie.[13] But Turkey's liberals were concerned that an autonomous state would eventually pursue policies that would harm their
interests. During the 1930s, that fear proved to be well grounded, as increased state control over the economy strengthened the arbitrary pow-

[8] Caglar Keyder, *State & Class in Turkey: A Study in Capitalist Development* (London: Verso, 1987), 26–30.

[9] Zafer Toprak, *Turkiye'de "Milli Iktisati," 1908–1918* (Ankara: Yurt Yayinlari, 1982).

[10] Feroz Ahmad persuasively argues that far from being liberal democrats, the founders of the party sought only a system allowing open competition between elites. See his "The Progressive Republican Party, 1924-1925," in *Political Parties and Democracy in Turkey,* ed. Metin Heper and Jacob Landau (London: I. B. Tauris, 1991), 74. The party was outlawed in 1925.

[11] Relevant passages of the party's program are quoted in Yerasimos, "The Monoparty Period," 83.

[12] Dating back to the conclusion of World War I, the Treaty of Lausanne dictated the maintenance of tariffs at their pre–World War I levels, prohibited the levying of differential rates of excise taxes on imported and locally produced commodities, and forced Turkey to eliminate all quantitative trade restrictions.

[13] For details, see Caglar Keyder, *The Definition of a Peripheral Economy: Turkey, 1923–1929* (Cambridge: Cambridge University Press, 1981); and his "The Political Economy of Turkish Democracy," *New Left Review* 115 (May–June 1979), 10.

ers of the state and increasingly impinged on the interests of property-owning classes, producing far more intense elite conflict.

With the lapsing of the Lausanne Treaty and the onset of the great Depression in 1929, the Turkish state initiated a new development program. Based on an ideology of autonomous national development, new policies created a relatively closed economy, emphasized capital accumulation through high taxes and transferring funds out of agriculture, and channeled investment to state-owned industries according to a Soviet-inspired five-year plan.[14] Employing extensive authority to set the price of goods and salaries, state policies imposed new controls and restrictions on private industry, setting the stage for heightened elite conflict.[15] Lacking a party, opponents of etatism worked through members of the government sympathetic to the concerns of private businessmen. The leader of this wing of the elite was Celal Bayar who, on assuming the office of Prime Minister in 1937, urged the replacement of etatism with policies privileging market forces and encouraging the private sector to play a leading role in development.[16]

Although Turkey remained neutral throughout World War II, state policies of resource mobilization caused hardships for almost all sectors of society and exacerbated the growing tensions between the state and the private sector. The National Defense Law of 1940 conferred on the state extensive powers of intervention in the marketplace to control the price and supply of goods, creating a black market that enriched many businessmen. But the position of businessmen was undermined by a capital levy, introduced in 1942, taxing wartime wealth accumulations. Although this tax fell almost exclusively on non-Muslims, the arbitrary character in which it was enacted undermined business confidence in the state and accelerated the erosion of the bureaucrat-bourgeoisie alliance.[17] Finally, wartime policies brought the state and private-sector industry, concentrated in textiles and cement manufacturing, into direct conflict. During the war, the state requisitioned all the output of private-sector textile concerns and resold them at an estimated 80 million Turkish Lira (TL) profit. In addition, the state nationalized two private sector-cement plants for over two years. After the war, private industrialists

[14] The standard text for the period is Korkut Boratav, *Turkiye'de Devletcilik* (Istanbul: Gercek Yayinevi, 1974). For a more concise summary, see his *Turkiye Iktisat Tarihi, 1908–1985* (Istanbul: Gercek Yayinevi, 1988), 45–62.

[15] Omer Celal Sarc, "Economic Policy of the New Turkey," *The Middle East Journal* 2 (October 1948), 444.

[16] See Korel Goymen, "Stages of Etatist Development in Turkey: The Interaction of Single-Party Politics and Economic Policy in the 'Etatist Decade,' 1930–1939," *Gelisme Dergisi* 10 (Winter 1976): 89–114. Bayar would be one of the founders of the Democrat Party in 1946.

[17] Keyder, *State & Class in Turkey*, 112–14.

expressed concern that the state had grown accustomed to monopoly profits gained by control of the private sector, and they feared that the state would "make the wartime situation permanent by expropriation of private plants."[18]

Other government policies created potential popular-class allies for the private sector. In the early 1930s, the government responded to several years of rapidly declining agricultural prices by initiating price-support policies for wheat, paying middle peasants—those who owned sufficient land to market a surplus and used primarily family labor—above-market prices to expand output and create a market for manufactured goods. At the same time, by adding taxes to imports and by maintaining high prices for products of the state manufacturing sector, the state turned the internal terms of trade sharply against the agrarian sector and thus transferred surplus out of the rural sector. At mid-decade, agricultural prices again turned up, boosting rural incomes, but by the end of the decade and persisting through the war years, the state again manipulated terms of trade to acquire a greater share of agricultural surplus at the expense of rural incomes: between 1939 and 1945, as the general price level increased by 450 percent, the government maintained constant purchasing prices for agricultural output.[19] Other state policies of requisitioning food supplies through direct state control of surplus, drafting peasants into the army, requisitioning farm animals, and new taxation policies, such as the Law on Taxation of Agricultural Products of 1943, all combined to create fertile ground for a new social coalition between large farmers, middle peasants, and a new state elite that promised a less heavy-handed approach to the rural sector.[20] Turkey's small working class also suffered during the period 1930–1945, with real wages declining with minimal interruption throughout the period.[21] Legislation enacted in 1936 and 1938 in response to growing labor discontent banned the right to strike or to form labor unions or any organizations based on class.[22]

[18] Robert W. Kerwin, "Private Sector Enterprise in Turkish Industrial Development," *Middle East Journal* 5 (Winter 1951), 30.

[19] Taking 1929 as the base year, by 1933, the internal terms of trade had declined from 100 to 48. Faruk Birtek and Caglar Keyder, "Agriculture and the State: An Inquiry into Agricultural Differentiation and Political Alliances: The Case of Turkey," *Journal of Peasant Studies,* 12 (July 1975), 456, 459.

[20] Sevket Pamuk, "Ikinci Dunya Savasi Yillarinda Devlet, Tarimsal Yapilar ve Bolusum," in *Turkiye'de Tarimsal Yapilar, 1923–2000,* ed. Sevket Pamuk and Zafer Toprak (Ankara: Yurt Yayinlari, 1988), 91–112.

[21] Boratav, *Turkiye Iktisat Tarihi,* 58, estimates that the index of private-sector wages declined from 100 in 1932 to 88 in 1939. Keyder reports a 25 percent decline in real wages in the largest manufacturing firms between 1934 and 1938, and, despite a short increase in 1938 and 1939, a further decline of 40 percent in all wages in Istanbul between 1938 and 1943. *State & Class in Turkey,* 104–5.

[22] William M. Hale, "Labour Unions in Turkey: Progress and Problems," in *Aspects of Modern Turkey,* ed. William M. Hale (London: Bowker, 1976), 61.

While policies that disadvantaged businessmen could be attributed to the exigencies of wartime mobilization, postwar policies that hurt the private sector could be attributed only to an arbitrary and predatory state exercising unrestricted control over the economy. State textile industries, for example, responded to reduced demand by dropping prices below costs, creating heightened competition with private firms. Capitalists again demanded that the state restrict its economic intervention, opening greater space for private initiative.[23] It was not only the competition from expanding public-sector industries that concerned private entrepreneurs, however, but also continued fears that the state would soon expropriate private-sector plants. It was not simply what the state had done, in other words, but what it might do in the future, given its arbitrary nature and lack of accountability.[24] Business insecurity was manifested as "a tendency to avoid investments, to keep capital liquid, and to show interest only in short-term undertakings."[25]

As strained relations with the private sector further eroded the basis of authoritarian rule, the government took steps toward cultivating a mass political base. In 1946, the government repealed the ban on trade unions and, in 1947, enacted more conciliatory labor laws, without, however, granting labor the right to strike or to engage in political activities, but the right to engage in collective bargaining was never enforced.[26] In 1946, the RPP introduced a land-reform bill into parliament that sought to integrate small and landless peasants into a coalition supporting the party. These measures provoked strong opposition and prompted four members of parliament to issue a report expressing strong opposition to land-reform legislation. When such legislation was passed over their opposition, the four began to operate as an opposition movement within the RPP. Faced with tremendous hostility, they left the RPP and established the DP, which quickly won the support of the urban bourgeoisie and rural elites. As Ilkay Sunar put it, the coalition that formed the DP and challenged bureaucratic rule had concluded that challenging state policies was insufficient; a change of government was called for.[27]

Conflict within the Turkish political elite emerged as other circumstances were pushing the RPP to allow multiparty politics. Immediately after the conclusion of World War II, the Soviet Union demanded conces-

[23] Kemal Karpat, *Turkey's Politics: The Transition to a Multi-Party System* (Princeton: Princeton University Press, 1959), 296.

[24] By the end of the decade, "Private Turkish industry [had] come to distrust the government to a considerable extent." Kerwin, "Private Sector Enterprise in Turkish Industrial Development," 29.

[25] Sarc, "Economic Policy of the New Turkey," 445.

[26] Maksut Mumcuoglu, "Political Activities of Trade Unions and Income Distribution," in *The Political Economy of Income Distribution in Turkey,* ed. Ergun Ozbudun and Aydin Ulusan (New York: Holmes & Meier, Inc, 1980), 382.

[27] *State and Society in the Politics of Turkey's Development*, 81.

sions from Turkey, including participation in the supervision of the Bosphorous and Dardanelles Straits and a military presence in eastern Turkey. President Inonu responded by seeking a stronger alliance with the West, an alliance that he believed required Turkey's transition to a democratic polity as well. The identification of democracy with westernization helped ruling bureaucrats accept the new polity, since a fundamental goal of the bureaucratic elite had been the westernization of the country. The bureaucratic elite thus believed that the transition to multiparty politics would deflect threats to their rule from internal dissent and external threat: the passage to a democratic system would channel the discontent of peasants and labor into a manageable framework, and the extension of greater political participation to businessmen would reassure them of the security of their property from state depradations while inducing them to cooperate with the state in the next stage of development.[28] At the same time, Inonu forged a pact with DP leaders, according to which the latter gave assurances that if they came to power, they would not change any fundamental elements of the Kemalist model of modernization.[29] Turkey's elites thus agreed to resolve their conflicts through open elections. The DP won the 1950 elections, obtaining 53 percent of the votes and 408 of 507 parliamentary seats, and on May 22, 1950, the party's leaders assumed control of the government.

The Construction of a Cross-Class Coalitions in Turkey

The DP won the 1950 election by constructing a cross-class coalition, which embraced private businessmen, large and medium-sized rural producers, and workers, predominantly from the public sector. The DP was a center-right party; opposed to state intervention that restricted private economic activity, not to mention private control over property, the party was amenable to healthy doses of state intervention, particularly to assist the private sector, which they envisioned as the leading economic sector. Moreover, the new governing elite used state intervention to construct and sustain their cross-class coalition. This coalition provided a powerful social base from which center-right parties dominated electoral politics

---

[28] For a more extensive discussion of the immediate causes of the transition to democracy, see Cem Erogul, *Demokrat Parti: Tarihi ve Ideolojisi* (Ankara: Imge Kitabevi, 1990), 46–48; and Taner Timur, *Turkiye'de Cok Partili Hayata Gecis* (Istanbul: Iletisim Yayinlari, 1991), 18–27, 38–50.

[29] DP promises on this accord led to Inonu's promulgation of the July 12, 1947, presidential decree that called the DP a loyal opposition party, a move that exposed the DP to the charge that it was not truly an independent political party. See Erogul, *Demokrat Parti*, 30–31.

for more than forty years. Their rule was continuously challenged; inter-elite conflict continued, becoming particularly antagonistic in the late 1950s. Indeed, the RPP supported the 1960 military coup, which initially returned the bureaucratic elite to political power. With the return to democracy in 1963, the Justice Party (JP), a center-right party replacing the outlawed DP, dominated politics, basing its rule on the same cross-class coalition established in 1950 by the DP. Subsequent military interventions in 1971 and 1980 again removed center-right parties from power. But after the return to electoral politics in 1973, center-right parties garnered the majority of electoral votes, the JP remained a powerful party, and only the fragmentation of parties of the right gave their challengers opportunities to form governments.[30] Following the 1980 military coup, the JP was disbanded, but with the return to electoral politics in 1983, two center-right parties, the True Path Party and the Motherland Party, dominated Turkish politics into the 1990s. As we shall see in Chapter 9, however, the Motherland Party attempted to construct a new coalition supportive of a restructured political economy.

Bringing these disparate groups into a single coalition required making side-payments. Ilkay Sunar deftly captures the nature of side-payments in his description of Turkish state intervention in the DP period: "Compelled to enhance private capitalization and populist distribution simultaneously, the Turkish populists had to intervene once and then intervene again, once to enhance private market production, and a second time to counteract the effects of market distribution that would have divided their social base of support."[31] The following sections detail the bargains that attained and retained the allegiance of peasants, workers, and capitalists.

State and Peasants in Turkey, 1950–1980

When discontent with the increasingly arbitrary exercise of power by his government sparked urban unrest in 1958, Prime Minister Adnan Menderes sought solace in the rural basis of DP rule, proclaiming, "Who cares what the intellectuals in Istanbul think, we have the peasants on our side." Menderes may have miscalculated the value of rural support in protecting him from his opponents—peasant loyalty to the regime posed no obstacle to the military coup that overthrew him two years later—but his

---

[30] In the 1973 elections, the RPP gained a plurality with only 33 percent of votes; all center-right parties together received 63 percent of votes.

[31] "The Politics of State Interventionism in 'Populist' Egypt and Turkey," in *Developmentalism and Beyond: Society and Politics in Egypt and Turkey,* ed. Ayse Oncu, Caglar Keyder, and Saad Eddin Ibrahim (Cairo: American University in Cairo Press, 1994), 96.

confidence in rural support was not misplaced, as the DP had conscientiously solicited peasant votes since 1950.

The 1950 DP campaign slogan, "It is enough," promised a new relationship between the state and common citizens. In their campaign speeches to villagers, DP candidates pledged to improve rural standards of living once they reached office.[32] Peasants responded to these pledges with enthusiasm. For the first time, villagers made the connection between the conditions of their quotidian lives and national politics, and they followed election campaigns with great interest. Coming to power with overwhelming peasant support, the DP fulfilled its promises. Indeed, from 1950 to 1980, all center-right political parties solicited peasant support through campaign pledges to pursue favorable policies, pledges that were diligently fulfilled.

Payoffs to peasants took various forms often consisting of private goods or goods that predominantly affected single villages. There are many instances, for example, of the DP building roads, schools, or factories in villages that voted for it, while discriminating against villages that voted for the RPP. This form of payoff has led many observers of Turkish politics to describe the relations of the DP to villagers in conventional patron-client terms.[33]

More generally, however, the relationship of the state to villagers took the form of a class coalition, where the state provided payoffs in the form of public goods that were available to peasants and large farmers regardless of party affiliation. Above-market prices for agricultural goods, for example, provide benefits to all peasants marketing a surplus. Turkey's pro-farmer bias in public policy emerges clearly through comparison of prices paid for agricultural goods with prices paid for industrial goods, a statistic known as *the internal terms of trade*. Boratav concludes that the terms of trade favored rural producers consistently over the period 1960 to 1976, a finding based on Varlier's analysis demonstrating the same trend dating back to 1951.[34] Indeed, detailed studies of prices for particular crops reveal that agrarian prices were raised substantially in periods of intense party competition, and there is some indirect evidence of gov-

---

[32] For examples, see Arnold Leder, "Party Competition in Rural Turkey: Agent of Change or Defender of Traditional Rule?" *Middle Eastern Studies* 15 (January 1979), 86.

[33] Sabri Sayari, "Some Notes on the Beginning of Mass Political Participation in Turkey," in *Political Participation in Turkey*, ed. Engin Akarli and Gabriel Ben-Dor (Istanbul: Bogazici University Press, 1975), 121–33; and Ergun Ozbudun, "Turkey: The Politics of Political Clientelism," in *Political Clientelism, Patronage, and Development*, ed. S. N. Eisenstadt and Rene Lemarchand (Beverly Hills, Calif.: Sage, 1981), 249–68.

[34] Korkut Boratav, "Turkiye'de Populizm: 1962–1976 Donemi Uzerine Notlar," *Yapit* 46 (Ekim 1983), 9; O. Varlier, *Turkiye'de Ic Ticaret Hadleri* (Ankara: Devlet Planlama Taskilati, 1978), 7. During periods of military rule, the terms of trade were turned against the rural sector.

ernments raising prices in anticipation of upcoming elections.[35] Thus, whereas many developing countries extract resources from agriculture to fund industrialization, a strategy Turkish governments pursued in the 1930s and 1940s, Turkish governments after 1950 have consistently used public policy to raise the incomes of rural producers.[36] Rising peasant incomes increased demand for industrial products and so spurred industrialization.[37]

Of course, policies designed to raise rural incomes did not affect all peasants equally. Price-support policies raise the price of food and so disadvantage rural labor or smaller farmers who must purchase some of their food on the market. The unequal distribution of benefits explains the geographic distribution of DP support; the DP consistently garnered more support in coastal regions and in western Anatolia, where large commercial farm and medium-sized peasant holdings producing surplus for the market were concentrated. The RPP, on the other hand, did best in the eastern regions, where it had earlier forged ties with large landlords who maintained domination over sharecropping peasants.[38]

As the state made side-payments to peasants, it removed moneylenders and merchants and local notables from their positions as intermediaries between peasants, markets, and the state; side-payments constituted a direct link between the state and medium-sized peasants. In addition, new administrative agencies replaced local notables as intermediaries between state and peasant.[39] The strategies of survival of peasants became more directly dependent on state policies, and control over peasant incomes proved to be a potent form of social control.[40] Local notables did not disappear, but their capacity to dominate local politics and economics was sharply reduced.[41] Moreover, traditional patrons were increasingly integrated into a national party structure, and their local authority rested "more on their roles as party functionaries than on their control of tradi-

[35] Ustun Erguder, "Politics of Agricultural Price Policy in Turkey," in *Political Economy of Income Distribution in Turkey*, 169–95; and A. A. Gurkan and H. Kasnakoglu, "The Political Economics of Agricultural Price Support in Turkey: An Empirical Assessment," *Public Choice* 70 (1991): 277–98.

[36] Alan Richards, "Introduction," in *Food, States and Peasants: Analyses of the Agrarian Question in the Middle East*, ed. Alan Richards (Boulder: Westview Press, 1986), 9.

[37] Kutlu Somel, "Agricultural Support Policies in Turkey, 1950–1980: An Overview," in *Food, States and Peasants*, 116–18.

[38] Cem Cakmak, "Turkiye'de 1950'li Yillardaki Genel Secimler Uzerine bir Deneme," *Gelisme Dergisi* 13 (1985): 245–83; Sayari, "Some Notes on the Beginning of Mass Political Participation in Turkey," 128–29.

[39] Serdar Turgut, *Demokrat Parti Doneminde Turkiye Ekonomisi: Ekonomik Kalkinma Surecleri Uzerine Bir Deneme* (Ankara: Adalet Matbaacilik, 1991), 154–64.

[40] Nukhet Sirman-Eralp, "Pamuk Uretiminde Aile Isletmeleri," in *Turkiye'de Tarimsal Yapilar*, 209–32.

[41] Mardin, "Center-Periphery Relations," 185.

tional patronage resources. . . ."[42] Over time, a new group of brokers from non-elite backgrounds challenged the traditional notables to assume control of party organizations.[43] Direct state rule, in other words, implied institutional links between state and society, displacing elites whose power stemmed from autonomous control over social resources.

Improvements in rural standards of living, however, were not accompanied by the development of political organizations representing rural interests, and rural producers played a largely passive role in the formulation of policy. The largest interest organization representing rural producers, the Turkish Union of Chambers of Agriculture (TUCA), is a state-sponsored organization and an instrument of control and management of agriculture. Farmers in the highly capitalized southern Mediterranean and western Aegean regions established the most important voluntary organization, the Turkish Federation of Farmers (TFF). But the TFF has not adopted any policy positions different from those of the TUCA and was indeed dominated by farmers also active in the latter organization.[44] In sum, the price of policies beneficial to rural producers has been organizational weakness and passivity in the policy-making process.

State and Organized Labor in Turkey

Three features of state-labor relations resemble state-peasant relations. First, the formation of an alliance with labor was the project of state elites seeking societal support and not a response to the demands of a powerful labor movement.[45] Second, the alliance rested on state provision of material benefits in the form of public goods. Third, labor unions were compelled to accept organizational weakness and political marginality as the price of these material benefits. One important difference is that elements of the labor movement left out of the bargain refused to accept their marginalization, leading to the radicalization and fragmentation of the labor movement and often to intensely conflictual relations with the state.

Although the RPP introduced some measures to cultivate the support of labor in the immediate postwar period, the DP won the support of la-

[42] Sabri Sayari, "Political Patronage in Turkey," in *Patrons and Clients in Mediterranean Societies,* ed. Ernest Gellner and John Waterbury (London: Duckworth, 1977), 108.

[43] Ayse Gunes-Ayata, "Class and Clientelism in the Republican People's Party," in *Turkish State, Turkish Society,* ed. Andrew Finkel and Nukhet Sirman (New York: Routledge, 1990), 159–83.

[44] Ustun Erguder, "Agriculture: The Forgotten Sector," in *Strong State and Economic Interest Groups: The Post–1980 Turkish Experience,* ed. Metin Heper (Berlin: Walter de Gruyter, 1991), 72–3.

[45] Alpaslan Isikli highlights the passivity of Turkish labor until the mid-1960s in his "Wage Labor and Unionization," in *Turkey in Transition,* 309.

bor leaders by encouraging the creation of a single peak labor confederation, Turk-Is, and by promising to grant labor the right to strike. Once in power, however, the DP moved to curtail the organizational effectiveness of Turk-Is by placing institutional constraints on its autonomy and influence and by "denying any credit to union intermediation for even transitory improvements in workers material conditions. . . ."[46] Instead, the DP appealed to workers by providing material benefits directly to them in the form of public policies supplying class-specific goods. DP patronage toward workers conferred real material benefits, including the construction of low-cost housing, the establishment of minimum wage levels, grants of pay bonuses and tax exemptions, and other fringe benefits that amounted to about 25 percent of the salaries of workers in the public sector.[47] Deteriorating economic conditions in the latter half of the decade reversed some of these gains, however, as wages declined by about three percent between 1955 and 1959.[48]

In the 1960s, competition between political parties enhanced the value of labor as an electoral constituency and thus ratcheted up the benefits granted to labor. Despite provisions in the new 1961 Constitution that promised to grant labor significant organizational power, efforts to restrict labor's capacity to participate in decision making again accompanied policies that significantly raised workers' incomes. Turk-Is was forced to agree to state-imposed constraints on its ability to make demands, leadership selection, and internal governance in exchange for official recognition and monopoly representation, as well as important financial subsidies. Turk-Is thus remained highly dependent on the state to satisfy bread-and-butter demands of its members in exchange for political acquiescence. As Sakallioglu summarized, "What the politics of labour incorporation served to secure was union quiescence and compliance in maintaining social peace, by simultaneous enforcement of legal and de facto constraints on one hand, and material inducements on the other."[49] Public policies in the 1960s and 1970s raised wages and expanded employment, and legislation was passed covering new social security payments, pensions, and benefits for health, family, and housing.[50] In 1974, for example, Turkish manufacturing wages were three times higher than the South Korean level; in 1977 they were twice as high; and in 1979, al-

[46] Robert Bianchi, *Interest Groups and Political Development in Turkey* (Princeton: Princeton University Press, 1984), 215.

[47] Umit Cizre-Sakallioglu, "Labour and the State in Turkey," *Middle Eastern Studies* 28 (October 1992), 716.

[48] Korkut Boratav, *Turkiye Iktisat Tarihi*, 92.

[49] Umit Cizre-Sakallioglu, "Labour: The Battered Community," in *Strong State and Economic Interest Groups,* 58.

[50] Cizre-Sakallioglu, "Labour and the State in Turkey," 718.

though the Korean wage level increased and the Turkish decreased, Turkish wages were still 50 percent higher.[51]

Despite these arrangements, state-labor relations became increasingly conflictual in the late 1960s and early 1970s. Membership in Turk-Is was concentrated in the public industrial sector, with the second largest contingent drawn from large-scale private manufacturing plants. In these sectors, side-payments to public-sector managers and industrialists reduced their opposition to improved wages and working conditions. Labor militancy emerged especially in the construction and service sectors and in smaller manufacturing plants, where collective bargaining was opposed by public and private employers. Workers in these sectors became an increasingly important segment of Turkish labor in the 1960s. Consequently, the labor movement fragmented with the founding of new confederations, especially the Confederation of Revolutionary Workers' Syndicates, which opposed Turk-Is's strategy of "abstaining from partisan activity and alliances."[52] The fragmentation of organized labor and growing worker support for the center-left RPP contributed to the polarization of Turkish politics in the 1970s.

State and Business in Turkey

The postwar discontent of workers and peasants lent urgency to the need to placate businessmen chafing under the constraints of etatist economic policy and unhappy about their inability to influence public policy. As the party defending private property, the DP placed a premium on reconciling the interests of the state and of the private sector, but this project was rendered difficult by the need to accommodate the interests of popular classes. After a few years of experimentation, the DP discovered that policies of import-substituting industrialization (ISI) addressed the political function of maintaining a coalition and the economic function of propelling industrial development. The benefits conferred on businessmen by ISI differed in two ways from those granted to popular classes. First, although public goods such as tariffs and exchange-rate policies formed the core of patronage directed to businessmen, private goods such as import licenses and selective access to foreign exchange that directly benefited individual businessmen also played a large role. Second, due to their superior bargaining position, businessmen received greater organizational inducements along with their material benefits. Consequently, Turkish businessmen were organized into a relatively strong corporatist

[51] Keyder, *State and Class in Turkey*, 161.

[52] Bianchi provides extensive coverage of these developments in his *Interest Groups and Political Development in Turkey*, 212–48. Citation from 216.

interest organization that provided businessmen with some input into policy making, and, more important, tremendous leverage over the allocation and distribution of patronage resources within the business community. Subsequent conflicts over access to rents, however, exacerbated cleavages within the business community, resulting in substantial polarization that paralleled the fragmentation of the labor movement and injected considerable instability into Turkish politics in the 1970s.

Between 1950 and 1953, the DP maintained a relatively liberal trade regime and emphasized expanded agricultural production and exports.[53] An ambitious program of agricultural mechanization, road building to facilitate marketing, cheap credits, and high support prices, all helped by the high prices for agricultural products caused by the Korean War, made possible 10 percent annual gross national product growth in the first three years. Merchants made huge profits and accumulated capital for potential future investment during this period.[54] The end of the Korean War and the subsequent decline in the price and quantity of agricultural exports forced a change in this policy. Between 1953 and 1958, the liberal trade regime was replaced with policies to control imports such as licensing, taxation of imports, and multiple foreign exchange rates. By protecting the domestic market, these policies favorably altered business calculations of risk and profitability and thus elicited new industrial investments. Protectionist trade policies also reconciled the interests of businessmen with the other two pillars of the DP's governing coalition, peasants and workers: side-payments made to lower classes expanded the size of the domestic market, making further private investment possible. In this period, the ranks of Turkish industrialists swelled, particularly as merchants began to invest in manufacturing.[55]

The new alliance between state and business was also expressed organizationally. Recognizing the need to consult with businessmen, but loathe to cede any real control over policy making, the RPP began in 1948 to consult with merchants' associations about creating a peak association, the Turkish Union of Chambers of Commerce (Turkiye Odalar Birligi, or TOB), which united the various chambers of commerce and created separate chambers of industry. Provisions of the law establishing the TOB included legal recognition of the association, compulsory membership, codified means of election, and the delegation to the confederation of several administrative functions such as allocating import quotas and de-

[53] I explore the relationship between side-payments and trade policy more extensively in Chapter 5.

[54] Ayse Oncu, "Chambers of Industry in Turkey: An Inquiry into State-Industry Relations as a Distributive Domain," in *Political Economy of Income Distribution in Turkey*, 466.

[55] Alec P. Alexander, "Industrial Entrepreneurship in Turkey: Origins and Growth," *Economic Development and Cultural Change* 8 (July 1960): 349–61.

termining prices. The new law went into effect on March 15, 1950, before the DP came to power. By the time the General Assembly of the TOB was inaugurated, however, the DP had come to power, and the inaugural address was given by the DP Minister of Economy and Commerce. For the next thirty years, the TOB would be closely associated with the DP and its successor party, the Justice Party.

Although the structure of the TOB embraced merchants, industrialists, and commodity brokers, it was created in a period when the vast majority of large private businessmen were merchants and even small merchants enjoyed membership: consequently, merchants dominated the TOB, and its policies generally reflected their interests.[56] This bias in the organizational structure of the TOB privileged merchants and opened cleavages within the business community, particularly between industrialists and importers.[57] The overvalued exchange rate and quotas on imports combined to render importing profitable and virtually risk free. Merchants thus competed with industrialists for access to foreign exchange and import licenses, while working to ensure that quotas were not transformed into absolute restrictions. Although in principle importers and industrialists could have compromised on the allocation of profits accruing from the new trade regime, the hegemony of commercial interests in the TOB supported an uncompromising posture on the part of importers. In response, the Chambers of Industry lobbied the government to transfer control over import licenses to them, arguing that industrialists should directly import the goods they needed for industry, but their protests were largely ineffectual until after 1960.[58]

By 1958, as the Turkish economy went into a tailspin, Turkish industrialists had concluded that successful industrialization—and profits for industrialists—required renegotiation of the bargain linking private businessmen to the state. Industrialists lobbied for the replacement of ad hoc ISI policies with a project of planned ISI that would devote more attention to promoting private-sector industrialization. The military officers behind the 1960 coup supported this project, and so, beginning in 1963, comprehensive five-year plans were drafted that included all sectors of the economy but paid particular attention to industrial development in which the public sector would complement the private sector by investing in more capital-intensive industries providing industrial inputs. The new ISI regime clearly benefited industrialists over importers: customs duties, access to foreign exchange, and guaranteed deposit rates on imports

---

[56] Henri J. Barkey, *The State and the Industrialization Crisis in Turkey* (Boulder, Colo.: Westview Press, 1990), 111; and Oncu, "Chambers of Industry," 459.

[57] This was only one of several overlapping cleavages. For more extensive discussion, see Barkey, *State and the Industrialization Crisis in Turkey,* 109–48.

[58] Oncu, "Chambers of Industry in Turkey," 465–67.

were all more favorable to industrialists, and loan rates for industrialists were also kept below the rate of inflation.[59]

Despite this policy bias, the TOB continued to be an arena of competition between industrialists, commercial interests, and the state. While broad policy favored industrialists, the merchant-dominated TOB controlled the implementation of policy, such as allocating foreign exchange and altering the quota lists that determined the level of importable goods. Industrialists, for example, preferred placing goods they produced on the restricted import list, whereas merchants preferred to keep them on the limited import list.[60] Control of the TOB became the object of intense political contest because business profitability was predicated on access to state benefits and control of the TOB provided the most direct access to the state.

By combining policies biased in favor of industry with a representational organization biased in favor of commerce, the state guaranteed that the instrument it had established to exert control over the bourgeoisie would be transformed into a conduit channeling private-sector cleavages into the state itself. Eventually, as these separate competing wings of private business publicly voiced their complaints, development strategy took on a more overtly political character, contributing to the overall fragmentation of the Turkish polity in the 1970s. As the private sector splintered, the alliance between businessmen and the JP became unmanageable.[61] The resulting political polarization and attendant private-sector mistrust of Prime Minister Suleyman Demirel led to the abandonment, in 1974, of the 1970 stabilization program that had temporarily put Turkey on the path of export-led growth. By the end of the 1970s, political cleavages within the bourgeoisie were leading to a proliferation of political parties and interest groups. As Eralp summarizes, "What had in the late seventies been a private struggle waged between various groups within the bourgeoisie under the umbrella issue of state regulation, transformed itself into a publicly waged war between organized bodies."[62]

State-business relations take on even greater complexity when we consider small businessmen—retail merchants, small enterprises employing low-wage labor and incorporating a rudimentary division of labor, and artisan production based on family labor—who were almost completely ex-

---

[59] Barkey, *State and Industrialization Crisis in Turkey*, 59–63, 70–74.

[60] Atila Eralp, "The Politics of Turkish Development Strategy," in *Turkish State, Turkish Society*, 225–26.

[61] The most important organizational expression of this fragmentation was the formation, in 1971, of the Turkish Industrialists' and Businessmen's Association (TUSIAD) by the twelve leading Turkish industrialists. For details, see Yesim Arat, "Politics and Big Business: Janus-Faced Link to the State," in *Strong State and Economic Interest Groups*, 135–41.

[62] "Politics of Turkish Development Strategy," 234.

cluded from the center-right coalition. Some members of the Turkish petit bourgeoisie benefited from modernization. Large-scale production of consumer durables, for example, created the need for small repair workshops and the proliferation of small production workshops in new fields of activity.[63] Furthermore, rising peasant incomes created new demand for artisan products and expanded markets for small merchants. Despite these gains, however, the petit bourgeoisie were the primary losers in the development process; their exclusion from the social coalition initially forged by the DP burdened them with organizational weakness and political marginalization for which they received no material compensation. Consequently, the Turkish petit bourgeoisie have been the major social group sustaining the Islamist revival challenging the state in Turkey.[64]

The main representative of the Anatolian petit bourgeoisie constituting the bulk of TOB membership was Necmettin Erbakan, who engineered a surprising electoral victory and became Secretary General of the TOB in 1969. Erbakan gained office by promising a more equitable distribution of state patronage and industrial policy that would favor smaller Anatolian businessmen. After Prime Minister Demirel removed him from his position, Erbakan became, in 1972, the unofficial leader of a new party, the National Salvation Party (NSP).[65] The NSP stressed two themes: securing the moral and material progress of Turkey through the adoption of an Islamic state and reordering the process of development to benefit small businessmen. On the latter theme, the party program called for greater respect for private property, the cessation of wasteful expenditure and exploitation, fair taxation (i.e., more taxes to be paid by big business), and more balanced social and geographical development. This last measure was a response to the concentration of large capital in the region surrounding Istanbul and to the relative neglect of Anatolian capital and businessmen. In the 1973 National Assembly elections, the NSP was

[63] Sencer Ayata, "Economic Growth and Petty Commodity Production in Turkey," *Social Analysis* 20 (December 1986), 81.

[64] Bianchi, *Interest Groups and Political Development in Turkey*, 250, writes that petit bourgeois "feelings of powerlessness are compounded by the preoccupation of the major parties with the problems of labor and big business, leaving the [petit bourgeoisie] with no reliable political allies other than those who carry the label of religious extremism." Of course, the resurgence of Islamism in both Syria and Turkey is expressed in a range of actions far wider than direct challenges to the state. More broadly, we can consider the Islamic resurgence to be an example of what Richart Rorty has called the contest of vocabularies. Vocabularies are methods of redescribing "lots and lots of things in new ways, until you have created a pattern of linguistic behavior which will tempt the rising generation to adopt it, thereby causing them to look for appropriate new forms of nonlinguistic behavior, for example, the adoption of . . . new social institutions." All modern Islamist movements, then, represent "a contest between an entrenched vocabulary which has become a nuisance and a half-formed new vocabulary which vaguely promises new things." See his *Contingency, Irony, and Solidarity* (Cambridge: Cambridge University Press, 1989), 9.

[65] Barkey, *State and the Industrialization Crisis*, 131–32.

the third largest party, receiving just under 12 percent of the votes and 48 of 450 seats. The majority of NSP supporters came from the lesser-developed provinces in Central and Eastern Anatolia. More specifically, the NSP garnered the most support in towns with a population over 100,000 in the least developed provinces of the country and in sections of larger cities populated by small-scale artisan-traders.[66]

Political Elites and Bureaucrats in Turkey

As self-designated agents of modernization since the nineteenth century, bureaucrats had assimilated an ethos legitimating their monopoly of national political power. Throughout the Ataturk era, the bureaucracy remained "a closely-knit elite corps, in which the traditional system of bonds of school, family, and elitist solidarity still operated despite increasingly formal laws and regulations."[67] These informal techniques of bureaucratic cohesion were reinforced by a series of laws and regulations insulating the civil service from interference by the political executive. The DP came to power opposing both the developmental project pursued by the Kemalist elite and the increasingly arbitrary rule that allowed the elite to threaten the interests of property-owning elites. The new DP elite thus worked to shift the locus of political power from the bureaucracy to the party-based government, resulting in ongoing antagonistic relations between the elected political elite and their bureaucratic agents.[68]

The DP (and its successor, the JP) pursued a three-pronged strategy to transfer political power from the bureaucracy to the party-based polity.[69] First, the incomes of civil servants, which had been quite high before 1950, were allowed to lag behind inflation to make the civil service a less attractive occupation. Between 1950 and 1960, while the wholesale price index rose from 97 to 255 (1948 = 100), the index of real income of the highest level of civil servants decreased from 103 to 73 (1948 = 100), and the real income of middle-level civil servants decreased from 103 to 75.[70] Moreover, the DP enacted legislation permitting the dismissal of civil ser-

---

[66] On the demographics of NSP support, see Jacob M. Landau, "The National Salvation Party," *Asian and African Studies* 11 (1976): 20–27. As Turkish politics became increasingly polarized in the 1970s, even the small number of NSP parliamentary deputies became important, and so the party joined several short-lived coalition governments. The NSP was disbanded after the 1980 coup, and, with the subsequent return to democracy, was reborn as the Welfare Party.

[67] Metin Heper, *The State Tradition in Turkey* (Northgate, England: Eothen Press, 1985), 68.

[68] Leslie L. Roos and Noralou Roos, *Managers of Modernization: Organizations and Elites in Turkey, 1950–1969* (Cambridge: Harvard University Press, 1971).

[69] Metin Heper, "The State and Debureaucratization: The Case of Turkey," *International Social Science Journal* 126 (November, 1990), 609.

[70] Figen Altug, "Devlet Memurlarinin Mali Durumlarindaki Gelismeler, 1948–1960 Donemi," *Bilim ve Toplum* 13 (Bahar 1981), 72.

vants from their executive positions.[71] Second, the DP excluded civil servants from policy making by ignoring their counsel, repealing decisions that ran counter to DP preferences, and circumscribing their sphere of influence. In particular, by establishing clientelist relations with businessmen, government ministers circumvented the bureaucracy.[72] Finally, the DP attempted to create an alternative structure of economic administration more firmly under their control. In particular, the DP expanded the State Economic Enterprises, staffed with their appointees, and established the Middle East Technical University to train bureaucrats faithful to the DP program.[73]

Bureaucrats defended their prerogatives tenaciously. Following the 1960 coup, for example, the 1961 Constitution created a number of autonomous "constitutional" agencies staffed by bureaucrats, while bureaucrats in the Ministry of Finance worked to impede projects assisting the private sector.[74] Bureaucrats made a similar comeback following the 1971 military intervention. Indeed, into the early 1970s, regulations still hampered the JP from staffing the existing bureaucracy with its supporters.[75] A new phase in the gradual erosion of bureaucratic autonomy began with the coalition governments that ruled Turkey after the 1973 elections. The RPP was the largest party in the 1973 elections, based on a new, left-populist position appealing to workers and urban small merchants. As the political preferences of individual civil servants diversified, relations with the RPP became strained, and the bureaucracy gradually lost cohesion. Consequently, new coalition governments were able to staff the bureaucracies with their own followers. In the negotiations that created coalition governments, each party was given control over a different ministry, fragmenting the bureaucracy. In addition, the parties relied heavily on unrestrained patronage, not only reshuffling civil servants but also creating thousands of new posts with little attention paid to meritocratic appointment. Between January 17, 1978, and August 1, 1978, during a coalition of the RPP with Independents, 206 high-ranking civil servants were removed from their posts and replaced with 320 new appointees; under a

[71] Metin Heper, "The Recalcitrance of the Turkish Public Bureaucracy to 'Bourgeois Politics,'" *Middle East Journal* 30 (Autumn 1976), 489.

[72] As one businessman related the effect of this on the bureaucracy, "When the Central Bank says that the funds are not available, the minister gives orders to transfer funds from one budget to the other. This leads to interferences at all levels of the bureaucratic process. . . . the institutions cannot function under these circumstances, the State Planning Organization cannot function, the Treasury and the Central Bank cannot function." Quoted in Ayse Bugra, *State and Business in Modern Turkey: A Comparative Study* (Albany: SUNY Press, 1994), 164.

[73] Heper, *State Tradition in Turkey*, 111.

[74] Heper, "Recalcitrance of the Turkish Public Bureaucracy," 489.

[75] Metin Heper, "Negative Bureaucratic Politics in a Modernizing Context: The Turkish Case," *Journal of South Asian and Middle Eastern Studies* 1 (1977), 81.

JP minority government that lasted from December 1, 1979, to May 1, 1980, the corresponding figures were 1,223 and 1,367.[76]

Over a thirty-year period, the politicization of the Turkish state apparatus was completed. This politicization even extended into the police and security services, effectively crippling the state. In the 1980s, when Turgut Ozal attempted to transform Turkey's precocious Keynesian state, one of his first tasks was to recast the relationship between political elites and the state bureaucracy to create a bureaucratic apparatus capable of administering his new economic strategy.

This chapter uses the Turkish case to illustrate the first two stages of my argument, the independent variable and the first causal mechanism. The independent variable is the emergence of intense and escalating interelite conflict over the proper relationship of centralized state authority to decentralized economic activity. In Turkey, that conflict dates back to the nineteenth century but took on new dimensions during the 1930s industrialization drive, which added burdens to social groups that had previously been allied to the regime, and particularly during the 1940s, when almost all social classes were alienated from the regime by the harsh economic policies implemented during World War II. The resulting deterioration of social support for the Kemalist regime of the RPP strained beyond repair the political arrangements undergirding mediated state rule. In response, political elites prepared new coalitional strategies. The second half of this chapter addresses the formation of new social coalitions as the first causal mechanism of the overall argument, linking the independent variable to the intervening variable—the new institutional profile of the unmediated state. In building a new, more inclusive coalition, the DP struck a bargain with family peasants, organized labor in the public sector, and large businessmen but largely excluded civil servants and the petit bourgeoisie. In the process, state elites established the new political and economic arrangements composing the Turkish political economy. These arrangements are the subject of Chapter 5. But first, the emergence of elite conflict and state building in Syria is surveyed in Chapter 4.

---

[76] Heper, *State Tradition in Turkey*, 115.

CHAPTER FOUR

Constructing Coalitions and Building States: Syria

In this chapter, the same ground is covered for Syria that was covered in Chapter 3 for Turkey. The Syrian mediated state, the emergence of inter-elite conflict over the proper relationship of the state to the economy, and the resolution of that conflict through the incorporation of popular classes into a cross-class coalition are discussed. The dynamics of elite conflict and conflict resolution differed in Syria, where an antioligarchic movement overthrew a state dominated by landed elites. Consequently, important features of the Syrian political economy that resulted from coalition building and the transition to an unmediated state differ from features of the Turkish political economy. Two features stand out: Turkey went from an authoritarian to a democratic regime, and Syria went from a parliamentary to an authoritarian regime. Furthermore, whereas Turkey went from a statist development policy that threatened the private sector with nationalization to a development policy that assigned a major role to the private sector, Syria went from private-sector–led development to a statist development project by way of nationalization and land reform.

For explaining some dependent variables, or for closely narrating the contemporary history of Syria and Turkey, these differences might matter greatly, but for the purposes of theorizing outcomes of economic development, they do not. In both Syria and Turkey, intense elite conflict caused state transformation to occur simultaneously with popular-sector incorporation into cross-class coalitions. The creation of cross-class coalitions through high levels of side-payments has similar consequences for late-developing nations despite differences in political and property regimes. This is discussed in subsequent chapters. The goal of this chapter is simply to chronicle the construction of a cross-class coalition in Syria.

The key actors in the pages that follow are state elites and social classes, not ethnic groups or religious sects. This cast of characters requires some justification, for many studies of modern Syria deny the salience of class analysis and claim that the fundamental building block of Syrian politics is some form of identity—ethnicity, clan, or religious sect—and that Syrian politics consists of ongoing competition for political or economic advantage between groups formed on ascriptive identities.[1] The two approaches are not, however, mutually exclusive, and there are grounds for conceptual cooperation. It is perfectly possible to agree that the Syrian political elite is predominantly Alawi, and that being Alawi confers certain privileges (and risks), without drawing any conclusions about the substance or the style of state-society relations. In other words, a state dominated by men of Alawi origins is only nominally an Alawi state and need not necessarily be construed as a state in which power is exercised on behalf of the Alawi community.[2]

A central story in late-developing societies is conflict over the proper relationship between the state and the economy. That does not mean that ethnic cleavages or religious differences are unimportant; in many respects they are important, and a full account of Syrian political life could not ignore them. There is no doubt, for example, that the key positions in the Asad regime, particularly in the security services, are held by men of Alawi origin.[3] But there is no reason to believe that positions on state-economy relations correlate with ethnicity or religious differences. Furthermore, when one looks at public policies, as we do in the second half of the chapter, it will be clear that critical policies are directed toward social classes, not primordial groups. The argument, then, is not that all of Syrian politics can be reduced to class politics but that for the purposes of analyzing economic development, we can largely ignore issues of ethnicity and religious differences. The resulting analysis is *not* a model of Syr-

---

[1] The classic example is Nikolaos Van Dam, *The Struggle for Power in Syria: Sectarianism, Regionalism, and Tribalism in Politics, 1961–1978* (New York: St. Martin's Press, 1979). The debate between identity-based and interest-based approaches is well illustrated in Volker Perthes, "The Political Sociology of Syria: A Bibliographical Essay," *Beirut Review* 4 (Fall 1992): 105–13; Joshua Landis, "The Political Sociology of Syria Reconsidered: A Response to Volker Perthes," *Beirut Review* 5 (Spring 1993): 143–51; and Perthes "Volker Perthes Responds to Joshua Landis," *Beirut Review* 6 (Fall 1993): 137–40.

[2] Daniel Pipes argues without much evidence that the Syrian state deliberately serves the interests of the greater Alawi community. See his *Greater Syria: The History of an Ambition* (New York: Oxford University Press, 1990), 176–77. For a more careful and detailed exploration of this topic, see Alisdair Drysdale, "The Regional Equalization of Health Care and Education Since the Ba`thi Revolution," *International Journal of Middle East Studies* 13 (1981): 93–111.

[3] For a survey, see Hanna Batatu, "Some Observations on the Social Roots of Syria's Ruling, Military Group and the Causes for Its Dominance," *Middle East Journal* 35 (Summer 1982): 331–44.

ian politics, but rather the application of a conceptual framework to the Syrian case.

The Meditated Oligarchic State in Syria, 1946–1963

Local elites played a central role in ruling Ottoman Syria.[4] Throughout the eighteenth and nineteenth centuries, local elites purchased large tracts of land and negotiated tenancy or sharecropping agreements with peasants. After 1920, French colonial officials considered creating an unmediated state. But facing widespread unrest in the 1920s, culminating in the large-scale revolt of 1925–1927, the French colonial administration struck a new bargain with local elites, recreating a mediated state through which it ruled Syria until independence.[5] From independence until 1963, the structure of the Syrian state continued to be one of indirect rule. Patron-client ties connected peasants to traditional notables, who were in turn connected to magnate politicians in the cities.[6] Elite control over land conferred control over people and, thus, political power. Consequently, Syrian politics, as depicted by Raymond Hinnebusch, "Was an urban game of competition for the spoils of office between small groups of landlord-notables and their followers. With the majority of the populace largely outside the political arena, the traditional elite presided over a narrowly based fragile state incapable of coping with . . . the internal crisis it soon faced."[7]

Agrarian elites transformed their control of land and people into political power in a number of ways. Primarily, they mobilized patronage ties to ensure their election to parliament.[8] Control of parliament allowed the agrarian elite to pass legislation deterring social mobilization while

[4] See Albert Hourani's seminal article, "Ottoman Reform and the Politics of Notables," in *The Beginnings of Modernization in the Middle East: The Nineteenth Century,* ed. William R. Polk and Richard L. Chambers (Chicago: University of Chicago Press, 1968), 41–68. For a revision of Hourani's thesis that still stresses the features of a mediated state, see Elizabeth Thompson, "Ottoman Political Reform in the Provinces: The Damascus Advisory Council, 1844–45," *International Journal of Middle East Studies* 25 (August 1993): 457–75.

[5] See Elizabeth Thompson, "Engendering the Nation: Statebuilding, Imperialism and Women in Syria and Lebanon, 1920–1945," Ph.D. dissertation, Columbia University, 1995, 76–132. See also Wajih Kuthrani, *Bilad al-Sham: al-Sukkan, al-Iqtisad, wa al-Siyasa al-Fransiyya* (Beirut: Maʿahad al-Inma al-Arabi, 1980), 119.

[6] The best study of the urban notables who dominated Syrian politics until 1963 is Philip S. Khoury, *Syria and the French Mandate: The Politics of Arab Nationalism, 1920–1945* (Princeton: Princeton University Press, 1987).

[7] Raymond A. Hinnebusch, *Peasant and Bureaucracy in Baʿthist Syria: The Political Economy of Rural Development* (Boulder, Colo.: Westview Press, 1989), 17.

[8] On the composition of members of the Syrian parliament during the post-independence period, see R. Bayley Winder, "Syrian Deputies and Cabinet Ministers, 1919–1959," 2 parts, *Middle East Journal* 16 (Autumn 1962): 407–29, and 17 (Winter-Spring, 1963): 35–54.

impeding the state bureaucracy from pursuing projects jeopardizing their elite privileges. Supplementing this, they worked to place their own clients into the state bureaucracy. Finally, they manipulated family ties to create alliances with the growing manufacturing bourgeoisie to forestall a Latin American–style, antioligarchic movement.

The Emergence of Inter-Elite Conflict in Syria

Conflict over fundamental political-economic issues and the role of the state in resolving them fueled elite conflict in Syria. Expanded state economic intervention was in large part a response to swelling demands from various social classes. The voices of property-owning classes were the loudest, as both agrarian elites and owners of industrial and commercial capital sought state assistance for economic expansion. During the French Mandate, economic policies largely served French interests. Syrian businessmen established factories in the 1930s, but French policies, including pegging the Syrian lira to the French franc, creating a customs union with Lebanon, and neglecting infrastructure spending, left the Syrian bourgeoisie with great visions but little capacity to further capitalist development.[9] After independence, the Syrian property-owning classes perceived great economic opportunities, but achieving their goals required large public investments in infrastructure, rationalization of the legal system, and state assistance in the creation of credit networks and in controlling labor.[10]

In the period 1946–1950, state intervention was restricted to broad areas in which there was general agreement on the need for state intervention, and there were no clear winners and losers. These early state projects, however, elicited new demands for state intervention, to provide goods entailing a more politically divisive distribution of costs and benefits. In the 1950s, compelling the state to take action was no longer the sole aim of political activity; increasingly, major actors sought to harness state power on behalf of more partisan projects that pinned costs on other major actors. Political conflict in Syria, then, was fundamentally an issue of defining the allocation of costs and benefits of increased state economic intervention.[11]

[9] See Khoury, *Syria and the French Mandate*, 85-93.

[10] Yahya Sadowski, "Political Power and Economic Organization in Syria: The Course of State Intervention, 1946–1958," Ph.D. dissertation, University of California, Los Angeles, 1984, esp. Chap. 3.

[11] In addition to Sadowski, "Political Power and Economic Organization," this account of elite conflict in Syria relies heavily on Steven Heydemann, "Successful Authoritarianism: The Social and Structural Origins of Populist Authoritarian Rule in Syria, 1946–1963," Ph.D. dissertation, University of Chicago, 1990.

Unlike Turkish lower classes, Syrian subordinate classes were not disinterested and passive bystanders to elite conflict, and rival positions over how to address the emerging "social question" increasingly influenced the terms of political conflict. The twin issues of defining the proper boundaries and functions of the state and addressing the grievances of lower classes intersected and fueled conflict. While the Syrian upper classes were lobbying state officials and political parties to enact new policies, workers and peasants were organizing to advance their own interests. Moreover, political parties established by middle-class intellectuals began to incorporate lower-class interests into their visions of a new Syrian political economy. Over the course of the 1950s, all sectors of Syrian society increasingly targeted control of the state as the necessary condition for either maintaining the status quo or reshaping Syrian society and economy. Participation in policymaking ceased to be the exclusive monopoly of the traditional elite, and a new elite claiming to represent popular classes emerged as a rival to the agrarian oligarchs. Issues of economic policy were quickly translated into questions about the basic structures of the Syrian polity.

Despite the efforts of the agrarian elite to consolidate their position, their control over the state became increasingly tenuous over the next decade. With the expansion of state regulatory activities, it became necessary to recruit new civil servants from among the educated middle classes, eroding the tight connections that had previously existed between economic elites and bureaucrats. Middle-class civil servants increasingly identified their interests—and the national interest—in opposition to the hegemony of the agrarian oligarchy, and these new bureaucratic cadres attempted to enact civil service legislation that would forge a meritocratic bureaucracy, insulating administrators from the demands of the traditional elite.[12] At the same time, however, bureaucrats from middle-class backgrounds became highly politicized and were often affiliated with anti-elite movements. More substantively, the traditional elite clashed with state administrators over issues such as the allocation of tax burdens to finance growing state economic intervention.[13] Thus, in the course of the 1950s, tension between the agrarian oligarchy and large sectors of the civil service reduced the control of the former over the state apparatus.

Between 1950 and 1963, three alternative political-economic projects jockeyed for supremacy. The first of these was the continued domination of the traditional agrarian elite, which required that notables continue to dominate the state apparatus and the peasantry. But reformist parties opposed this outcome. These parties increasingly gained seats in parliament

---

[12] For the details of these reforms, see Ralph Crow, "The Civil Service of Independent Syria," Ph.D. dissertation, University of Michigan, 1964.

[13] Heydemann, "Successful Authoritarianism," 73.

and were strengthened by the extraparliamentary activities of peasants and workers to gain rights and make demands on the state. Thus, an alternative political settlement was some form of reformist coalition that neither included nor sought to dispossess completely the traditional elite. In the first half of the 1950s, members of the Syrian elite made a tentative commitment to the creation of a social pact "based on the integration of peasants into the country's economic life and a more limited accommodation of workers' organizational and economic demands."[14] The key actors in this potential coalition were a handful of government officials from non-elite backgrounds, some members of the bourgeoisie who saw Syria's future as linked to the creation of a large domestic market, and the Ba`th party.[15]

Khalid al-Azm was the most visible of Syria's reformist bourgeoisie and the leader of a group of independent parliamentary deputies known as the Democratic Bloc. Al-Azm believed that because private capitalists were ill-equipped to undertake the costly social overhead projects necessary for economic growth, further development would require close public-private cooperation. The program of the loosely knit group of businessmen that he headed was to modernize the traditional system of rule and advance industrialization under the leadership of the bourgeoisie but with substantial state assistance. This project entailed broadening the political coalition through some political concessions to labor and enacting moderate measures addressing peasant needs for land, education, and an improved standard of living.[16]

During the 1950s, al-Azm and his collaborators often worked in tandem with the Ba`th party, creating a reformist alliance that bears resemblance to the modernizing, antioligarchic alliances that pursued populist incorporation and import-substituting industrialization in Latin America. In the 1960s, the Ba`th party became associated with radical, authoritarian regimes seeking socialist transformation at home and an anti-imperialist, anti-Zionist foreign policy. But the Ba`th initially advocated only moderate reforms, contesting the 1947 elections, for example, on a platform calling for direct elections of deputies, neutral poll watchers, and the abolition of the system of allocating parliamentary seats to religious groups. Over the course of the 1950s, the Ba`th party increasingly

[14] Heydemann, "Successful Authoritarianism," is the best discussion of this reformist coalition. Quotation from page 48.

[15] On reformist bureaucrats, see Sadowski, "Political Power and Economic Organization," 237–38. On smaller landowners and their links to the Ba`th party, see C. Ernest Dawn, "Ottoman Affinities of 20th Century Regimes in Syria," in *Palestine in the Late Ottoman Period: Political, Social, and Economic Transformation,* ed. David Kushner (Leiden: E. J. Brill, 1986), 183–85.

[16] On al-Azm's political and economic program, see Tabitha Petran, *Syria* (London: Ernest Benn, 1972), 107, 113.

stressed social reform, especially after the party joined with Akram Hawrani's Arab Socialist Party, which had begun to mobilize peasants against large landowners in the region of Hama.[17] The peak of their reformist influence came after the September 1954 elections when 16 of 30 Ba`thist candidates were elected to Parliament along with 50 independents (most of whom were affiliated with al-Azm's Democratic Bloc) who supported reform of Syria's political economy. Consequently, the conservative government of Sabri al-Asali, needing the support of the reformers to win a vote of confidence, accepted social welfare reforms advocated by the Ba`th, while the latter was able to place its adherents into government positions.[18]

The reformist coalition, however, was never able to garner enough support and influence to decisively translate its program into policy. Although the Ba`th and the progressive independents were able to place supporters in the government apparatus, and they were able to make or break governments, they could not make a new social pact. Landed interests remained opposed to land reform, the extension of economic and political rights to peasants, or new taxes on exports to fund public programs and were able to block reformist initiatives while passing legislation protecting landlord de facto ownership of state domains. As Petran summarized the stalemate, "Displacement of the old guard had begun, but the new forces were not united and no party was strong enough to impose its control. The old guard still held its command posts, as Azm's inability to form a government representing the modernizing forces demonstrated."[19] Furthermore, because reformist parties perceived oligarchic control of parliament as illegitimately obtained, parliament itself was increasingly seen as an illegitimate mechanism for political change, fueling polarization and the radicalization of the opposition. Reflecting this radicalization, Marxist intellectuals and military officers from provincial rural towns who were less inclined to compromise with the oligarchy began to play a more visible role within the Ba`th party. In addition, between 1954 and 1958, the Syrian Communist Party gained noticeable popular support.[20] In response, even members of the bourgeoisie who initially supported reform became increasingly concerned that social re-

[17] See John F. Devlin, *The Ba`th Party: A History from Its Origins to 1966* (Stanford: Hoover Institution Press, 1976), 28–52.

[18] Ibid., 68–70.

[19] Petran, *Syria,* 108.

[20] One should not exaggerate the depths of popular support for the Communists: in 1958, they had only one seat in parliament, held by their leader, Khalid Baqdash. Their strength came instead from three sources: approximately 18,000 well-organized cadres; important allies within the state, including the Minister of Defense and the Chief of Staff; and the capacity—real or perceived—to tap political resources in Moscow. See Sadowski, "Political Power and Economic Organization," 271–72.

forms, once initiated, would spiral out of control and eventually threaten their own property rights and claims on economic surplus. The bourgeoisie elected to continue to support landed interests despite their knowledge that this would act as a drag on development.[21] The inability to reach a compromise, in other words, altered the preferences of major actors, making future compromise and a negotiated transition to new arrangements highly unlikely.

In 1958, the stalemate between the landed elite and the reformist alliance was temporarily broken and political conflict was temporarily muted by a surprising move: the dissolution of the Syrian Arab Republic and the creation of a political union with Egypt, the United Arab Republic (UAR). Ostensibly dedicated to advancing the cause of Arab nationalism, Syrians supported the union, however reluctantly, for a variety of reasons. The military officers who took the lead in pushing for union represented opposing tendencies; some supported the Ba`th, some the Communists, and some the conservative military officer Shishakli associated with the landed elite. Support for union came from politicians and military officers who saw union with Egypt as the only way to avert civil war.[22] Indeed, in the months before the union, the Ba`th party had begun to cooperate with the oligarchic parties out of fear of increasing Communist influence.[23]

Syrians might have perceived union with Egypt as the remedy to their domestic polarization, but that is not how Egyptian President Nasir understood the situation. In his view, ending Syrian political instability, which he saw as potentially threatening to his own tenure in office, required more than just political union; it required the imposition of a new political-economic formula that would eradicate the causes of instability at their source. To this end, one of the first decrees of the new UAR was issued on March 13, 1958, dissolving all political parties. In September 1958, the UAR government enacted the Agrarian Reform and Agricultural Relations Laws.[24] In July 1961, Nasir issued the "Socialist Decrees," applied to both Egypt and Syria. In Syria, the decrees nationalized banks, insurance companies, and a small number of industrial firms. Finally, the UAR regime established the foundations for a comprehensive system of corporatist organization of business, peasants, and labor.

[21] Heydemann, "Successful Authoritarianism," 142–74.

[22] Chief of Staff Colonel Afif al-Bizri, who was affiliated with the Communists, remarked, "We have a choice between Nasser and a civil war which may restore imperialism." Cited in Sadowski, "Political Power and Economic Organization," 273.

[23] Malcolm Kerr, *The Arab Cold War: Gamal `Abd al-Nasir and His Rivals, 1958-1970,* 3d ed. (London: Oxford University Press, 1971), 10.

[24] Implementation of the measures was scarcely carried out, with less than 5 percent of the land subject to reform actually distributed to about 5,000 families. See Petran, *Syria,* 136–37.

Nasir's reforms created many enemies and few friends. Over time, peasants might have been mobilized as support for the UAR regime, but in the interim, Nasir faced the opposition not only of the old landowning and commercial classes, but of the Ba'th party itself, which, contrary to its expectations in 1958, was thoroughly excluded from power. Even army officers who had initially supported the union were alienated by policies subordinating the Syrian officer corps to Egyptian control. Thus, when a group of military officers acting in concert with the traditional oligarchy staged a coup on September 1961, Nasir had no allies to draw on.

Although most of Nasir's policies were reversed between September 1961 and the Ba'th party coup of 1963, his regime left an important legacy in Syria. Most important, he experimented with and demonstrated the feasibility of a third potential settlement of Syria's political-economic conflicts: rule by an antioligarchic movement with the support of popular classes. Furthermore, by dissolving civil associations and establishing controls over labor and peasants, the UAR government created political space within which the Ba'th party could operate more freely in 1963.[25] It was simply easier for the Ba'th to remove its opponents from power and establish control of state, society, and economy in 1963 than it would have been in 1958 when its competitors were still organized and active.

Constructing a Cross-Class Coalition in Syria

The 1963 coup was not made by the party itself, but by a small core of military officers who were members of the Ba'th. They did so without the assistance of the older civilian leaders of the party and without the participation of the popular classes they claimed to represent. After the coup, as Ba'thist leaders assumed control of the government, the old civilian founders of the party, with their mystical attachments to the Arab nation, their respect for private property, and their willingness to compromise with the urban and rural bourgeoisie, still held important positions. But the party now contained diverse factions that disagreed on issues ranging from whether to pursue immediate union with Egypt to, more important, the related issues of building domestic alliances and promoting economic development, as younger, more radical members vied for power on behalf of pursuing more fundamental socialist transformation.[26] Programmatic cleavages overlapped with factional, often ethnic struggles for

[25] Heydemann, "Successful Authoritarianism," 227–39.

[26] The best account of these various factions and their struggle for supremacy is found in Itamar Rabinovitch, *Syria under the Ba'th, 1963–66: The Army-Party Symbiosis* (Jerusalem: Israel University Press, 1972).

power within the regime, producing successive internal coups. In 1966, the old guard lost their formal positions in the party and the more radical elements consolidated their control over the state apparatus. In 1970, these party members were pushed out of power by military officers who successfully incorporated Syrian businessmen into a cross-class alliance with peasants and workers.

Because the struggle for power by rival factions within the regime is already well covered in the literature, the remainder of this chapter discusses exclusively the construction of the Syrian cross-class coalition.[27]

State and Peasant in Syria

Just as the incorporation of peasants into a cross-class coalition created a durable basis for the dominance of center-right parties in Turkey, the construction of an alliance with Syrian peasants created a stable basis for the new state elites of the center-left Ba`th party. In particular, the implementation of land reform stripped the old elite of a major source of social power while wedding peasant loyalties to the new regime. The state forged a tacit bargain with peasants, linking state power to the welfare of peasants: in return for eradicating their dependence on traditional elites and providing for their welfare, the state called on the peasantry to accept a new position of dependence on the state, to provide symbolic support through participation in the state's legitimating institutions, to provide its sons and daughters for service in the state bureaucracy and armed forces, and to cooperate with state agricultural policies. Peasant compliance with this bargain has made a major contribution to regime stability.[28]

While before 1963 the state bureaucracy barely penetrated the countryside, the Ba`th party complemented land reform with vigorous institution building, supplanting elite mediation by landowners, merchants, and moneylenders with direct state rule over peasants. As Francoise Metral summarizes the transition to direct rule in the countryside, "By stabilizing prices and granting credit at a 5 percent interest rate, the state limits not only the farmers' risks but also his profits. It frees him from traditional patterns of dependency on landowners, merchants and moneylenders, but it imposes a number of bureaucratic controls on him. The system thus places the state with a bureaucratic apparatus in direct

---

[27] On factional conflict, see, for example, Van Dam, *Struggle for Power in Syria.*

[28] See Ghassan Salame, *al-Mujtama` wa al-Dawla fi al-Mashriq al-Arabi* (Beirut: Center for the Study of Arab Unity, 1987), 191, who writes of the "political covenant" (*mithaq siyasi*) resulting in peasant identification with and support for the regime.

contact with a mass of small cultivators."[29] The major institutional innovations linking the state to peasants were agricultural cooperatives in charge of the distribution of inputs and marketing of output, and the General Federation of Peasants, which to some extent represented peasant interests within the state, but more important, exercised control over peasant political and economic behavior.[30] At the local level, village notables continued to influence relations between their fellow villagers and local agencies of national authority. But the capacity of local notables to mediate was rooted not in the autonomous control over social resources, but in their position within patronage networks controlled by the state and executed through bureaucratic offices.[31]

The state fortified institution building with welfare-enhancing public policies. Working through the cooperatives, the state intervened in the provision of inputs, the process of production, and the marketing of surplus. In some instances, the state set agricultural prices below world-market prices, as in the case of cotton, an export crop that was a major source of foreign currency. More generally, however, the state set generous prices for agricultural products while subsidizing inputs and making massive investments in agricultural infrastructure.

As in Turkey, however, the benefits of the agrarian reform and subsequent public policies were not equally divisible among all peasants. Instead, we find systematic bias in favor of the creation and sustenance of a class of middle peasants. This is most obvious from the pattern of appropriation and distribution of land. Before the reform, large landowners, holding more than 100 hectares, represented less than 1 percent of the agrarian population, yet controlled about 50 percent of the land. Middle peasants, whose landholdings ranged from 10 to 100 hectares, were about 9 percent of the agrarian population and controlled 37 percent of total lands. Small holders farming less than 10 hectares constituted about one-third of the agrarian population and possessed about 13 percent of the land. Landless peasants, finally, were about 60 percent of the population. Substantial inequality of landholdings continued after the agrarian

---

[29] See her "State and Peasants in Syria: A Local View of a Government Irrigation Project," in *Arab Society: Social Science Perspectives,* ed. Nicholas Hopkins (Cairo: American University in Cairo, 1977), 340–41. Ziad Keilany's discussion of land reform and its effects on the Syrian transition to an unmediated state in the countryside notes, however, that although their power had been sharply curtailed, rural notables have not been completely eliminated. See his "Land Reform in Syria," *Middle Eastern Studies* 16 (October 1980), esp. 220–23.

[30] Hinnebusch, *Peasant and Bureaucracy,* 66–76.

[31] Yahya Sadowski, "Ba'thist Ethics and the Spirit of State Capitalism; Patronage and the Party in Contemporary Syria," in *Ideology and Power in the Middle East: Studies in the Honor of George Lenczowski,* ed. Peter J. Chelkowski and Robert J. Pranger (Durham: Duke University Press, 1988), 168.

reform. Large holdings were not fully eradicated but constituted just under 18 percent of total land. Small holdings proliferated and made up 75 percent of all holdings but just 24 percent of total land. Medium-sized holdings, on the other hand, constituted 24 percent of all holdings and almost 59 percent of all land owned. Meanwhile, in 1970, about 170,000 peasants remained landless.[32] Furthermore, richer peasants and capitalist farmers have benefited disproportionately from state largess.[33] The goal of land reform, then, seems to have been not social justice, but the creation of a stratum of independent peasants who would be political clients of the state, produce a surplus to feed the cities, and provide crops for export and raw materials for industry, while maintaining the maximum number of large surplus-producing farms which would not pose a political threat to the regime.

State and Labor in Syria

As in Turkey, the creation of an alliance between the Syrian state and urban labor posed more intractable problems than did winning the support of peasants. In Turkey, the initial inclusion of labor into the cross-class coalition proceeded smoothly, but as the labor force diversified, maintaining a stable alliance proved impossible. In Syria, on the other hand, the initial incorporation of labor was quite difficult. Factions within the regime sought different and competing accommodations with labor, with left-wing members championing a program of democratic administration of the means of production and the preservation of labor organizations autonomous from the state.[34] Moreover, independent labor leaders stood between the new regime and workers, contesting the incorporating bargain offered to workers. Syrian labor had mobilized and organized before 1963, and although labor organizations were sharply controlled and demobilized during the UAR period, an independent labor leadership existed in 1963 whose members spanned the political spectrum yet did not have close ties to the Ba`th party. These leaders viewed the new regime with suspicion and resisted Ba`th efforts to impose their own cadres in leadership positions.[35]

---

[32] Hinnebusch, *Peasant and Bureaucracy*, 88, 108.

[33] For example, undistributed state lands in the Hassake region were rented only to members of upper classes: tribal shaykhs, rich farmers, and members of the old and new bourgeoisie. See Adnan Musallam, *al-Masala al-Zira`iyya fi al-Qutr al-Arabi al-Suri* (Damascus: Matba`a Dar al-Ilm, 1983), 43.

[34] Elisabeth Picard, "Une Crise Syrienne en 1965," *Soual* 8 (February 1988), 84.

[35] Elisabeth Longuenesse, "Labor in Syria: The Emergence of New Identities," in *The Social History of Labor in the Middle East*, ed. Ellis Jay Goldberg (Boulder, Colo.: Westview Press, 1996), 107–11.

The new regime bargained from a weakened position, because it needed the support of labor in its efforts to tame the opposition of small merchants demonstrating in Aleppo, Hama, and Hums in 1964. When suppression of the demonstrators by regular army units led only to the spread of the demonstrations to Damascus and the inclusion of urban professionals in the demonstrations, the government permitted the trade-union leader Khalid al-Jundi to organize workers from the more militant trade unions into workers' militias that helped to break the strikes of the merchants and to combat the Muslim Brotherhood in Damascus.[36] The regime's dependence on labor was reflected in new labor legislation, passed in 1964, that repealed previous antilabor regulations and granted wide privileges to labor and in the 1964 Constitution, which called for an independent labor confederation. When these measures failed to elicit union support, however, military officers within the regime launched an assault on the union leadership. Over the next few months, they expelled radical cadres from the party, suspended the new liberal labor law, and imposed Ba`thist cadres in the middle levels of the union administration. In the union elections of December 1964 and January 1965, Ba`thist candidates took control of the syndicates from Nasserists, communists, and independents, and strikes were prohibited. By 1968, the Ba`thist regime had completed the corporatization of the Syrian labor movement.[37]

Thus, by 1970, a new relationship between the state and the union movement had solidified. The institutional infrastructure of the labor movement was transformed from a means for workers to press demands on capitalists and the state, to a means for controlled mobilization of labor.[38] Labor unions were grouped into a national-level syndicate controlled by the state, which imposed on union elections a single electoral list composed almost completely of party members.[39] Furthermore, the regime took particular pains to cultivate the loyalty of union cadres to prevent the emergence of an independent union leadership.[40] Finally, at the level of the shop floor, public-sector workers were effectively controlled through the triad of the party, the syndicates, and administrators. This triad is exemplified in the case of a director general of a public-

[36] See Petran, *Syria,* 176; and Fred H. Lawson, "Class Politics and State Power in Ba`thi Syria," in *Power and Stability in the Middle East,* ed. Berch Berberoglu (London: Zed Books, 1989), 18.

[37] Picard, "Crise Syrienne" 86–87.

[38] Jean Hannoyer and Michel Seurat, *Etat et Secteur Public Industriel en Syrie* (Beirut: CERMOC, 1979), Chap. 2.

[39] Elisabeth Longuenesse, "Etat et Syndicalisme en Syria: Discours et Pratiques," *Soual* 8 (February 1988), 103–4.

[40] Sadowski, "Ba`thist Ethics," 171.

sector factory who was not only a party member but also sat on the worker council of the factory.[41]

The regime complemented the cooptation and political marginalization of the union movement with efforts to win the loyalty of workers themselves. Material privileges granted to workers included an income policy that kept wages growing well above the inflation rate, widespread subsidization of basic consumption needs, and deliberate policies of overemployment in public-sector industries. These policies are discussed further in Chapter 5. The exchange of material benefits for loyalty and acquiescence in organizational weakness has refashioned urban labor into a stable base of support for the regime over the past three decades.[42]

State and Bourgeoisie in Syria

Divisions within the new regime over the scope of economic transformation and the composition of new alliances were most clearly reflected in policy toward Syrian capitalists. In May 1963, the new government nationalized local banks and insurance companies. The new Agrarian Reform Law followed in June. But these measures were accompanied by assurances to the private sector that these nationalizations were designed to facilitate private-sector growth by removing control over capital from firms unwilling to invest in productive industrial investment. In early 1964, demonstrations in northern cities by shopkeepers and other opponents of the regime were met by a combination of coercion and assurances from Salah al-Din al-Bitar, one of the founders of the Ba`th party, that the private sector would be assigned an important role in the transition to a more egalitarian economic order. The government proposed creating a "common sector" in which state and private ownership would be combined to manage firms. At the same time, moderates within the party gained control over agrarian policy and agrarian cooperatives began to take precedence over state farms. But the private sector was not appeased, and members of the bourgeoisie began to organize to overturn the rising wave of nationalization while increasing the transfer of their capital abroad.[43]

Faced with bourgeois opposition and determined to end decisively lingering divisions within the regime, the military wing of the party pushed

[41] Hannoyer and Seurat, *Etat et Secteur Public Industriel*, 32.

[42] Fred Lawson, "External versus Internal Pressures for Liberalization in Syria and Iraq," *Journal of Arab Affairs* 11 (1992): 1–33.

[43] Fred Lawson, "Political-Economic Trends in Ba`thi Syria: A Reinterpretation," *Orient* 29 (1988), 580.

through a series of nationalization measures in late 1964 and early 1965. Included in the nationalized firms were 130 industrial establishments, 60 commercial establishments, and all cotton-ginning mills. In addition, the state took direct control of foreign trade in strategic materials such as pharmaceuticals, mineral oil, cotton, grains, and cars. In response, a large number of Syrian industrialists left the country. Those who stayed generally refused to manage the new state sector and turned to the commercial areas left for the private sector. As Volker Perthes summarizes the results of the nationalizations, "After 1965, the Syrian bourgeoisie, or what was left of it, was much more commercial and less industrial than in the pre-Ba`thi period; private industry for the next two decades was limited mostly to artisanry and small-scale manufacturing."[44] The supporters of these measures—left-wing regionalists, commonly referred to as *neo-Ba`thists*—removed their more moderate competitors from positions of power in a February 1966 coup.

Combined with land reform, nationalization of the large-scale private sector completely removed the old notables from positions of power. But factions within the regime continued to call for a more radical social transformation, threatening potential supporters of the regime. Wealthy peasants, who had benefited from the agrarian reform, were made uneasy by statements calling for the creation of collective farms. Ba`thist control over foreign trade and particularly over the import of luxury goods angered merchants and the middle class. Bureaucrats and managers of the state sector were angered by the arbitrary powers of party members. Finally, military officers were alienated by approval of Palestinian commando activity that created tensions with Israel prior to the 1967 war and by calls to create popular militias to combat Israel after the war.[45]

In 1970, Hafiz al-Asad overthrew the neo-Ba`th in a coup celebrated in Syria as the Corrective Movement. Asad sought to maintain Ba`thist domination over the state and public-sector domination over the economy while minimizing the number of people who were opposed to Ba`thist rule. Alongside measures to appease kulaks, bureaucrats, and military officers, Asad liberalized sections of the economy, particularly foreign trade, and offered a new deal to Syrian businessmen. Asad, in other words, consolidated his rule by reincorporating private capital into his cross-class coalition. Although the state continued to control strategic areas of foreign trade, to play a leading role in industry, and to determine the course of development through its expenditures, Asad's overtures created new possibilities for private businessmen to cooperate with the

---

[44] "The Syrian Private Industrial and Commercial Sectors and the State," *International Journal of Middle East Studies* 24 (May 1992), 209.
[45] Sadowski, "Ba`thist Ethics and the Spirit of State Capitalism," 170.

state. This invitation to the private sector was realized during a decade of enormous capital inflows, as Arab oil states financed the rebuilding of Syria's economic infrastructure destroyed in the 1973 war. Private businessmen established small firms that acted as subcontractors in construction and agents of the government in negotiating foreign tenders or public purchases.[46] By lifting restrictions on several imports while maintaining an overvalued exchange rate, the state began to subsidize private-sector imports. Private-sector investment in tourism and transportation was encouraged, as was the repatriation of Syrian capital. In all these domains of activity, private businessmen had no reason to complain about payments made to peasants and workers.

In exchange for these favors, private businessmen were explicitly ordered, often in individual meetings with top state officials, to remain politically passive. In the 1970s, business influence was not expressed through organized collective action. Instead, individual businessmen cultivated ties with members of the government to direct more patronage in their direction. Subsequently, numerous government officials became involved in business ventures. This convergence of interests of public- and private-sector elites created what Syrians have called the "new bourgeoisie." The new bourgeoisie embraces those businessmen whose loyalty to the regime is purchased by a similar set of public policies: an overvalued exchange rate, lax import restrictions, and participation in public-private shared enterprises.

As in Turkey, Syria's Islamists have posed the most effective opposition to the regime, currying support from social classes excluded from bargains extended by the state, especially members of the petit bourgeoisie.[47] Some members of the small business sector flourished under Ba`thist rule, especially owners of small manufacturing workshops producing goods not supplied by large-scale industrial plants, and merchants controlling retail marketing. Artisans and merchants increased their numbers, both absolutely and as a share of the active labor force, leading one scholar to label Syria a "petit-bourgeois regime."[48] But these benefits for the petit bourgeoisie were unintended consequences of state policy; in terms of explicit policy, the Syrian urban petit bourgeoisie was the major social group excluded from relations of constituency clientelism or other forms of patronage, while many public policies earned the regime the enmity of smaller businessmen. Since 1963, for example, small

---

[46] Ibid., 172.

[47] For a history of Islamic movements in Syria, see Habib al-Janhani, "al-Sahwa al-Islamiyya fi Bilad al-Sham: Mithal Suriya," in *al-Haraka al-Islamiyya fi al-Watan al-Arabi* (Beirut: Markaz Dirasat al-Wahda al-Arabiyya, 1987), 107–22.

[48] See Elisabeth Longuenesse, "The Class Nature of the State in Syria," *MERIP Reports* 77 (May 1979): 3–11.

traders have had to deal with state administrators, many of whom are of recent rural origin and are either hostile to urban merchants or ignorant of their business practices. Moreover, state industrialization projects have threatened the material well-being of small-scale manufacturers through policies raising the wages of state factory workers relative to inflation and through competition from cheap factory-made textiles.[49] Finally, various marketing schemes, including marketing cooperatives, consumer cooperatives, and price controls, have pushed merchants out of some market segments and increased competitive pressures on them in others, while wealthier peasants who have prospered under the Ba`th have competed with urban merchants in the transport and marketing of agricultural produce.[50]

Excluded from circuits of state distribution, the Syrian urban petit bourgeoisie has become staunch opponents of the regime, couching their resistance in the idiom of Islamic fundamentalism. Islamic fundamentalism has provided the petit bourgeoisie with an alternative development program that clearly supports private property while appealing to their sense of dignity as a status group.[51] Throughout the 1960s, small-scale merchants and artisans, particularly in northern cities, led protests against the regime. In the 1970s, members of urban lower-middle-class families joined with urban professionals to constitute a new Islamist movement that posed a significant threat to the regime between 1976 and 1982.[52] The largest sector of the population not coopted by the regime—with their families, small-scale urban manufacturers, and merchants composing about one-sixth of the population in 1970—became the core of support for the only credible alternative to the regime.

This emphasis on the class nature of the Islamist revolt in Syria is not meant to deny the salience of religious cleavages. The ideology of the Muslim Brotherhood portrayed the conflict as one between Sunni Muslims and heterodox Alawis, and there is no reason to believe that participants did not perceive it in those terms.[53] But evidence supporting a class-based interpretation is too strong to be denied. In the 1980 Muslim

[49] Fred Lawson, "Roots of the Hama Revolt," *MERIP Reports* 110 (November 1982): 24–28.

[50] Hanna Batatu, "Syria's Muslim Brethren," *MERIP Reports* 110 (November 1982); and Sadowski, "Ba`thist Ethics and the Spirit of State Capitalism," 174.

[51] Batatu, "Syria's Muslim Brethren."

[52] Raymond Hinnebusch, *Authoritarian Power and State Formation in Ba`thist Syria: Army, Party, and Peasant* (Boulder, Colo.: Westview Press, 1990), 286. Detailed information on the role of urban professionals is lacking. For some idea of the causes and scope of their participation in antiregime activities, see Stanley Reed, "Dateline Syria: Fin de Regime?" *Foreign Policy* 39 (Summer 1980), 181; and Eric Rouleau, "Le Palais du Peuple" *Le Monde*, June 29, 1983, 4

[53] For an analysis of the ideology of the Muslim Brotherhood from an Islamist activist, see Umar Abd al-Allah, *The Islamic Struggle in Syria* (Berkeley: Mizan Press, 1983).

Brotherhood uprising in Aleppo, for example, socialist cooperative stores were the first targets to be destroyed.[54] Equally striking is the relative quiescence of the Damascene large and small bourgeoisie, in stark contrast to the bloody events in the north of the country, where businessmen participated in general strikes. In general, even small Damascene businessmen had benefited from the regime far more than northern businessmen. Consequently, in March 1980, at the height of the rebellion, leaflets were distributed in Damascus calling on the merchants of Hamidiyya, the largest bazaar, to go on strike. Damascene merchants did not comply. The critical variable in determining whether merchants would support or oppose the regime was their inclusion or exclusion from the circuits of patronage that compose constituency clientelism in Syria.

State and Bureaucrats in Syria

As we saw earlier, during the 1950s both the landed elite and rising middle-class parties infiltrated government bureaucracies. This politicization of the bureaucracy ran counter to efforts from within the civil service to establish meritocratic norms of recruitment and operation. On coming to power, the new regime accelerated the colonization of the bureaucracy, adding to previous tendencies the massive deployment of civil service jobs as a tool of patronage with which to cultivate support among urban middle classes while giving rural constituencies opportunities for urban employment and social mobility. Civil servants have accepted this bargain, trading expanded employment and job security, tacit acceptance of corruption, and the absence of job performance standards for their support of the regime. Consequently, employment in the state bureaucracy expanded from 24,000 civil servants in the 1950s to almost 475,000 by 1983.[55]

The Ba`th regime has not merely won the support of individual civil servants; it has also reshaped the state bureaucracy into a compliant instrument of the political elite. The first step in the domestication of the state was to purge the bureaucracy of any incumbents opposed to the Ba`thist land reform begun in 1963. This was followed by the channeling of rural migrants, who were strong supporters of the regime, into the bureaucracy, popular organizations, and army, leading to a phenomenon Ghassan Salame referred to as "the ruralization of [state] power."[56] When Hafiz al-Asad came to power in 1970, he made two major modifications

---

[54] Batatu, "Syria's Muslim Brethren," 16.

[55] Hinnebusch, *Authoritarian Power and State Formation,* 191. This figure includes teachers and public-sector workers, but excludes the military.

[56] See his *al-Mujtama` wa al-Dawla,* 191.

to this system of bureaucratic control. First, party control over the bureaucracy was reduced; experts began to take some precedence over reds.[57] In addition, as part of a larger strategy of winning the support of urban, Sunni, middle classes, Asad "deliberately coopted significant numbers of Damascenes into the top ranks of party and state and many nonparty technocrats into government."[58] Despite Asad's introduction of a degree of technocratic rationality into the bureaucracy, however, bureaucratic autonomy has never been part of the bargain linking civil servants to the political elite.

State Transformation in Syria and Turkey Compared

Syria and Turkey represent both similar and different values of variables important to political-economic analysis. Most striking among the latter are their differences in political and property regimes. While Turkish governments have been democratically elected and have protected private property, Syria's authoritarian government nationalized the large-scale private sector and instituted a major program of agrarian reform. Consequently, while Turkish development projects have assigned a large role to the private sector, Syrian development projects, while not neglecting the private sector, have assigned the largest role to the public sector.

These differences are surely important. But do they explain outcomes of economic development, understood in terms of changes in the capacity to create value? Subsequent chapters argue that they do not. For amidst the differences distinguishing Syria and Turkey, key similarities justify placing them in the same analytic category. Both Syria and Turkey were mediated states in the postwar period. In both countries, intense inter-elite conflict, the independent variable of my argument, broke out over the proper relationship of the state to the economy. In both countries, that conflict was resolved only when one section of the elite cultivated the mass support needed to defeat decisively its rivals. In each country, sectors of the elite won the right to implement their vision of the political-economic future by constructing cross-class coalitions, incorporating workers and peasants into alliances that included private business-

---

[57] Despite this, Maoist-inspired attacks on the bureaucracy continued. In 1972, one analysis of the Syrian bureaucracy concluded that the bureaucracy will continue to expand and govern the society in accordance with its own interests unless "a revolutionary vanguard takes control of the administration of the state and extirpates the division between manual laborers and the intelligentsia so that a yawning gap no longer divides the masses from their government." Samir Abduh, *Dirasa fi Buruqratiya al-Suriya* (Damascus: Dar Dimashq, 1972), 45.

[58] Hinnebusch, *Peasant and Bureaucracy*, 24.

men and managers of public-sector enterprises. The construction of cross-class coalitions is the first causal mechanism of my argument. Chapter 5 explores the impact of cross-class coalitions on the institutional capacity of the state to promote development.

Why did high levels of inter-elite conflict produce different political and property regimes in Syria and Turkey? In both countries, building cross-class coalitions primarily entailed incorporating peasants. But the costs to divided elites of incorporating peasants differed in the two cases, because different structures of agrarian landholdings in regions of the Ottoman Empire produced correspondingly different relations of agrarian elites to the state in the first half of the twentieth century. Consequently, whereas property-owning elites incorporated a mass base in Turkey, in Syria it was an antioligarchic movement that captured political power and transformed the state.

Consider first agrarian property structures. In most provinces of western Anatolia, a small-holding peasantry secure in its possession of the right of usufruct can be traced back to the Byzantine Empire. Throughout the centuries of Ottoman rule, the Ottoman state successfully maintained this small peasantry as a bulwark against the consolidation of power by a landowning aristocracy. In the second half of the nineteenth century, large estates were formed, not in areas of smallholder dominance, but in reclaimed wastelands, as in the Cukurova province, and in the Kurdish tribal lands in the east. A large class of small-holding peasants thus persisted into the twentieth century.[59] In the provinces constituting Syria, on the other hand, state control was attenuated, and, beginning in the eighteenth century, urban notables gradually took control of large tracts of land, transforming independent peasants into sharecroppers.[60]

Differences in landholding patterns produced different elite structures. Throughout Ottoman history, the state elite derived its power, privilege, and prestige by holding offices within the state, not from autonomous control over sources of social power. During the Kemalist period, the structure of the Turkish political elite largely replicated that of the Ottoman Empire, as senior members of the state bureaucracy, the party, and the military ruled in alliance with landowners, provincial notables, and businessmen who were distinctly junior members of the al-

[59] The seminal work on this topic is Haim Gerber, *Social Origins of the Modern Middle East* (Boulder, Colo.: Lynne Rienner, 1987), esp. 104–18

[60] For the emergence of large landholdings in the eighteenth century, see Abdel-Karim Rafeq, "Economic Relations between Damascus and the Dependent Countryside," in *The Islamic Middle East, 700–1900*, ed. A. L. Udovitch (Princeton, N.J.: Darwin Press, 1981), 653–86; and Gerber, *Social Origins of the Modern Middle East*, 95–101. While correctly stressing the regional distribution of large landownership in Syria, and the persistence of small ownership in many regions, Gerber affirms (116–18) the predominance of small landholders in Turkey and of large landowners in Syria.

liance. In independent Syria, on the other hand, large landholders established rule as an agrarian oligarchic elite.[61]

Given these different property and elite structures, what were the costs
to elites of incorporating peasants? In Turkey, costs were low to both sections of the divided elite. Bureaucrats and landowners might have preferred to continue excluding peasants, but incorporation did not directly
threaten the sources of their elite status: bureaucrats would still hold their
offices after peasant incorporation, and, because a large stratum of small
landowning peasants existed, landowners could appeal to them without
having to offer redistribution of land. It was therefore possible to negoti-
ate a transition to democratic politics without redistributing property.

Large Syrian landowners who controlled the oligarchic state could not
build a social coalition by including the peasantry, because this would
threaten the landed basis of their own claims on power, privilege, prestige, and wealth; the costs of incorporation were intolerably high for
them. Thus, as we have seen, they resisted efforts to pass legislation in
parliament that would have effected incorporation. Combined with political power allowing them to block social reforms, landlords' inability to
incorporate created a structural opening for antioligarchic movements
led by a counter-elite to appeal directly to peasants and threatened the
elite status of the agrarian oligarchy. While the costs of incorporation to
landlords were high, the cost of incorporation to an antioligarchic movement was low. Therefore, no negotiated transition was possible: incorporation was possible only by the nondemocratic capture of power and the
decisive removal of the sources of oligarchic power through land reform
and economic nationalization.

---

[61] Philip S. Khoury provides a detailed analysis of the rise of the landowning elite to political prominence in his *Urban Notables and Arab Nationalism: The Politics of Damascus,
1860–1920* (Cambridge: Cambridge University Press, 1983).

CHAPTER FIVE

Precocious Keynesianism in Practice

The material in this chapter covers the period of precocious Keynesianism—1950 to 1980 in Turkey and 1963 to 1980 in Syria. Chapter 9 discusses the post-1980 period, when Syria and Turkey experimented with new political-economic arrangements. Building mass coalitions by making high levels of side-payments creates durable patterns of interaction among state, society, and economy. In this chapter, the institutional features of the transformed Syrian and Turkish states are discussed, focusing on state-society relations, fiscal structures, the nature of the bureaucracy, and patterns of state economic intervention. This set of institutions and attendant policies does not exhaustively describe the Syrian and Turkish political economies; it does, as discussed in later chapters, define the developmental capacity of the state and thus best accounts for development outcomes. I demonstrate below how the construction of cross-class coalitions dictated institutional outcomes. In addition, I demonstrate that these four institutions are similar in Syria and Turkey, despite other differences in their political and economic systems. The political economies of Syria and Turkey are thus not identical; it surely matters for many reasons that Syria is authoritarian and Turkey is democratic. I argue instead that, given the similarities illustrated in this chapter and the causal effect these similarities have for developmental outcomes, the Syrian and Turkish political economies are best understood as analogous but not isomorphic.

Constituency Clientelism in Syria and Turkey

The differences between Syria and Turkey emerge nowhere more clearly than in the nature of their political regimes. Yet because definitions of regimes typically exclude public policies from their semantic purview, and because little evidence supports the hypothesis that authoritarian and democratic regimes implement predictably distinct policies or produce different levels of economic growth, regime type cannot account for development outcomes.[1] Viewed from the perspective of interest organization and articulation, Syria and Turkey present a more conflicting picture of similarities and differences. While the existence of legal parties and the slow emergence of autonomous interest groups distinguish Turkey from Syria, corporatist modes of interest organization are found in both. While the corporatist paradigm helps us to conceptualize important dimensions of Syrian and Turkish politics, we cannot resort to it to discover the direction of economic change in Syria and Turkey. Corporatist arrangements stem from a bargain between state agents and functional groups in which the terms of the bargain are a set of *organizational* inducements and constraints; by themselves, they tell us little about policies and economic outcomes.[2] The inducements offered to Syrian and Turkish lower classes in exchange for organizational weakness were not institutional benefits or regularized access to decision making, but material benefits offered directly to the constituent members of those groups so that interest organizations provide minimal capacity for popular classes to press their demands on the state.[3]

In both cases, state elites exploited their control over resources to build societal constituencies by forging patronage relations that created a relationship linking ruler and ruled that I call *constituency clientelism*. State elites in both countries established three types of relationships with major

---

[1] David Collier and Ruth Berins Collier write that "The regime is typically distinguished from the particular incumbents who occupy state and governmental roles, the political coalition that supports these incumbents, *and the public policies they adopt* (except of course policies that define or transform the regime itself)." See Ruth Berins Collier and David Collier, *Shaping the Political Arena: Critical Junctures, the Labor Movement, and Regime Dynamics in Latin America* (Princeton: Princeton University Press, 1991), 789 (emphasis added). For critical discussion of the hypothesized link between regime type and economic performance, see, for example, Stephan Haggard, *Pathways from the Periphery: The Politics of Growth in the Newly Industrializing Countries* (Ithaca: Cornell University Press, 1990), 261–65; Karen Remmer, "The Politics of Economic Stabilization: IMF Standby Programs in Latin America," *Comparative Politics* 19 (1986): 1–24; and Adam Przeworski and Fernando Limongi, "Political Regimes and Economic Growth," *Journal of Economic Perspectives* 7 (Summer 1993): 51–69.

[2] Ruth Berins Collier and David Collier, "Inducements versus Constraints: Disaggregating Corporatism," *American Political Science Review* 73 (December 1979): 967–86. See Chapter 2, footnote 70, for further discussion of the restricted utility of the corporatist paradigm for explaining economic outcomes.

[3] For excellent analyses of corporatist arrangements in Turkey and Syria, see Robert Bianchi, *Interest Groups and Political Development in Turkey* (Princeton: Princeton University Press, 1984); and Raymond A. Hinnebusch, *Authoritarian Power and State Formation in Ba`thist Syria: Army, Party, and Peasant* (Boulder, Colo.: Westview Press, 1990). Of course, state-appointed representatives of popular classes may, if only to serve their own interests, argue for more beneficial policies.

social classes. First, state officials gained the support of popular classes through the direct provision of indivisible goods, such as subsidized inputs and above-market prices for agrarian classes and above-market wages and high levels of secure employment for organized labor in the public sector. When state agencies, for example, purchase agricultural products at above-world prices, individual peasants do not have to appear before a patron and express fealty to benefit; all peasants who produce and market that good receive high prices, and therefore the good is characterized by nonexcludability. Furthermore, the benefits appropriated by one peasant do not affect the benefits available to other peasants, subject to the limits of the state treasury. The same logic of noncompetitiveness and nonexcludability applies to other forms of state patronage, such as subsidies for consumer goods and minimum wages. Finally, members of these included classes do not have to engage in collective action to receive their benefits; indeed, the provision of these incentives is predicated on their acceptance of political marginalization.

Second, state elites in both countries established relationships with larger businessmen based on a combination of divisible and indivisible goods. Again, businessmen do not have to engage in collective action to achieve these benefits, although they are the group with the highest potential to engage in collective action. Instead, the system encourages businessmen to act as individuals, exploiting political influence to direct state largesse in their direction.[4] But note that the value of many of these private goods is greatly enhanced by protectionist trade policies, which are a public good. Finally, in both cases, significant sectors of the population have been excluded from these relations of patronage. The only option available to these groups to gain access to state resources is to engage in collective action. In Turkey, this has occurred through the creation of small parties, including the National Salvation Party, which represented smaller Anatolian merchants and industrialists. In Syria, this collective action has taken the form of Islamist-inspired, antiregime violence.

Thus, a central similarity unites the two cases despite other differences in the institutional expression of state-society relations and the broader political regime. Constituency clientelism is, in other words, consistent with both democratic and authoritarian regimes. Furthermore, because the bargain yielding constituency clientelism entails the exchange of material benefits for organizational weakness and political quiescence, the concept covers corporatist institutions. Most important, in contrast to

---

[4] Even Turkish businessmen, who emerged as leading figures in civil society in the 1950–1980 period, enjoyed limited collective capacity to influence politics. See, for example, Serif Mardin, "The Transformation of an Economic Code," in *The Political Economy of Income Distribution in Turkey*, ed. Aydin Ulusan and Ergun Ozbudun (London: Holmes and Meier, 1980), 44.

other conceptualizations of political systems, constituency clientelism specifically incorporates public policy into its definition; indeed, the public goods offered by the state to its constituents make up the bulk of public policy.

Politicized versus Insulated Bureaucracies

In contrast to the autonomous bureaucracies of East Asian developmental states, bureaucracies in Syria and Turkey are politicized and thus heteronomous.[5] The Syrian and Turkish cases represent two different paths to the politicization of the bureaucracy. In Turkey, propertied elites mobilized popular support against an established bureaucratic elite, resulting in the erosion of bureaucratic autonomy and the marginalization of the bureaucracy as a locus of decision-making power. The Turkish case thus supports the claim advanced in Chapter 2 that the existence of a state apparatus with a history of autonomy from social forces and legal-rational procedural norms is not a sufficient condition for an effective bureaucracy. In Syria, on the other hand, civil servants participated in the new coalition fabricated by the military elite that assumed power in 1963. Civil servants did not, however, constitute a constituency for bureaucratic autonomy and were included in the coalition only on the condition that they acquiesce in the implementation of the basic platform of social transformation advocated by the new political leadership. The politician–civil servant alliance was predicated on the continued subordination of the administrative apparatus of the state to political logics, precluding the construction of an apparatus capable of acting in a developmental manner. The Syrian case thus supports the claim, advanced in Chapter 2, that unless the bargain between political elites and civil servants explicitly secures bureaucratic autonomy from political intervention, it will not create a developmentally competent administrative apparatus.

The Turkish Bureaucracy

In 1950, the Turkish bureaucracy enjoyed resources necessary for the embedded autonomy that in East Asia has permitted the formulation and implementation of long-term development strategy: a history dating back several centuries, a tradition of meritocratic recruitment and promotion,

---

[5] In light of Peter Evans's recent work, however, autonomy is only one necessary but not sufficient element of the developmental state apparatus. For elaboration of the need for "embeddedness," see his *Embedded Autonomy: States & Industrial Transformation* (Princeton: Princeton University Press, 1995).

and a high degree of esprit de corps.[6] Moreover, Turkish bureaucrats believed that only they possessed the rational vision required to modernize Turkey and that they, and not professional politicians, should rule.[7] But the exclusion of this constituency for bureaucratic constituency from the governing coalition undermined its claims to formulate and implement policy. As we saw in Chapter 3, the Democratic Party (DP) came to power dedicated to restraining the arbitrary power of the civil and military bureaucracy. Thus, a meritocratically recruited and highly educated bureaucratic elite that enjoys a high degree of social status and sustains its cohesion through informal networks is not a sufficient condition for bureaucratic autonomy.

One of the most critical periods in the erosion of bureaucratic autonomy in Turkey occurred in the period immediately following the 1960 coup, which was engineered by civilian and military officials angered by their exclusion from the governing coalition and the anarchic path of development being pursued by the DP. One mechanism designed to augment bureaucratic control over modernization was the institutionalization of the State Planning Office (SPO).[8] Inspired by the Japanese and French examples of technocrat supervision of economic adjustment and modernization, the founders of the SPO devised a plan for industrial deepening. Milor concludes that "had the SPO been able to insulate itself from political pressures it might have become a key bureau, in a way reminiscent of the Japanese MITI or the French planning *commissariat....* "[9] But two elements of the plan alienated the political leadership. First, planners sought to rationalize the State Economic Enterprises (SEEs) by introducing market reforms and removing the public sector from the realm of patronage politics. Second, planners sought to mobilize the funds required for their new five-year development plan by raising taxes. Both of these options were rejected by the political leadership. As a result of this conflict, the staff of the SPO collectively resigned. This did not signal an end to the SPO or to technocrat recruitment into the Turkish bureaucracy, but it did signal that precocious Keynesianism was inconsistent with the construction of a developmental state. Turkish political elites could not tolerate bureaucratic autonomy, not simply because the bureaucracy was a potential political challenger to their rule, but because

[6] Within a large literature detailing the history of the Turkish bureaucracy, Metin Heper, *State Tradition in Turkey* (Northgate, England: Eothen Press, 1985), provides a particularly good discussion.
[7] The most extensive discussion of the beliefs of Turkish bureaucrats is Gencay Saylan, *Turkiye'de Kapitalizm Burokrasi ve Siyasal Ideoloji* (Ankara: V Yayinlari, 1986).
[8] Information in this paragraph is taken from the excellent article by Vedat Milor, "The Genesis of Planning in Turkey," *New Perspectives on Turkey* 4 (Fall 1990): 1–30.
[9] Ibid., 26.

bureaucrats advocated economic reforms that clashed with the dictates of providing welfare benefits to coalition members.

The Syrian Bureaucracy

As we saw in Chapter 4, during the decade and a half between independence and the Ba`thi assumption of power, the Syrian civil service had become a "battleground of contending interests, with various factions of the old guard, cabinet ministers, parliamentary deputies, opposition political forces, and the military all involved in manipulating and corrupting bureaucratic procedures to their own advantage."[10] Thus, when the Ba`th came to power, no powerful constituency for bureaucratic insulation existed. Had such a constituency for bureaucratic autonomy existed, it is not a foregone conclusion that it could have maintained its position; throughout the 1960s, Ba`th party cadres were more interested in regime consolidation and social transformation than they were in ceding autonomy to civil servants. Bureaucrats that opposed land reform or nationalization were removed from their posts, and the decade was marked by the superiority of "reds" to "experts." But the fact remains that the alliance that was forged between the political elite and the administrative cadres was one devoid of measures designed to insulate the bureaucracy from political intervention; instead, employment in the bureaucracy was, as we have seen, a powerful tool for cultivating support. Reliance on patronage appointments in turn influenced the structure of authority within the bureaucracy; cabinet ministers refused to delegate authority to specialized agencies or even, in many cases, their deputies.[11] Moreover, politically motivated appointments and massive overstaffing of agencies combined to ensure that, although many bureaucrats were highly trained, large numbers of appointees were ill qualified for their jobs. Reviewing the evidence of administrative inefficiency, Volker Perthes concludes, "From a regime perspective, efficiency is not the only criterion by which the performance and value of the bureaucracy is to be judged."[12]

Thus, from the beginning, civil servants joined the Ba`thist coalition under the implicit understanding that the administrative apparatus of the

---

[10] Stephen Heydemann, "Successful Authoritarianism: The Social and Structural Origins of Populist Authoritarian Rule in Syria, 1946–1963," Ph.D. Dissertation, University of Chicago, 1990, 90.

[11] As Gerd Nonneman observes, the high turnover of bureaucrats in key agencies such as the State Planning Council bred inefficiency. See his *Development, Administration and Foreign Aid in the Middle East* (London: Routledge, 1988), 36.

[12] Volker Perthes, *The Political Economy of Syria under As`ad* (London: I.B. Tauris, 1995), 141–5, citation from 145.

state would respond to political, not developmental, requirements. The politicization of decision making is reflected in the composition of key agencies. The Supreme Planning Commission, responsible for resource allocation, includes members of popular organizations, as does the Economics Committee, which presides over the budget and public-sector investment.[13] Members of the Economic Committee in turn report directly to President Asad and the Ba`th party. Although the Ba`th party organization has no formal role in planning, the regime assiduously seeks the approval of the party's key cadres for changes in policy. Moreover, strategies are altered in response to political exigencies: the fifth five-year plan, issued in 1980, for example, gave much higher priority to agricultural investment at a time when the Islamist uprising was forcing the political leadership to consolidate its support among its key social support group.

Meanwhile, using the bureaucracy to respond to political exigencies sharply conflicted with the requisite of bureaucratic autonomy as a tool of development. The lack of bureaucratic control over long-term investment is evident in the huge discrepancies between five-year plans and actual investments. The absence of an industrial strategy reached an absurd level during the investment boom of the mid-1970s. Muhammad Haydar, vice-premier for economic affairs, recounts how he went to Saudi Arabia after the 1973 war to request funds for development projects. Saudi King Faysal asked him for a list of projects and figures, but Haydar had come unprepared and spent the night with his pocket calculator to put together a program.[14] Moreover, even when technocrats objected to particular projects on reasonable grounds, their protests were often ignored, leading to manifold economic deficiencies.[15] The political logic of bureaucratic inefficiency is exemplified in Hinnebusch's study of the agrarian bureaucracy, where he found that despite significant technocratic input into the policy process, "the subordination of economic rationality to the calculus of power is evident in policies such as the use of the bureaucracy to maximize employment and in the sacrifice of profitability in agro-industry to patronage and low priced output."[16]

When the regime elects to grant bureaucratic autonomy, however, Syrian agencies are quite capable. The parastatal engineering and construction firm, Milihouse, or the Military Housing Establishment, has performed well since its establishment in 1975. Deriving most of its business from civilian contracts, by the early 1980s Milihouse had expanded to in-

[13] Nonneman, *Development, Administration and Foreign Aid in the Middle East,* 44.

[14] See Patrick Seale, *Asad: The Struggle for the Middle East* (Berkeley: University of California Press, 1988), 447–48.

[15] Perthes, *Political Economy of Syria,* 44.

[16] Raymond A. Hinnebusch, "Bureaucracy and Development in Syria: The Case of Agriculture," *Journal of Asian and African Studies* 24 (January and April 1989), 80.

clude more than sixty factories and fifty subsidiary firms. The secret of Milihouse's success is that each subsidiary was given "its own management and a large degree of financial autonomy, and, most importantly, is permitted to operate as a private company, freeing it from the onerous bureaucracy of the public sector."[17]

Patterns of Taxation and Expenditure in Syria and Turkey

The effective deployment of fiscal resources is a potentially important mechanism of state-assisted development. But patterns of fiscal extraction and expenditure are highly sensitive to coalitional considerations. This section demonstrates that during the precocious Keynesian period, obligations to constituencies curbed state capacity to extract resources from society and forced reliance on indirect and invisible taxes far more than on direct taxes. At the same time, state expenditures, a large portion of which were devoted to welfare programs, regularly outstripped domestic receipts. The resulting budget deficits were partially covered by external transfers of economic and military aid but also by inflationary monetary policy, which stimulated destabilizing "state intervention" cycles—periods of expansionary state spending based on budget deficits, followed by periods of inflation and subsequent retrenchment. The positive contributions public investments made to development were thus constrained by the exigencies of coalition maintenance.

Turkey

Between 1923 and 1949, Turkish governments practiced fiscal conservatism, with budget surpluses occurring in 21 of 27 years. The onset of precocious Keynesianism in 1950 altered fiscal practices; as government expenditures steadily increased, both absolutely and as a share of national income, they quickly exceeded government revenues, producing persistent budget deficits in all but four years between 1950 and 1980.[18] Budget deficits averaged 3 percent of gross national product (GNP) between 1953 and 1957, declined to 2.3 percent through 1962, but then skyrocketed to 5.3 percent between 1963 and 1967 and to 6 percent

[17] As cited in Eliahu Kanovsky, *What's Behind Syria's Current Economic Problems* (Tel Aviv: The Dayan Center for Middle Eastern and African Studies, Occasional Papers, 1985), 20. Barbara Geddes refers to islands of bureaucratic autonomy in a sea of patronage-based administrations as "pockets of efficiency." See Barbara Geddes, "Building 'State' Autonomy in Brazil, 1930–1964." *Comparative Politics* 22 (January 1990): 217–35.

[18] Republic of Turkey, *Statistical Indicators, 1923–1990* (Ankara: State Institute of Statistics, 1991), 390–91.

through 1972.[19] By 1979–1980, the budget deficit had reached 12.2 percent of GNP.[20] But even these figures underestimate the deficits of the public sector, because they do not include the losses of several public agencies that finance their operations by borrowing from the Central Bank. The agricultural agency Toprak, for example, financed its purchases of agricultural goods at above-market prices by issuing bonds guaranteed by the Treasury. Because these bonds were never redeemed, the costs of maintaining an agricultural support policy were ultimately met simply by printing money.[21] Toprak's debt in the 1950s amounted to 45 percent of the decade's total increase in currency and 40 percent of the total currency in circulation by 1959.[22]

Just as political considerations dictated increased spending, they also forced politicians to reduce revenue extractions, exacerbating budget deficits. In 1954, for example, remaining taxes on agriculture were eliminated. As Dwight Simpson wryly observed, "However valuable such a step may have been politically, when 77 percent of a population and 40 percent of a gross national product is exempted from taxation it becomes very hard to finance a large investment program without a corresponding deficit."[23] Parliamentary debates in the 1960s demonstrated that Turkish politicians understood both the need to raise tax revenues and the political costs associated with the relevying of such taxes.[24] As a result, agricultural taxes were not reimposed until after the September 1980 military coup. Consequently, even as tax revenue rose from 15.3 percent of GNP in 1974 to its highest level of 19.2 percent in 1977, Turkey remained below the average of 19.6 percent for a sample of twenty middle-income countries.[25]

With political imperatives ruling out increased taxes, Turkish governments turned to external sources of income to finance their deficits. Capital inflows have been particularly important. U.S. military and economic aid commenced in 1946 and represented large capital inflows during the

---

[19] International Bank of Reconstruction and Development, *The Economic Development of Turkey*, Vol. II. Domestic and External Finance, 1974, Chapter 5, page 3.

[20] Bent Hansen, *Political Economy of Poverty, Equity, and Growth: Egypt and Turkey* (Oxford: Oxford University Press), 369.

[21] Aydin Ulusan, "Public Policy Toward Agriculture and Its Redistributive Implications," in *Political Economy of Income Distribution in Turkey*, 127.

[22] Zvi Hershlag, *Turkey: The Challenge of Growth* (Leiden: E. J. Brill, 1968), 164.

[23] "Development as a Process: The Menderes Phases in Turkey," *Middle East Journal* 19 (Spring 1965), 149.

[24] Ustun Erguder, "The Politics of Agricultural Taxation in Turkey, 1945–1965," Ph.D. Dissertation, Syracuse University, 1970.

[25] World Bank, *Turkey: Industrialization and Trade Strategy* (Washington, D.C.: The World Bank, 1982), 174.

1950s.[26] Total project and program assistance, along with grain aid, averaged 2 percent of GNP, 23 percent of imports, and almost 12 percent of fixed investments in the period 1950–1979.[27] After 1970, Turkey became increasingly indebted, as total debt increased from $1.9 billion in 1970 to $19 billion in 1980.[28] Finally, in the early 1970s, remittances from Turkish workers abroad amounted to 5 percent of gross domestic product (GDP), covering an average of 39 percent of Turkey's import bill between 1972 and 1974.[29] A second source of deficit financing was the Central Bank, which pursued loose monetary policies. Between 1950 and 1984, the rate of growth in the money supply was 26 percent, more than 20 points higher than growth in national income, yielding an inflationary expansion of the money supply averaging 20 percent annually.[30]

Analysis of expenditure patterns also indicates Turkey's commitment to precocious Keynesianism. Between 1972 and 1978, for example, transfer payments regularly outpaced investment, consuming on average 32 percent of government expenditures, whereas investment accounted for just under 20 percent. Government payments to public-sector enterprises and agencies to cover operating losses constituted a major share of transfer payments, but even these sums covered only one-half of public-sector debt.[31] Between 1973 and 1980, the total financial requirements of state enterprises averaged about 6.5 percent of GNP.[32]

Consequently, Turkey passed through regular state intervention cycles between 1950 and 1980, as expansionary monetary policies dictated by infirm fiscal practices resulted in high inflation and balance of payments deficits. Each episode of state-induced inflation was temporarily halted by the implementation of austerity programs. Not coincidentally, each episode was also accompanied by a military coup, and it was authoritarian governments that enacted painful reforms (1960–1961, 1970–1973, and

[26] Total economic and military aid was 2.6 billion dollars between 1953 and 1961; of this total, almost 90 percent took the form of grants. Atila Eralp, "Turkey in the Changing Post-War World Order: Strategies of Development and Westernization," in *Developmentalism and Beyond: Society and Politics in Egypt and Turkey*, ed. Ayse Oncu, Caglar Keyder, and Saad Eddin Ibrahim (Cairo: American University in Cairo Press, 1994), 208.

[27] Calculated from figures in Hansen, *Political Economy of Poverty, Equity, and Growth*, 377.

[28] Anne O. Krueger and Okan H. Aktan, *Swimming Against the Tide: Turkish Trade Reform in the 1980s* (San Francisco: Institute for Contemporary Studies, 1992), 28.

[29] Hansen, *Political Economy of Poverty, Equity, and Growth*, 392.

[30] Ibid., 372.

[31] World Bank, *Turkey: Policies and Prospects for Growth* (Washington, D.C.: The World Bank, 1980), 62–63. Transfer payments refer to payments by the state that are not in compensation for a good or service. The deficits of SEEs rose from 12.8 billion TL in 1975 to 47.7 billion TL in 1978. The difference was covered by other domestic sources such as borrowing from the Central Bank, and foreign borrowing.

[32] Averages calculated from data in John Waterbury, *Exposed to Innumerable Delusions* (Cambridge: Cambridge University Press, 1993), 122.

1980–1983). State intervention cycles recurred, however, with each return to civilian government.

Syria

Between 1931 and 1945, years of the French mandate in Syria, the budget registered a surplus in all but three years. Between 1946 and 1957, budgets were in the black for all but four years.[33] Beginning in 1958, official Syrian budgets have been balanced, and estimates of budget deficits vary. According to data reported to the World Bank, Syrian budget deficits climbed from 3.5 percent of GDP in 1972 to 10.8 percent of GDP in 1977, before dipping back down to 9 percent in 1978.[34] Analyzing the size of public-sector borrowing, Eliyahu Kanovsky found budget deficits for every year from 1968 to 1980, with the exception of 1979. The average budget deficit for this period was 7.8 percent of GDP, ranging from 3.7 percent in 1969 to 15.6 percent in 1976.[35] Lavy and Sheffer estimate that between 1974 and 1978, budget deficits averaged 34 percent of GDP; as external financing averaged 16 percent of GDP, domestic financing covered the remaining deficit of 18 percent of GDP.[36]

Official government data group Syrian tax revenue into five categories: taxes, state property, extrabudgetary receipts or nontax revenues from public agencies and enterprises, diverse receipts composed of international capital inflows, and finally exceptional receipts, which refer to domestic loans from the financial sector and are used primarily as a device to produce balanced budgets. As a percentage of GDP, tax revenues increased from 7.4 percent in 1964 to 11 percent in 1972, and then dipped slightly, averaging 10 percent through 1976.[37] As a share of total government resources, taxes contributed a declining share, from 61 percent in 1964 to 30 percent in 1970 and then down to 13 percent in 1979.[38] Ex-

---

[33] *Recueil des Statistiques Syriennes Comparées, 1928–1968* (Damascus: Office Arabe de Presse et de Documentation, 1970), 113.

[34] World Bank, *World Tables, 1989–1990* (Baltimore: Johns Hopkins University Press, 1990), 544.

[35] *What's Behind Syria's Current Economic Problems*, 25–7 and Table 5.

[36] Victor Lavy and Eliezer Sheffer, *Foreign Aid and Economic Development in the Middle East: Egypt, Syria, and Jordan* (New York: Praeger, 1990), 57.

[37] Figures for 1964 to 1977 from Eliahu Kanovsky, *The Economic Development of Syria* (Tel Aviv: University Publishing Projects, 1977), 106–107. Figures for 1973 to 1977 calculated from data on tax revenues taken from Hossein Askari, et al., *Taxation and Tax Policies in the Middle East* (London: Butterworth Scientific, 1982), 164; and GDP as reported in *World Tables, 1989–1990*, 544. In calculating tax revenues, I excluded both pipeline royalties and the contributions of state enterprises, most of which are taken from the sale of oil.

[38] Office Arabe de Presse et de Documentation, *Le Budget de la Syrie*, various years.

cluding capital inflows, the share of tax revenues in total government resources is higher, but still declined from 67 percent in 1966 to 34 percent in 1975. Tax revenues, furthermore, stem largely from indirect taxes: as a share of total government domestic resource mobilization, direct taxes on citizens averaged 12 percent between 1966 and 1977, ranging from a low of 7 percent in 1975 to a high of 15 percent in 1977. The corresponding average share of indirect taxes was 38 percent, ranging from 27 percent in 1975 to 54 percent in 1966.[39] In short, as one analyst put it, "Syria's taxpayers do not carry a particularly heavy load."[40]

To some extent, the surplus of state enterprises compensates for the low level of taxation; these funds have contributed as much as 30 percent of all government revenues in some years. Oil revenues constitute most of these funds, as public industrial enterprises seldom earn profits. Even with these funds, however, Syria depends on external sources of capital to underwrite budget deficits and to permit the state to sustain private and public consumption while financing a large military and an ambitious development program. External funds contributed less than 20 percent of total revenues in the 1960s, but in 1975 they chipped in for 29 percent, and they accounted for more than one-third of total revenues in 1979 and 1980.[41] Given these figures, some scholars have suggested that many features of the Syrian political economy can be accounted for by the rentier state thesis. The rentier state thesis (or sometimes the allocation state thesis) argues that states deriving most of their revenue from external sources, not from domestic resource mobilization, are characterized by a high degree of state autonomy, authoritarian governments, bureaucracies that are oriented toward distribution and not extraction, and an emphasis on consumption, not development.[42] Although originally developed in relation to oil-producing states of the Arab Gulf and Iran, the paradigm has been applied to states such as Syria, which are recipients of

---

[39] Askari et al., *Taxation and Tax Policies in the Middle East*, 164. The highest tax rate in Syria is 12 percent; civil servants, from whom taxes could easily be collected with minimal administrative effort, are taxed at a flat rate of only 4.4 percent. Given these low rates, income taxes amounted to just over 1 percent of total government revenues in the early and mid-1970s. Ibid., 286.

[40] Patrick Clawson, *Unaffordable Ambitions: Syria's Military Build-Up and Economic Crisis* (Washington, D.C.: The Washington Institute for Near East Policy, 1989), 12. In 1977, per capita tax revenues in Syria were $107, the fourth lowest of 16 Arab countries. Askari et al., *Taxation and Tax Policies in the Middle East*, 94.

[41] Calculated from Office Arabe de Presse et de Documentation, *Le Budget de la Syrie*, various years.

[42] The rentier state thesis was first articulated by Hossein Mahdavi, "The Pattern and Problems of Economic Development in Rentier States: The Case of Iran," in *Studies in the Economic History of the Middle East*, ed. M. A. Cook (London: Oxford University Press, 1972). More recent versions of the argument can be found in *The Rentier State*, ed. Hazem Beblawi and Giacomo Luciani (London: Croon Helm, 1987).

transfers from their wealthier neighbors, transforming them into "induced allocation states."[43]

Syria fits uneasily into this paradigm. Luciani, for example, defines allocation states as those receiving more than 40 percent of their revenues from external sources. According to this threshold, however, Syria was only temporarily an allocation state and slipped in and out of the category on a regular basis.[44] Moreover, Syria did not cross the 40 percent threshold until the mid-1970s. This raises a significant problem for the paradigm: the features of the Syrian political economy that are attributed to the presence of oil rents existed before the 1970s, so that the dependent variables predate the emergence of the independent variable. More fundamentally, the thesis fails to distinguish between constraining conditions and permissive conditions: the presence of externally derived wealth makes certain arrangements possible but does not dictate their establishment. Indeed, proponents of the approach have not grappled with countercases, such as democratic Venezuela, or substantial industrial development, such as in Indonesia.[45] The argument advanced here explains the origins of Syria's political-economic arrangements; the presence of huge rents partly explains the relative longevity of these features despite inefficient economic performance.

Even with generous external support, Syria ran persistent budget deficits through 1980, which were financed by expansionary monetary policy. Indeed, the average annual rate of expansion in the money supply was almost completely governed by financing the budget deficit left over after accounting for external transfers. Thus, between 1963 and 1967, the money supply expanded by 9.2 percent annually, and bank financing of budget deficits increased by 9.1 percent annually. Between 1967 and 1972, while the money supply was expanding at a rate of 14.9 percent, bank financing of budget deficits increased by 25.5 percent per annum, and financing of public enterprises expanded at the rate of 18.6 percent annually.[46]

Syrian budget data do not directly indicate the total size of transfer payments, as a substantial portion of subsidies, particularly for essential consumer goods, are financed by the Stabilization Fund and thus do not ap-

[43] For discussion of "induced allocation states, see Giacomo Luciani, "Allocation vs. Production States: A Theoretical Framework," in *The Rentier State*, 63–82; and Michel Chatelus and Yves Schemeil, "Towards a New Political Economy of State Industrialization in the Arab Middle East," *International Journal of Middle East Studies* 16 (May 1984): 251–65.

[44] Luciani, "Allocation vs. Production States," 72, 74.

[45] For an important statement of the rentier state thesis that attempts to account for deviations from the modal outcome stressed in the earlier literature, see Terry Lynn Karl, *The Paradox of Plenty: Oil Booms and Petro-States* (Berkeley: University of California Press, 1997).

[46] Kanovsky, *The Economic Development of Syria*, 106–10.

pear in the budget. Still, available data do support the contention that precocious Keynesian states dedicate large shares of state funds to transfer payments, as subsidies for both consumers and producers, and to finance losses of public-sector enterprises. As a percentage of total expenditure in the consolidated budget, internal subsidies and other transfer payments climbed from 10 to 21 percent between 1974 and 1980, averaging about 14 percent during this period.[47] A substantial portion of these funds comprised official transfers to the public sector, which rose from $410 million in 1974 to $1.5 billion in 1980. In 1981, total reported costs of the controlled price and subsidy system, including these transfer payments to the public sector, was Syrian lira (LS) 4.5 billion, or roughly 7 percent of GDP.[48]

As in Turkey, Syria's fiscal structures produce state intervention cycles. The index of wholesale prices, for example, rose from 100 in 1963 to almost 173 in 1973, while the corresponding consumer price index rose to 152 in 1973.[49] By 1976, the huge influx of transfers from the oil-producing countries had added to the monetary sources of inflation, driving the inflation rate up to around 30 percent. Deterioration of the balance of payments kept pace with inflation; in constant dollars, the trade deficit in the period 1980–1983 was more than 400 percent greater than the trade deficit of 1968–1972.[50] By the end of the 1970s, the government was forced to introduce drastic measures designed to combat inflation and reduce imports while scaling back government investments in certain sectors.

State Economic Intervention in Turkey and Syria

In Syria and Turkey, coalitional dynamics produced patterns of state economic intervention that insulated constituencies from world-market forces while enhancing their position within protected domestic markets. Because enhancing the position of each class pins costs on other classes, the state had to comprehensively intervene through side-payments to compensate for these costs. This section examines state economic intervention in markets for agricultural inputs and products, labor, credit, and trade policy.

[47] International Monetary Fund, *Government Finance Statistics Yearbook*, vol. 13, 1989, 581.
[48] Lavy and Sheffer, *Foreign Aid and Economic Development in the Middle East*, 32, 50. Because some state-owned enterprises have their losses financed by state-owned banks, even these numbers understate the magnitude of transfer payments.
[49] These figures probably underestimate the actual rate of inflation by 3 to 6 percent annually. Kanovsky, *The Economic Development of Syria*, 108–11.
[50] Kanovsky, *What's Behind Syria's Current Economic Problems*, 35.

Turkish Agricultural Markets

As we saw in Chapter 3, whereas state intervention in agricultural markets before 1950 siphoned rural surplus into the urban industrial sector, after 1950 Turkish governments assiduously cultivated peasant electoral support by transferring funds to the rural sector, thereby increasing peasant incomes. These policies also compensated peasants for the antirural bias of import-substituting industrialization (ISI), although their benefits are unequal and tied to farm size. State intervention worked through various SEEs, whose operations were in turn financed by the Central Bank. Indeed, in many years, agricultural SEEs received more than half of all credits issued by the Central Bank to the public sector, indicating the importance successive governments have placed on agricultural policy.[51] SEEs incurred these debts by regularly purchasing agricultural commodities at above world-market prices, resulting in terms of trade that consistently favored agriculture, while providing key inputs such as fertilizers at below world prices and cost.[52] State subsidies for bread, milk, and meat in turn partially compensated urban consumers for higher agricultural prices.[53]

Because they played such an important political role, policies subsidizing farmers remained in place even as they produced economically inefficient behavior, as graphically illustrated in Christopher Hann's study of tea production in the Black Sea region.[54] Production of tea is undertaken by a large number of small farmers whose well-being is guaranteed by state subsidies granted by agencies that monopolize the purchasing and processing of tea, buying it at above market prices and then selling it at subsidized prices to consumers. The entire industry is under state control: permission to extend cultivation, for example, must be granted by the authorities. The status of the state as the monopsonistic purchaser of the tea harvest and its control over the process of production have not translated into state capacity to rationalize the tea industry or make Turkish tea competitive on the international market. Well aware that the state will purchase whatever they produce, Turkish peasants have tenaciously worked to escape state control to expand production beyond what the domestic market would bear. Boosting domestic demand would have required reducing the price paid to producers, which was politically unfea-

---

[51] World Bank, *Turkey: Policies and Prospects for Growth*, 69.

[52] Ismail Bulmus, "Türkiye'de Tarimsal Taban Fiyat Politikasi ve Etkileri," *METU Studies in Development* (1981): 541–573; Kutlu Somel, "Agricultural Support Policies in Turkey, 1950–1980: An Overview," in *Food, States, and Peasants in the Middle East: Analyses of the Agrarian Question*, ed. Alan Richards (Boulder, Colo.: Westview Press, 1986), 98.

[53] World Bank, *Turkey: Policies and Prospects for Growth*, 69.

[54] C.M. Hann, *Tea and the Domestication of the Turkish State* (Huntington, England: The Eothen Press, 1990).

sible. Exporting the excess production was ruled out due to the low quality of Turkish tea: quality control was completely lacking because during periods of intense party competition, state agencies were instructed to avoid antagonizing rural supporters. Furthermore, the monopsonistic structure, which paid a uniform purchase price, precluded competition between factories and so guaranteed that no market mechanism would serve to penalize inefficient behavior. As a result, excess production was merely dumped into the Black Sea.

Turkish Labor Markets

Public enterprises also played a major role in the incorporation of urban labor into the cross-class coalition. The price of labor support has been the overstaffing of SEEs and wage increases that were decoupled from productivity increases. Despite the greater concentration of capital-intensive industries in the public sector, employment practices driven by political considerations have greatly inflated the size of the public-sector workforce. In 1968, for example, the nine largest state manufacturing concerns had combined sales of Turkish lira (TL) 6.1 billion while employing a labor force of 91,000 workers. At the same time, the ninety largest private-sector firms, concentrated in labor-intensive industries, had sales of TL 9.5 billion, while employing only 86,000 workers.[55] Despite continued investment in heavy, capital-intensive industry in the public sector, the labor intensity of the public sector relative to that of the private sector continued to increase. One study estimated that as the share of the public industrial sector in total output declined from about 51 percent in 1970 to 30 percent in 1979, its share in manufacturing employment remained constant at 36 percent.[56] According to a second analysis, as the size of the industrial labor force increased at an annual rate of 4.3 percent between 1970 and 1977, labor employed in the SEEs increased at an average annual rate of 11.1 percent.[57] Although the figures from the two studies are only rough estimates, they both indicate a general magnitude of overemployment, corroborating the conclusion reached by Vedat Milor in his study of the (non)developmental role of the Turkish public sector: that due to political pressures, "the SEEs supply jobs of zero and even negative marginal productivity to the unemployed and thus

---

[55] Bertil Walstedt, *State Manufacturing Enterprise in a Mixed Economy: The Turkish Case* (Baltimore: Johns Hopkins University Press, 1980), 31–32.

[56] World Bank, *Turkey: Industrialization and Trade Strategy*, 248.

[57] World Bank, *Turkey: Policies and Prospects*, 66.

contribute negatively to economic growth by locking (human) resources in low value-added fields. . . ."[58]

Because of the admission of public-sector labor into the cross-class coalition and the exclusion of civil servants, the wage levels of even unskilled public-sector labor rose above both administrative staff in the public sector and skilled labor in the private sector. In 1980, for example, the average annual pay for the 39,000 workers of Sumerbank, a large textile concern that sells directly to consumers, was TL 386,000 ($5,100), while the average annual pay for the 7,932 managerial staff was only TL 308,000 ($4,100).[59] Furthermore, in a sample of 16 industries, the average ratio of real wages of public-sector versus private-sector workers was 1.33; the only industry in which public-sector wages were lower than private wages was printing and publishing, where the ratio was 0.99; in tobacco processing, on the other hand, the ratio was 1.83.[60] By the end of the 1970s, the wage level in all Turkish manufacturing industries was more than 50 percent higher than Korean wages.[61] These data indicate clear links between the distribution of benefits and inclusion in the cross-class coalition.

Turkish Credit Markets

The Turkish state intervened extensively in the financial system, in part to provide subsidized credit, an important tool of state-led development. The developmental effectiveness of state intervention in credit markets, however, is related to the degree of control state officials exercise over borrowers. States exercise the greatest potential leverage in credit-based financial systems with government-administered prices; leverage is reduced when the financial system is based on decentralized capital markets or when credit-based systems are dominated by financial systems owning large equity shares in the industrial firms they finance.[62] The

---

[58] Vedat Halit Milor "A Comparative Study of Planning and Economic Development in Turkey and France: Bringing the State Back In," Ph.D. Dissertation, University of California, Berkeley, 1989, 251.

[59] World Bank, *Turkey: Industrialization and Trade Strategy*, 263.

[60] Ibid., 263–64.

[61] Turkish wages were estimated to be $12.68 per day in 1978 and $15.64 in 1979; the corresponding daily wage in Korea was $8.00 and $10.29. Ibid., 226.

[62] John Zysman, *Governments, Markets, and Growth: Financial Systems and the Politics of Industrial Change* (Ithaca: Cornell University Press, 1983), 18. In addition to France and Japan, both Korea and Taiwan have credit-based financial systems with government-administered prices. In all three countries, the ratio of debt to equity in the corporate sector is high—300 to 400 percent in Japan from the 1950s through the 1970s and in Korea in the 1970s, and between 160 and 200 percent in Taiwan in the 1970s—securities markets are weak, firms resist going public, and banks are by far the most important sources of credit at

leverage stemming from credit-based systems with administered prices is in turn most effectively realized when the growth in the money supply is restricted, so that the state can keep demand greater than supply; when private banks rely on state financing, so that states can effectively set the price of money; and when enterprises rely on sources of finance external to the firm, so that state control over the price and allocation of credit can be translated into state manipulation of calculations of risk, cost, and profitability.[63]

During the period of precocious Keynesianism, the Turkish financial system was overwhelmingly credit-based; in 1980, transactions on securities markets were equal to about 1 percent of the total assets of the banking system.[64] Furthermore, the state exercised discretionary power to set differential interest rates, maintaining, for example, interest rates for medium- and long-term loans for priority industrial sectors below market rates to encourage industrial investment.[65] Thus, there was some potential for the Turkish state to exercise control over investment for developmental purposes, but this potential was not realized.

The Turkish Central Bank's control over the banking system was due to its overwhelming control over assets, relative to domestic commercial deposit banks.[66] Control over assets was derived in part from the authority to expand the money supply. As we saw earlier, however, the Central Bank deliberately inflated the money supply to underwrite government deficits. A second source of Central Bank control over assets was the determination of relatively high reserve deposits required for private banks. According to a World Bank study, however, the system of required reserves allowed the Central Bank to mobilize at low cost "a substantial proportion of the financial resources collected by deposit money banks for the financing of budgetary deficits, public enterprises, and selective credits."[67] Between 1975 and 1980, the share of total assets of the banking sector absorbed by loans to the government and to public-sector enterprises increased from 48 to 61 percent, substantially crowding out private invest-

---

administered prices. See Robert Wade, "The Role of Government in Overcoming Market Failure: Taiwan, Rpublic of Korea, and Japan," in *Achieving Industrialization in East Asia*, ed. Helen Hughes (Cambridge: Cambridge Universe Press, 1988), 131–39.

[63] Sylvia Maxfield, "The Politics of Mexican Financial Policy," in *The Politics of Finance in Developing Countries*, ed. Stephan Haggard, Chung H. Lee, and Sylvia Maxfield (Ithaca: Cornell University Press, 1993), 246.

[64] World Bank, *Turkey: Industrialization and Trade Strategy*, 122.

[65] Ayse Oncu, "Chambers of Industry in Turkey: An Inquiry into State-Industry Relations as a Distributive Domain," in *The Political Economy of Income Distribution in Turkey*, 471.

[66] The Central Bank, public deposit banks, and public investment and development banks together accounted for almost 71 percent of the total assets of the banking system in 1975. World Bank, *Turkey: Industrialization and Trade Strategy*, 134.

[67] Ibid., 127.

ment.[68] Thus, rather than acting as a catalyst for private capital accumulation and as a conduit directing investment into strategic industries, the Central Bank used its control over the financial system to finance precocious Keynesianism. Given the need to finance its own operations, the state preferred to work through the private sector to allocate subsidized medium- and long-term credit to industrial firms.[69] But because private banks preferred higher-interest, short-term commercial loans, the state subsidized longer-term industrial loans by rediscounting borrowers' bills. Because of the state's lack of credibility in rediscounting bills and caps placed on rediscounting, however, private banks generally disdained making the longer-term loans.[70]

Finally, Turkish businessmen had recourse to several practices that reduced state leverage. Unlike their East Asian counterparts, Turkish businessmen relied heavily on self-financing through reinvested profits. Between 1965 and 1971, for example, 61 percent of investment was financed by the resources of the investors; the figure might be as high as 66 percent for industry and as low as 36 percent for agriculture.[71] Even when Turkish firms resorted to credit, however, their access to private financial institutions buffered them from state control. Although legally banks were prohibited from loaning more than 10 percent of their capital to any one firm, this decree was waived for banks holding more than 25 percent equity in the firm. Capitalists responded by creating vertically integrated holding companies consisting of commercial and industrial enterprises and commercial banks.[72] In general, private banks made state-subsidized, long-term industrial loans only to firms in which they were shareholders. In practice, then, the largest firms had easy access to credit, some of which was subsidized by the state. As a result, the state had highly restricted leverage over the allocation of credit.[73] Minimal state control coupled with a differential interest rate system that provided incentives for banks to loan to commercial firms led banks to channel credit into commerce rather than into industrial undertakings. Between 1962 and

[68] Ibid., 149–50.

[69] Public investment banks constituted only 11.6 percent of the total banking system in 1975, declining to under 5 percent in 1980. Ibid., 134.

[70] Oncu, "Chambers of Industry in Turkey," 471–72.

[71] World Bank, *Turkey: Prospects and Problems of an Expanding Economy* (Washington, D.C.: The World Bank, 1980), 87.

[72] Oncu, "Chambers of Industry in Turkey," 471, argues that because the 1957 law that gave rise to these conglomerates applied to both public and private banks, it cannot be understood as a deliberate measure to increase private investments. Yet the fact remains that this law was part of a broader package of policies specifically designed to encourage private investments and is thus best interpreted as a side-payment offered to the private sector.

[73] Ayse Bugra, *State and Business in Modern Turkey: A Comparative Study* (Albany: SUNY Press, 1994), 222–23.

1978, the majority of bank credits financed commercial operations, whereas only a minuscule amount went to industry.[74]

In summary, massive state intervention in the financial system subsidized borrowers without rendering the state capable of promoting capital accumulation and guiding new investments into targeted sectors, partially because the state used its control over the banking system to offset its continuous budget deficits. Furthermore, the policy of printing money to cover deficit spending meant that the money supply was insufficiently restricted to provide the state leverage over the entire banking system. In addition, the hybrid nature of the Turkish financial system did not render bureaucrats capable of guiding industrial investment into sectors promising rapid mobility. Instead, commercial banks, responding to the incentive structures that the state established, lent their funds to commercial sectors (i.e., to sectors that did not directly contribute to development). Even the policy of industrial incentives was not combined with adequate planning to ensure that these incentives would be allocated in a discriminatory manner. As one study concluded, "The industrial incentives system only serves as a means of transferring moneys from the Government's Budget to investors without contributing to the channeling of investments into the activities whose promotion is envisaged by the Development Plans and without contributing to the optimal allocation of the scarce resources of the society."[75] Thus, in direct contrast to the Korean and Taiwanese states, Turkish state control over the financial system was relatively infirm and did not render the state capable of promoting development.

Turkish Trade Strategy

Because side-payments to peasants and workers impose costs on industrialists, and the deficit financing of these side-payments causes significant inflation, the state must compensate industrialists through mechanisms such as subsidized credit or intermediate inputs sold below cost by public enterprises to the private sector. Turkish state enterprises producing intermediate inputs for private-sector firms, for example, sold their output at prices ranging from 1 to 46 percent below cost.[76] In addition, by increasing factor costs and fueling inflation (given a fixed exchange

---

[74] In 1962, 51 percent of all credits went to private-sector commerce, and only 3 percent to private-sector industry. By 1978, the share of commerce had risen to almost 63 percent whereas the share of industry remained under 5 percent. The public sector, on the other hand, received 14 percent of all bank credits in 1962, and 9 percent in 1978. Yakup Kepenek, *Turkiye Ekonomisi: Gelisimi, Uretim Yapisi, ve Sorunlariyla* (Ankara: Savas Yayinlari, 1983), 153. See also Oncu, "Chambers of Industry in Turkey," 471.

[75] Hasan Olgun, "The Structure of Protection in Turkish Manufacturing Industries," *Gelisme Dergisi* 6 (Kis 1975), 147.

[76] Milor, "Comparative Study of Planning and Economic Development," 246–48.

rate), side-payments price locally manufactured goods out of international and unprotected local markets. Therefore, states will compensate local industrialists through protection; the construction of cross-class coalitions in late-developing economies is a sufficient but not necessary cause of ISI.[77] Coalition-building elites could maintain open markets while using other forms of direct subsidies to compensate industrialists. There are two reasons why this strategy is not likely to be chosen, however. First, protection is a relatively inexpensive way for the state to compensate industrialists. Not only does a protected market induce investment, but the mechanisms of protection generate state revenues. Barring protection, much higher levels of subsidies would be required to coax investment from industrialists facing international competition, placing additional burdens on state budgets already strapped by the loss of tariff revenues. Second, a feasible economic logic underpins the strategy of compensating industrialists through protection. In principle, payments made to lower classes expand the size of the domestic market, providing increased demand for the products of protected industries.[78]

Turkish trade strategy between 1950 and 1980 supports this proposition, albeit with the proviso that although policy elites may experiment with other trade strategies, these will be unsustainable. Between 1950 and 1953, for example, Turkey maintained liberal trade and payments policies while encouraging agricultural exports. As many have noted, this strategy was initially consistent with basing political incumbency on the support of rural farmers and urban commercial interests, but its deficiencies became readily apparent. Beginning in 1950, agricultural price supports created strong inflationary pressures.[79] By 1954, inflation induced by precocious Keynesianism began pricing Turkish agricultural goods out of foreign markets, resulting in a decline in exports, an unsustainable balance-of-payments deficit, and critical shortages in imported materials needed for industrial output.[80] In response, Turkish manufacturers joined a handful of American firms convinced that exporting was not a viable strategy in calling for compensatory protectionist tariffs.[81]

---

[77] Note that ISI is consistent with pinning the costs of development on popular classes. But once a decision has been made *not* to pin those costs on constituencies, ISI becomes almost inevitable.

[78] For discussion of this logic in reference to Turkey, see Somel, "Agricultural Support Policies in Turkey," 117.

[79] Anne O. Krueger, *Foreign Trade Regimes and Economic Development: Turkey* (New York: Columbia University Press, 1974), 40–47, also lists rising government expenditures and losses of state economic enterprises selling goods at below cost as contributing to inflation.

[80] William Hale, *The Political and Economic Development of Modern Turkey* (London: Croon Helm, 1981), 104–6.

[81] Sylvia Maxfield and James H. Nolt, "Protectionism and the Internationalization of Capital: U.S. Sponsorship of Import Substitution Industrialization in the Philippines, Turkey, and Argentina," *International Studies Quarterly* 34 (1990), 70, note that even Ameri-

The Menderes government resolutely opposed currency devaluations that might have offset domestic inflation and made Turkish goods more competitive. Devaluation made little political or economic sense. Given the state's commitment to precocious Keynesianism, devaluations would have been continually offset by high inflation.[82] Devaluation, furthermore, would have disadvantaged urban merchants and farmers, two key constituencies, while inflation disadvantaged civil servants, who were not members of the DP coalition, and urban workers, who were secondary members of the DP coalition.[83] Thus, by late 1953, Turkey began to shift toward ISI, a strategy that promised to promote industrialization while satisfying capitalists, workers, and farmers.[84] High levels of side-payments incurred through the construction of cross-class coalitions, in other words, ultimately compels policy makers to choose ISI.

In 1970, Turkey's second "precocious Keynesian cycle" forced the Justice Party (JP) government headed by Suleyman Demirel to implement stabilization measures. Along with devaluing the lira, Demirel levied new taxes designed "to boost the manufacturing sector's competitiveness and to force the assembly industries to seek domestic sourcing for their imported components."[85] Demirel's measures quickly produced a burst of exports, led by a dramatic increase in manufactured exports. Industrialists, however, objected vociferously to these measures, and the Demirel government ultimately succumbed to business opposition.

Barkey argues that the tax on assembly industries was not unbearable and that private-sector opposition was a response to Demirel's failure to consult with businessmen before implementing his policy package. Business opposition also stemmed, however, from the failure to reform precocious Keynesianism. By the late 1960s, rising wages and continued labor militancy had led many industrialists to adopt a more militant, antilabor

---

can manufacturers with state-of-the-art manufacturing facilities were soon dissuaded from exporting.

[82] The government offered premium rates for selected export goods amounting to a 13 percent devaluation between 1953 and 1957, but this was more than offset by continued increases in the domestic prices of these goods. Hale, *Political and Economic Development*, 106.

[83] Maxfield and Nolt, "Protectionism and the Internationalization of Capital," 71.

[84] As Haggard observes, *Pathways from the Periphery*, 35, in relatively resource-rich countries, devaluation benefits the agro-export sector without advancing industrialization. An overvalued exchange rate combined with agricultural subsidies, on the other hand, benefits the countryside without biasing against industrialization and lowers the domestic price of capital good imports. Note that ISI did not become an explicitly articulated development strategy in Turkey until 1961. The 1953 measures, however, were clearly aimed at promoting import-substituting industrialization: for example, they licensed and taxed nonessential imports, while permitting unlicensed imports of machinery, industrial raw materials, and spare parts.

[85] Henri J. Barkey, *The State and the Industrialization Crisis in Turkey* (Boulder, Colo.: Westview Press, 1990), 154. Note also that the wide-ranging tax increases spared the agricultural sector, where JP electoral support was concentrated.

policy.[86] Furthermore, industrialists began to voice complaints about Demirel's prorural policies when the manufacturing terms of trade noticeably deteriorated. They argued for reduced support for farmers to check inflation and to boost capital accumulation.[87] Businessmen were thus clearly displeased with an economic package that pinned extra costs on them while sparing the agrarian sector from any reductions in their privileges. That Demirel heeded industrialists' calls to scrap the new policies is not an indication of business strength; business could not, after all, force Demirel to reduce payments to the agrarian sector.[88] Instead, Demirel simply adhered to the logic of side-payments. Either he would have to cut payments to workers and farmers to compensate businessmen for reductions in their privileges or he would have to restore side-payments to industrialists; because the former threatened political disaster, Demirel chose the latter. As in the 1950s, then, a return to ISI was necessary to hold the state's social coalition together. Not surprisingly, Turkey's decisive shift to export-led growth (ELG) in the 1980s was accompanied by the dismantling of the cross-class coalition.[89] In sum, Turkey supports the proposition that in countries in the early stages of industrial development, the construction of cross-class coalitions renders ELG infeasible and is thus a sufficient condition for ISI; elites can experiment with other policies, but high levels of side-payments constitute a structural constraint that will quickly and automatically force them to return to ISI.

State Economic Intervention in Syria

Syrian Agricultural Markets

As in Turkey, economic intervention in agricultural markets for credit, inputs, and products gives the state the capacity to determine peasant incomes; given the centrality of peasants to coalitional calculations, the Syrian state has largely supported incomes of peasants.[90] The price of fuel for tractors and irrigation pumps, for example, was kept low and stable through 1974, and even after subsequent price increases in 1975–1976, it

---

[86] Bianchi, *Interest Groups and Political Development in Turkey*, 264–65.

[87] Barkey, *State and the Industrialization Crisis in Turkey*, 129.

[88] Following the 1971 military intervention, the three leading business organizations proclaimed their support for the military government's new agenda, "starting," as one leading businessman put it, "with agricultural and fiscal reforms." These latter reforms did not materialize, however, until late 1980. Barkey, *State and Industrialization Crisis*, 129.

[89] See Chapter 9 for details.

[90] In contrast, prior to 1963, state intervention in agricultural markets was designed only to stabilize prices and was largely ineffectual, in part because of the lack of administrative capacity. See Samir Makdisi, "Syria: The Public Sector and Economic Growth, 1945–1957," Ph.D. Dissertation, Columbia University, 1961, 111–18.

was well below world prices. Over the course of the 1970s, prices paid by peasants for fertilizers averaged 65 to 95 percent of world prices, and the price of fertilizer expressed in wheat declined by over one-half between 1963 and 1976.[91] The state also subsidized credit: individuals paid 5.5 percent on short-term, seasonal loans, and cooperative members paid only 4 percent. For medium-term loans, the rate dropped to 3 and 2 percent respectively.[92] Evidence demonstrates that the state paid peasants above-market prices for farm products as well. Peasant unrest in response to a downturn of prices on world markets in 1964–1965 led the regime to install a new marketing system that stabilized prices and incomes while maintaining above world prices for many farm products.[93] The "fair" rate of profit that is the stated goal of public policy was set at 10 percent in the 1960s; in the 1970s, it was raised to 20 to 25 percent.[94]

Prices paid to peasants vary by crop, and wheat receives the most support. A comparison of state-determined producer prices for wheat in Syria with equivalent prices in Turkey reveals that the average producer price as a percentage of world market prices has been two points higher in Syria than in Turkey, a country in which state support for peasants is well documented and often quoted. With the exception of the years 1974–1976, when prices plummeted, the Syrian government paid peasants well above world market prices for wheat, as much as 26 percent above in 1973.[95] Indeed, in 1977–1978, when U.S. farmers received $85.58 for a metric ton of grain, Syrian growers received $153.84.[96] Moreover, the state purchased sugar beets from producers at above world market prices and sold refined sugars at subsidized prices.[97]

The state has, on the other hand, clearly extracted profits from the sale of cotton, paying particularly low prices between 1974 and 1976 and allowing price increases to lag behind inflation over the course of the 1970s. Cotton is probably the exception, however. Surveying the general trend of agricultural prices, Hinnebusch found that to the extent that the state extracted a surplus for crops other than cotton, the magnitude of resource transfer declined over the 1960s and 1970s and was extremely

---

[91] Raymond A. Hinnebusch, *Peasant and Bureaucracy in Ba`thist Syria: The Political Economy of Rural Development* (Boulder, Colo.: Westview Press, 1989), 140, 135.

[92] Ibid., 126.

[93] Hinnebusch, *Authoritarian Power and State Formation*, 135.

[94] Hinnebusch, *Peasant and Bureaucracy*, 148.

[95] Alan Richards and John Waterbury, *A Political Economy of the Modern Middle East* (Boulder: Westview Press, 1990), 158.

[96] Hinnebusch, *Peasant and Bureaucracy*, 159. By the late 1970s, prices for sugar beets were among the highest in the world.

[97] Oussama S. al-Dimashki, "Endogenizing Government's Price Policies: Sugar Price Policy in Syria," Ph.D. Dissertation, University of Nebraska, 1990.

modest compared to the 50 to 100 percent profit margins enjoyed by landowners, merchants, and moneylenders before 1963.[98] Combined with subsidized inputs, state intervention clearly benefited its middle-peasant base. Hinnebusch estimates that after a decline in the late 1960s, per capita agricultural incomes in 1981 increased 76 percent over the average income for 1960–1963.[99]

Syrian Labor Markets

After the Ba`thist assumption of power, bureaucratic employment ballooned as the new elite used public employment as a patronage resource. A similar trend is apparent in industrial employment. Hinnebusch, who studied agricultural industrialization, found a vegetable oil plant where 250 workers were employed to do the work that could have easily been done by 15.[100] In a 1972 study, Tabitha Petran wrote, "The greatest drain on the profitability of the nationalized firms resulted from overstaffing in both the production and administrative departments."[101] Longuenesse's survey of the public industrial sector in the late 1970s echoes this conclusion.[102] Anecdotal evidence of particular projects regularly confirms these assessments.[103]

By most accounts, living standards of urban labor in the public sector increased throughout the precocious Keynesian period. According to one estimate, while salaries of industrial workers increased 15 percent between 1954 and 1964, prices rose by 25 percent, resulting in a decline in real incomes. In contrast, between 1965 and 1977, salaries increased by 156 percent and prices rose only 131 percent, resulting in real increases of workers' standard of living of 25 percent.[104] Although overall wages in the public sector are lower than in the private sector, wages of the inflated labor forces are still a significant drain on the government budget, and public-sector employment can be quite attractive for unskilled la-

---

[98] Hinnebusch, *Peasant and Bureaucracy*, 150.

[99] Ibid., 276.

[100] Ibid., 165.

[101] Tabitha Petran, *Syria* (London: Ernest Benn, 1972), 210.

[102] Elisabeth Longuenesse, "L'Industrialisation et sa Signification Sociale," in *La Syrie d'Aujourd'hui*, ed. André Raymond (Paris: Centre National de la Recherche Scientifique, 1980), 349. Longuenesse also notes extremely high rates of absenteeism, apparently tacitly accepted by management.

[103] A frequently cited case is that of the paper and pulp mill, whose 800 workers were kept on the payroll during a lengthy conversion process.

[104] Salim Nasr, "Les Travailleurs de l'Industrie Manufacturiere au Machrek: Irak, Jordanie, Palestine, Liban, Syrie," in *Industrialisation et Changements Sociaux dans l'Orient Arabe*, ed. Andre Bourgey (Beirut: Centre d'Etudes et de Recherches sur le Moyen Orient Contemporain, 1982), 159.

bor.[105] Furthermore, employment in many public-sector establishments provides other benefits for workers: secure employment, pensions, and free medical care, child care, and transportation.[106] Finally, the public sector acts as a school for training unskilled labor, often new migrants from the countryside, who then move as skilled labor either to the Gulf, where wages are five times higher than in Syria, or to the private sector. In other words, the public sector acts as employment of last resort for unskilled labor and as a vocational school for the private sector.

Subsidizing Consumers

A third area of state economic intervention that answers to political considerations is the high level of subsidies for basic commodities. Subsidized goods include bread, sugar, tea, cooking oil, fuel oil, and electricity. By subsidizing these goods, the state raises living standards of civil servants, labor, and peasants. Indeed, Law 158 of 1969 set prices of basic consumption goods at below cost.[107] For example, although undersupply of electricity necessitates daily power cutoffs, the price of electricity has fallen in real terms since 1975, currently covering only two-thirds of operating costs. The prices of kerosene and gasoline are both kept at 20 percent below international prices. Indeed, in many instances, the state subsidizes both consumers and producers. Lavy and Sheffer report that at one point, Syria was paying farmers LS 1,230 for soft wheat, importing flour at LS 1,070, and selling flour to state bakeries at only LS 142.5. These bakeries in turn sold bread to the public at a price equal to roughly 13 percent of the imported flour.[108]

The political logic underlying state intervention in agricultural, labor, and basic commodity markets became apparent in 1980, in the midst of the uprising by the Muslim Brotherhood, when the state decided it was time to call in its markers. The regime finally quelled the rebellion in 1982, but only after the Syrian army laid siege to the city of Hama, where the Brotherhood had declared a general uprising. The subsequent destruction of the city resulted in an estimated 20,000 deaths.[109]

[105] When public sector salaries were raised by 10 to 20 percent in 1978, it was estimated that the increase alone would cost the state 159 million dollars. *Middle East Economic Digest (MEED)*, January 20, 1978.

[106] Perthes, *Political Economy of Syria*, 97.

[107] Munir Hamash, *al-Tijara al-Dakhiliyya: al-Suq wa al-Tanmiya* (Damascus: al-Ahali, 1988), 81.

[108] Lavy and Sheffer, *Foreign Aid and Economic Development*, 51. State employees are regularly given bonuses to cover energy costs.

[109] See the chapter on "The Great Repression, 1976 to 1982," in Middle East Watch, *Syria Unmasked: The Suppression of Human Rights by the Asad Regime* (New Haven: Yale University Press, 1991), 8–21.

While unleashing the apparatus of coercion, the regime also took steps to consolidate support with its coalitional constituencies. Peasants, organized labor, and civil servants, as well as the Damascene bourgeoisie, remained loyal to the regime. Their loyalty was ensured by increased payoffs to them. In 1980, when the Syrian army was beginning to go on the offensive against the Muslim Brotherhood, the state also deployed the weapons of precocious Keynesianism: the fifth five-year plan allocated 30 percent of all investments to rural services including new programs of electrification, drinking water infrastructure, roads, schools, and health clinics,[110] and government employees were given pay raises ranging from 10 to 75 percent, the fourth increase in seven years.[111] Following attacks on government stores that sold subsidized goods, subsidies for essential foodstuffs were raised from LS 600 million ($153 million) to LS 900 million ($229.2 million).[112] Further, the government announced a tightening of the system of price controls, a policy that the Muslim Brotherhood denounced to stir up resentment among merchants.[113] In May 1980, a presidential decree lowered limits on landholdings and distributed an additional 28,000 hectares to peasants.[114] Finally, subsidies for university students were increased. By 1981, at the height of the Muslim Brotherhood uprising, it was reported that total subsidies for food and fuel amounted to $1.53 billion, or $150 per capita, a sum equivalent to all revenues earned from oil exports that year.[115]

By this time, however, the state was asking for more than passive loyalty. Pursuing the strategy of using the countryside to surround the cities, Asad addressed a special session of the Peasants Union, saying, "I am first and last a peasant and the son of a peasant." Shortly thereafter, the regime armed and organized peasant battalions to use as a strike force against the "feudalists" who were conspiring to overturn the socialist revolution.[116] Labor unions, student organizations, and other popular organizations also formed militias.

In a democratic system such as Turkey's, the political rationale underpinning public policy can be inferred from numerous sources, and election returns can be used to demonstrate how these policies produce elec-

---

[110] See "Syria Puts the Farmer at Heart of Economy," *MEED*, June 1, 1979.

[111] *MEED*, January 25, 1980.

[112] *MEED*, March 14, 1980.

[113] *MEED*, April 11, 1980.

[114] *MEED*, May 23, 1980.

[115] Alistair Drysdale, "The Asad Regime and Its Troubles," *Merip Reports* 110 (November-December 1982), 6.

[116] These peasant squadrons, as well as a series of reforms designed to shore up support for the regime among peasants, were well covered in the newspaper of the Peasant's Union, *Nidal al-Fallahin*, throughout 1980 and 1981. For Asad's remarks, see *Nidal al-Fallahin*, March 12, 1980.

toral victories. In an authoritarian system like Syria's, making manifest the politics of state economic intervention is more difficult. The crisis confronting the regime in the late 1970s and early 1980s provides one such window onto regime calculations. During that period, the level of state spending directed toward the regime's constituents increased dramatically. These policies were not initiated during the crisis period, only intensified. Available evidence suggests a durable pattern of using state control over pricing policy to channel benefits to selected groups. That pattern spans agricultural markets, labor markets, and markets for final consumption goods. The Ba`th regime, like the center-right political parties governing Turkey, made a concerted effort to protect its constituents from the vagaries of the international market, while enhancing their positions within the domestic market.

The Syrian Banking System

Since the nationalization of banks in the 1960s, the banking system has been reduced to an appendage of the state budget. Loans to the private sector were two-thirds of net domestic credit in 1962 and just under 50 percent in 1963; in the aftermath of the nationalizations, however, loans to the private sector have been negligible. Moreover, one 1972 study found that "short-term commercial credits are very privileged in comparison with medium- and long-term credits essential for industrial and other productive activities."[117] With new public investments financed directly from the budget, the primary role of the banking system was financing budget deficits and the losses of public enterprises, largely through monetary expansion.[118]

The Syrian Foreign Trade Regime

Like most other developing countries in the twentieth century, Syrian industry in 1963 was highly concentrated in light industries transforming agricultural products into finished consumer goods. In 1965, for example, almost three-fourths of total industrial production, in the food-processing, textiles, hides, and tobacco industries, used agricultural products as raw materials.[119] Given the labor intensity of these industries, factor costs loom large in the level of competitiveness. Moreover, much of subsequent industrialization produced products such as fertilizers and tractors for the agrarian sector. In general, then, the profitability and international competitiveness of Syrian industry were highly sensitive to levels of

---

[117] Petran, *Syria,* 216.

[118] Kanovsky, *The Economic Development of Syria,* 105–9 and Table 22A.

[119] Yahya Arudqi, *al-Iqtisad al-Suri al-Hadith,* vol. 1 (Damascus: Ministry of Culture, 1972), 223.

side-payments made to peasants and workers. Rapidly increasing prices for many raw materials, overstaffing of administrative and production personnel, and forced sale of many products at prices near or below cost combined to reduce profitability and international competitiveness, so that public industries were unable to finance the establishment of new plants, technical upgrading, or even the replacement of obsolete plants from their own revenues.[120]

Because industrial development spoke to multiple and competing political and economic goals, which hampered competitiveness, the state had little choice but to pursue ISI.[121] Moreover, the use of foreign resources to fund industrial investments brought about further appreciation of local currency, resulting in a marked bias against exports and toward growth of the nontradables sector and a growing import bill that in turn produced large balance-of-payments deficits.[122] High levels of side-payments effectively precluded ELG and virtually imposed ISI. But high levels of side-payments are not a necessary condition of ISI: as in Turkey, Syrian governments imposed protectionist measures before the precocious Keynesian period.[123] Furthermore, the link between side-payments and ISI is overdetermined in Syria; whereas Turkish governments occasionally experimented with outward-oriented strategies that proved unsustainable, given high levels of side-payments, the Syrian government remained wedded to ISI for multiple reasons, and so the effect of side-payments on trade policy is less visible. Still, the Syrian case supports the proposition that high levels of side-payments rendered ELG infeasible and dictated an ISI regime, even though the recipients of protection were almost exclusively public-sector enterprises, not private capitalists.

The link between side-payments and ISI continued in the 1970s, when the state reincorporated larger businessmen into their coalition. Not surprisingly, the Asad regime elicited the support of businessmen in the 1970s by offering opportunities to earn high profits by exploiting the trade regime; these opportunities included import and export licenses and supervision of government contracts, especially for imports and construction.[124] Consequently, in the 1970s, larger businessmen concen-

---

[120] Hinnebusch, *Peasant and Bureaucracy*, 166.

[121] One report stated these multiple goals as follows: "Syria views import substitution (almost regardless of cost), the decentralization of industry (i.e., establishing plants in various parts of the country), and the employment of a rapidly growing population as being in some cases as important as strict profitability." Cited in Kanovsky, *What's Behind Syria's Current Economic Problems*, 19.

[122] Lavy and Sheffer, *Foreign Aid and Economic Development in the Middle East*, 40–41.

[123] For discussion of Syrian ISI prior to 1963, see Arudqi, *al-Iqtisad al-Suri al-Hadith*, vol. 2, 92–100; and Makdisi, "Syria," 183–92.

[124] These opportunities also included illegal means, such as access to state property, bribes, and illicit commissions. See Volker Perthes, "The Bourgeoisie and the Ba'th," *MERIP Reports* (May-June 1991), 34.

trated their activities in the nontradables sector.[125] Private manufacturing establishments were overwhelmingly small-scale: in 1972, private manufacturing accounted for one-third of total output but 60 percent of the industrial labor force.[126] Private enterprises dominated the real estate, construction, and commercial sectors and constituted significant shares of the transportation and service sectors.[127] For both political and ideological reasons, the regime preferred this division of labor. But even had the regime wanted to encourage large-scale private industrial investment, it would have found itself in the same position as the Turkish state: the exploitation of the financial system to finance budget deficits would have deprived the state of the primary mechanism by which developmental states have collaborated with private capital, the reliance of the private sector on its own sources of funding rendered it independent of the state, and the high level of side-payments effectively ruled out an outward-oriented trade strategy.

The set of political arrangements and institutions discussed in this chapter is the intervening variable of the overall argument. Taken together, they define the capacity of the state to resolve Gerschenkronian and Kaldorian collective dilemmas. The two cases are not strictly equivalent: indeed, the analysis reveals stark differences between them. But in both cases, creating and sustaining relations of constituency clientelism had a fundamental if not determinative impact on other critical institutions linking state, economy, and society. In both countries, bureaucracies were politicized and thus unable to act as effective agents of development; fiscal policies were distributive, rendering both states heavily dependent on a combination of unreliable external sources or inflationary monetary policy to finance budget deficits; and state economic intervention largely spoke to the demands of constituency clientelism by protecting constituencies from the vagaries of the market. Thus, although many of the particulars of the two cases differ, key elements of their respective political economies share fundamental properties. The Syrian and Turkish political economies are analogous, not isomorphic.

What remains to be proved is that these shared features can account for their developmental outcomes. Before turning to this argument in Chapters 7 and 8, however, Chapter 6 surveys state building in Korea and Taiwan to examine the consequences of low levels of elite conflict.

---

[125] The few exceptions are discussed in ibid., 33.

[126] Longuenesse, "L'Industrialisation et sa Signification Sociale," 345. In 1974, the 9,478 registered private manufacturing establishments employed on average only four workers.

[127] Michel Chatelus, "La Croissance Economique: Mutation des Structures et Dynamisme du Dèsèquilibre," in *La Syrie d'Aujourd'hui,* 241.

CHAPTER SIX

Elite Cohesion and State Building in East Asia

Like Syria and Turkey, Korea and Taiwan entered the twentieth century as mediated states: the political infrastructure of the Korean Yi dynasty, for example, combined a highly centralized and patrimonial political center, with an aristocracy-based bureaucracy sufficiently powerful to check royal power.[1] The transformation from mediated to unmediated states thus frames my argument concerning the origins of East Asian developmental states. Arguments about the subsequent emergence of the developmental state in Korea and Taiwan are rendered difficult by the unique colonial experiences of the two countries. Nineteenth- and twentieth-century British and French colonialism retained and ruled through mediated state structures, which characteristically took the form of a thin layer of colonial officials, who allied with local notables and thus had little capacity to actually penetrate the societies they ruled.[2] In contrast, the Japanese colonial administration in Korea and Taiwan built an unmediated state, in which "a highly articulated, disciplined, penetrating colonial bureaucracy substituted both for the traditional regimes and for indigenous groups and classes that under 'normal' conditions would have accomplished development themselves."[3]

---

[1] James Palais, *Politics and Policy in Traditional Korea* (Cambridge: Harvard University Press, 1991), 5. See also Gregory Henderson, *Korea: The Politics of the Vortex* (Cambridge: Harvard University Press, 1968), 13–35.

[2] For illustration of the European strategy of colonial rule through alliances with local elites, see Joel S. Migdal, *Strong Societies and Weak States: State-Society Relations and State Capabilities in the Third World* (Princeton: Princeton University Press, 1988).

[3] Bruce Cumings, "The Origins and Development of the Northeast Asian Political Economy: Industrial Sectors, Product Cycles, and Political Consequences," in *The Political Economy of the New Asian Industrialism*, ed. Frederic C. Deyo (Ithaca: Cornell University Press, 1987), 54. More specifically, Japanese central administrators relied on provincial officials who in turn collaborated with landlords who continued to rule peasants directly. But local landlords had little autonomy from local officials and so little choice but to collaborate

This historical specificity of Korea and Taiwan is the point of departure for two accounts of the origins of developmental states. One line of argument uses a class-power model, arguing that in Korea and Taiwan, the effects of Japanese colonialism, postwar military conflicts, and land reforms yielded weak class structures, particularly through the removal of the old agrarian elite, that were unable to constrain the state or contend for rival development strategies. Hagen Koo exemplifies this position when he writes, "When [Korea and Taiwan] decided to pursue outward-looking industrialization, consequently, they encountered no effective class opposition."[4] Alternatively, Atul Kohli argues that the Japanese actually created a developmental state in their colonies and that the postwar developmental state was merely a continuation of this legacy.[5] In making this argument, Kohli largely dismisses the 1950s regime of Syngman Rhee as anomalous and argues, somewhat metaphorically, that the Park Chung Hee regime, which came to power following a 1961 military coup, simply chose to reimpose the Japanese system: "South Korea under Park Chung Hee did not so much "switch" as it fell back into the grooves of colonial origins, or, more precisely, chose one of the two or three main alternatives that was available to it from its complex historical legacy. . . . The key elements of the eventual path it adopted—a Japanese-style, state-driven export economy—were deeply etched into the social fabric."[6]

These arguments raise many questions. The class power model presents an image of a powerful state unconstrained by weak social classes and thus able to shift toward export-led growth (ELG). But rather than opposing outward-looking industrialization, strong agricultural interests might be expected to support it, as import-substituting industrialization (ISI) frequently produces bias *against* agricultural interests. Indeed, Haggard argues that the weakness of agricultural interests in Korea and Taiwan facilitated the earlier shift to ISI.[7] It is thus not clear from Koo's account why a weakened landlord class was a prerequisite for outward-oriented policies. Furthermore, there are limits to the utility of analyses assessing class power to make demands on the state. Syrian and Turkish

---

closely with colonial directives. As Robert Bullock observes, "Where persuasion failed, various sanctions were readily at hand." See his "Agricultural Development in Korea and Taiwan," manuscript, University of California, Berkeley, n.d., 14.

[4] Hagen Koo, "The Interplay of State, Social Class, and World System in East Asian Development," in *Political Economy of the New Asian Industrialism*, 171.

[5] Atul Kohli, "Where do High Growth Political Economies Come From? The Japanese Lineage of Korea's 'Developmental State'," *World Development* 22 (September 1994): 1269–93. According to Kohli, the three features of the Japanese state that have persisted into the contemporary era are a highly authoritarian and penetrating state, alliances between the state and industrialists, and tight control over labor.

[6] Ibid., 1286.

[7] Stephan Haggard, *Pathways from the Periphery: The Politics of Growth in the Newly Industrializing Countries* (Ithaca: Cornell University Press, 1990), 35–36.

workers and peasants were quite weak when they began receiving privileges from the state, and neither the Syrian nor the Turkish bourgeoisie was strong enough to make binding claims on the state. State elites themselves initiated policies for their own political reasons.

The continuity thesis, on the other hand, slights the striking discontinuities the 1950s represent.[8] With the removal of the Japanese colonial administration, the institutions of the unmediated Korean state virtually disappeared.[9] Furthermore, in the early days of independence, the landlord class made a political comeback, "recapturing the state in 1945 and 1946, under American auspices, and us[ing] it in traditional fashion to protect social privilege rather than to foster growth."[10] Following the outbreak of the Korean War, American forces under MacArthur pushed through numerous reform programs, including the rebuilding of the army and civilian bureaucracy and implementation of land reform. During the 1950s, however, Korea under the Rhee regime was anything but a developmental state; even close ties to industrialists took the more common form of directly unproductive, rent-seeking activities. These striking discontinuities do not necessarily mean that historical antecedents were unimportant, but they sensitize us to the need for careful delineation of the causal mechanism linking history to subsequent phenomena.[11]

Ultimately, I consider both accounts insufficient because they neglect the political dynamics and conflicts attending the transition to developmental states and ELG in the 1960s.[12] We can identify certain sociological

[8] Kohli, "Where do High Growth Political Economies Come From," writes (1270) of the anomolous 1950s, "While there were important discontinuities in the postcolonial period, the grooves that Japanese colonialism carved on the Korean social soil cut deep. The decade and a half following the Japanese departure was at least chaotic, and often tragic. When the dust settled, however, South Korea under Park Chung Hee fell back into the grooves of an earlier origin. . . ." Presumably, the argument also would apply to Taiwan, where the Kuomintang regime (KMT) did not simply inherit the Japanese regime, but brought a huge civil service apparatus with it from the mainland and, once established on the island, instituted numerous state-building measures, including a radical land reform that removed the social stratum that had acted as intermediaries in the past, and substantially reorganized party and administrative structures. See Thomas B. Gold, *State and Society in the Taiwan Miracle* (Armonk, N.Y.: M. E. Sharpe, 1986), 64–67; and Tun-jen Cheng, "Democratizing the Quasi-Leninist Regime in Taiwan," *World Politics* 41 (July 1989), 475.

[9] Henderson writes, "Administration virtually collapsed. With the uprooting of the Japanese, routine vanished. . . . The departure of 700,000 Japanese civilians removed almost all the country's technical and managerial skills and its industrial capital resources." *Politics of the Vortex*, 137.

[10] Cumings, "Origins and Development of the Northeast Asian Political Economy," 66.

[11] For further discussion of Kohli's provocative thesis, see Stephan Haggard, David Kang, and Chung-In Moon, "Japanese Colonialism and Korean Development: A Critique," *World Development* 25 (June 1997): 867-81, followed by Kohli's vigorous defense, "Japanese Colonialism and Korean Development: A Reply," 883–88.

[12] As David C. Kang critically remarks, "Some scholars write as if Korea—like Athena from the head of Zeus—sprang full-grown into development in the 1960s." See David Kang, "South Korean and Taiwanese Development and the New Institutional Economics," *International Organization* 49 (Summer 1995), 577.

and historical specificities that distinguish Korea and Taiwan from other late-developing nations, but we cannot move directly from these features to the rise of the developmental state. As we shall see later, elite conflicts rendered the transition to a developmental state particularly problematic in Korea. Thus, specific features of East Asian societies matter for the way in which they shaped elite conflict and produced distinctive resolutions to that conflict. The causes of relative elite cohesion in East Asia may be idiographic, but the consequences of that cohesion can be theorized.

The preceding three chapters detailed the coalitional consequences and institutional concomitants of high levels of elite conflict in Syria and Turkey. Low levels of elite conflict are a necessary but not sufficient condition for the construction of developmental states. Examining elite conflict in Korea and Taiwan, then, serves three functions: it provides a fuller account of the political antecedents of the developmental state; it establishes that different levels of elite conflict result in divergent state structures; and it offers some insights into the origins of different levels of elite conflict.

Elite Conflict in Taiwan and Korea

Taiwan

Taiwan represents a clear case of state building in the absence of elite conflict and popular-sector incorporation. The principal cause of the loss of the mainland, as the leadership of the Kuomintang (KMT) saw it, had been the party's alliance with larger landlords, which allowed Mao's Communist Party to mobilize peasant support. In response, when the KMT occupied Taiwan in 1949, its leaders were determined to build a strong state on Taiwan that would be based on direct links to the peasantry while circumventing the mediating role of landlords that might check state power. Consequently, the KMT excluded members of the Taiwanese elite from participation in public politics. The KMT faced only weak opposition to its state-building project and its efforts to exclude members of the indigenous Taiwanese elite from political participation. Japanese administrators of Taiwan had almost completely demobilized the population and disbanded the organizations of the leaders of labor or peasant movements. Under the KMT, political repression and organizational controls recreated state autonomy with respect to popular classes.[13] Similarly, local Tai-

---

[13] Although the most prominent political leaders had been neutralized by the Japanese, the KMT responded to antigovernment demonstrations in February 1947 by executing numerous, less prominent members of a potential counter-elite composed of urban intellectuals and some rural notables. See Edwin A. Winckler, "Elite Political Struggle, 1945–1985," in *Contending Approaches to the Political Economy of Taiwan*, ed. Edwin A. Winckler and Susan Greenhalgh (Armonk, N.Y.: M. E. Sharpe, 1988), 153–54.

wanese capitalists posed little opposition to the state and its new developmental projects. A small capitalist class, drawn from the native merchant
class and large landowners, had developed in Taiwan during the Japanese
occupation. But given the high level of economic and political control exercised by the Japanese state, the nascent Taiwanese bourgeoisie was
highly dependent on the state, and its potential for exercising political influence was correspondingly circumscribed.[14] With independence, the
KMT recreated this relationship; the state took a commanding role in rebuilding the devastated economy, while the political elite coopted and
neutralized the business elite, leaving the latter in a position in which
wealth depended on access to the state and acceptance of political marginalization. Hence, by 1950, the KMT faced little overt opposition to its
far-reaching land reform that created an agricultural sector of small holders in direct contact with the state and removed a landlord class that
could have checked state power, thereby decisively building an unmediated state. With the virtual absence of powerful social forces capable of
making binding claims for political inclusion or economic privilege, the
construction of a cross-class coalition could only have resulted from intense elite conflict.[15] As Edwin Winckler observes, however, the political
elite in Taiwan were convinced that "the masses should not be given divisive choices between competing elites.[16]

Elite cohesion, however, stemmed from more than conviction. The political elite of Taiwan was bound by few ties to existing social classes, its
members owed their status to organizational positions and thus placed little value on the economic, political, and social status quo, and they
shared political experiences that taught them lessons about how to consolidate rule and generate political power. The KMT elite was thus internally unified to a degree that no segment of the elite faced incentives to
consider popular incorporation as a political strategy for gaining hegemony.[17] Consequently, the KMT implemented a highly controlled and
gradual form of popular incorporation, and only in the 1970s, well after
the primary ingredients of rapid industrial growth were in place, did incorporation include populist policies designed to create a mass base.

[14] Thomas B. Gold, "Colonial Origins of Taiwanese Capitalism," in *Contending Approaches to the Political Economy of Taiwan*, 101–20.

[15] As Cumings observes, "the Kuomintang had finally found a part of China where its bureaucracy was not hamstrung by provincial warlords and landlords." "Origins and Development of the Northeast Asian Political Economy," 65.

[16] Edwin A. Winckler, "Mass Political Incorporation, 1500–2000," in *Contending Approaches to the Political Economy of Taiwan*, 60. Winckler's analysis is based on the proposition
(42) that "Common interests between elites enable elites to collude to exclude masses, while
conflicting interests between elites require elites to mobilize masses against other elites."

[17] Thomas Gold seconds the claim of KMT elite unity in his "Entrepreneurs, Multina-
tionals, and the State," in *Contending Approaches to the Political Economy of Taiwan*, 203.

Given a cohesive·elite and the absence of social pressure, the KMT political elite was able to delegate authority over economic affairs to a technocratic elite.[18] In the early 1950s, however, members of the economic bureaucracy divided over the appropriate scope for the private sector in development and the relative balance of state and market in the determination of prices and resource allocation. On one side of this cleavage stood socialist-oriented cadres who called for the continuation of state dominance in the economy, based on state ownership of confiscated Japanese industries. Their opponents favored market-oriented policies and advocated expanding the role of the private sector.[19] Similarly, toward the end of the decade, the state elite split over reforms leading to ELG.[20] In principle, battles over development policy could have split the KMT elite, provoking one contending faction to seek mass support as a strategy of conflict resolution.

In practice, however, both debates were resolved within the elite, largely through reference to pragmatic considerations. Thus, in the early part of the 1950s when the state came into ownership of remaining large industry, concerted state effort was needed to revive the economy, and unsettled political conditions dissuaded capitalists from making investments. Under these conditions, the position of the socialist cadres dominated. Subsequently, however, local capitalists rushed to make investments to benefit from protectionist trade policy; by the end of the decade, there was clear evidence that local businessmen could play a valuable role in development, strengthening the position of economic reformers who argued that controlled liberalization would stifle inflationary pressures. Furthermore, the policy of encouraging the private sector narrowed the cleavage separating the mainland political elite from the indigenous Taiwanese and thus bolstered regime stability. Finally, reformers were supported by American pressure and incentives to adopt a position giving greater latitude to market forces and private economic activity. By the end of the 1950s, American advisers were linking continued assistance to a retrenchment of the state from direct production and insisting on giving more freedom to private investors. We should not exaggerate the impact of this pressure: Taiwan did not adopt a particularly liberal system, and reforms did not include privatization of state-owned enterprises. But given the strength of technocratic arguments for incremental liberalization, the potential political benefits from cultivating allies among the native bourgeoisie, and the absence of challenges to state rule, American

---

[18] Ibid.

[19] Gold, *State and Society in the Taiwan Miracle*, 67–73.

[20] Tun-jen Cheng, "Political Regimes and Development Strategies: South Korea and Taiwan," in *Manufacturing Miracles: Paths of Industrialization in Latin America and East Asia*, ed. Gary Gereffi and Donald L. Wyman (Princeton: Princeton University Press, 1990), 153–57.

influence, expressed largely in financial terms, certainly eased the decision to give more weight to the position of liberal economists.[21]

Conflict over basic political-economic arrangements that resulted in precocious Keynesianism in Syria and Turkey was thus not absent in the Taiwanese case. For a number of reasons specific to the Taiwanese case, elite-level conflict was strikingly moderate and was resolved within the political elite without movement toward a more inclusive polity or populist economic policies. But historical specificity does not rule out incorporating Taiwan into a broader theoretical framework based on levels of elite conflict. Low levels of conflict there supplied the necessary condition permitting the construction of a developmental state. So far, I have described only the low level of elite conflict in Taiwan; later in this chapter, I explore the causes of different levels of conflict.

Korea

In the early years of Korean independence, politics was organized around the competition for power among three groups: members of the Korean independence movement centered around Syngman Rhee and, after Rhee's election to the presidency, concentrated in the bureaucratic apparatus; a conservative bloc, composed of landlords, Korean businessmen, and members of the judiciary and police force, that had collaborated with the Japanese colonial administration; and the Communists, the best-organized group in Korea, who also enjoyed mass support.[22] Repressive measures against the left were swiftly implemented. By the early 1950s, the main cleavage in Korean politics separated Rhee and his allies—organized first in the Korean National Party and after 1952 in the Liberal Party—from the conservative landlord bloc organized as the Democratic Nationalist Party (DNP). These two groups had collaborated in containing the left, but once this task was achieved, their interactions turned conflictual.

Land reform was the most contentious issue in postwar Korean politics. Leftist forces, inspired by the North Korean land reform of 1946, seized on the issue as a means of contesting state control over rural areas. By the end of the decade, the U.S. Military Government was pushing land reform as a preemptive, anticommunist measure. Land reform appealed to Rhee as a means of securing a rural base for his regime while appropriating the social base of his conservative rivals. But landlords used their domination of the National Assembly to block reform measures until af-

[21] According to Tun-jen Cheng, the political leadership used the carrot of American assistance to silence dissenting voices. Ibid., 155.

[22] Quee-Young Kim, *The Fall of Syngman Rhee* (Berkeley: Institute for East Asian Studies, 1983), 11–15; and Sungjoo Han, *The Failure of Democracy in South Korea* (Berkeley: University of California Press, 1974), 11–15.

ter the outbreak of the Korean War. When land reform was finally instituted during the Korean War, the conservative bloc lost a major source of
its power. In addition, Rhee's success at cultivating support among Korea's business class through political allocation of rents basically removed
contentious economic issues from the political agenda.[23] The DNP continued to act as an opposition party, but for the rest of the 1950s, inter-
elite conflict took the form of factional rivalries for power and prestige.
Instead, the main political cleavage in Korea pitted the authoritarian
state against groups in civil society protesting authoritarian rule and advocating democratization.[24]

Once a major fault line opened up, pitting the regime against increasingly mobilized elements of society, regime stability rested on reproducing elite consensus to preclude the possibility of any member of the elite
encouraging antiregime movements among society. In Taiwan, the KMT
elite succeeded in creating that unity, but in Korea, the elite was less
homogeneous; members of the elite came from diverse social and economic backgrounds, were not united by membership in a party organization or adherence to an ideology, had fought bitter struggles over land reform, and retained mutual suspicions dating back to the period of
Japanese colonialism. Even as members of the DNP lost power and influence relative to Rhee and his allies, their mutual antagonism and conflict
continued. As Rhee's popularity declined, factions within the DNP sought
to exploit popular discontent with the Rhee regime as a means to win the
1960 elections. Faced with this alliance, Rhee resolved to win the 1960
elections at all costs, squeezing businessmen for extra donations, rigging
the electoral system, and organizing anticommunist youth battalions to
terrorize the opposition. As efforts to rig the elections became apparent,
pro-opposition students organized demonstrations, culminating in the
April 19, 1960, student uprising that toppled the Rhee regime. The uprising was initially a protest against electoral fraud, but it also entailed
protests against government corruption and ineffectiveness, "pitting the
small urban middle class, represented by the university and the press,
against the entrenched administration and political elites."[25] Opposition
forces did not initially claim to speak for the economic grievances of
lower classes, although ultimately such grievances emerged, particularly
in the form of complaints against the illegal acquisition of wealth by businessmen allied to the Rhee regime.[26]

---

[23] Kim Kyoung-Dong, "Political Factors in the Formation of the Entrepreneurial Elite in
South Korea," *Asian Survey* 16 (May 1976): 465–77.
[24] Jang Jip Choi, "Political Cleavages in South Korea," in *State and Society in Contemporary
Korea*, ed. Hagen Koo (Ithaca: Cornell University Press, 1993), 18–28.
[25] Ibid., 25.
[26] Han, *Failure of Democracy in South Korea*, 165–70.

By the end of April, Rhee had announced his resignation, and in July, the first free elections to the National Assembly produced a new government headed by Chang Myon. The Chang Myon government was never able to consolidate its rule, however, remaining caught between supporters of the Rhee regime and more radical parties and students. Increasingly, as 1960 wore on, economic issues came to the forefront. Economic problems attributed to the Rhee regime were expected to be solved quickly by the new administration; when the new administration showed itself incapable of such rapid action, discontent rose, and leftist parties called for the nationalization of industry and the implementation of vast social insurance schemes.[27]

The government responded to economic stagnation and growing discontent with the first hint of a precocious Keynesian strategy in Korea, announcing, in December 1960, the initiation of a "New Deal" public works program that would employ a large number of the unemployed in the National Construction Service. The program was fairly modest, projecting spending of about $30 million for works in irrigation, forestation, road and dam construction, and building. Following the May 1961 coup, the plan was never implemented, but its existence indicates recognition by the Korean leadership that public policies oriented toward lower classes might be politically necessary.[28] This program was insufficient to build support for the regime, however; during the Second Republic, which was overthrown on May 16, 1961, there were more than 500 major demonstrations by university students and 45 by trade unions.[29] The final straw came when a faction of radical students called on their counterparts in North Korea to join them at Panmunjom to ignite a movement for reunification. Fearing a rise in communist influence from the north, elements of the military overthrew the Chang government.

Studies of the Korean developmental state have often neglected the period 1961–1965, during which the institutions of the developmental state were established along with new economic policies of outward-oriented industrialization.[30] By mid-decade, the essential elements of the Korean developmental state were in place. But this path of political development was not a foregone conclusion, for elite conflict was seemingly intense, al-

---

[27] Ibid., 91.

[28] Ibid., 209–11.

[29] David I. Steinberg, *The Republic of Korea: Economic Transformation and Social Change* (Boulder, Colo.: Westview Press, 1989), 55.

[30] Cumings, "Origins of the Northeast Asian Political Economy," 67, writes of the 1961 coup that brought Park to power in Korea, "The now-senile Rhee was toppled, the colonial-linked police and military came undone, and the way was clear for a dynamic authoritarian system." Haggard's *Pathways from the Periphery* is an important exception to this criticism, and he too notes the similarities of the early years of the Park regime to that of Syngman Rhee, while stressing different causal factors in the transition to ELG.

though it differed in dynamics and in intensity from elite conflict in Syria and Turkey. Economic and political reforms occurred during a turbulent period, "amidst strife and opposition, over the loud cries of special interest groups, and in the face of continuing and widespread pessimism and distrust."[31] The military regime was internally divided and faced opposition from political parties with far more social support than the military government enjoyed. The absence of elite cohesion enlarged the space for students, the academic intelligentsia, and the press to express opposition, and created the potential for Park's elite rivals to mobilize popular support against him.[32]

Stephan Haggard notes that the early years of the Park regime "seemed to mirror the Rhee pattern of building support by dispensing largesse."[33] In fact, Park's strategy more closely resembled the Syrian version of precocious Keynesianism than Rhee's exclusionary patronage system. Indeed, Park initially indicated that he would stabilize his rule through populist incorporation, a strategy that the Chang government had first entertained. Korea's largest businessmen, organized into vertical holding companies (*chaebol*), had exploited their close political ties with Rhee to engage in lucrative rent-seeking behavior, leading to a public outcry against illegal wealth in the early 1960s. As we saw, the illegal wealth accumulated by the *chaebol* elicited discontent among urban middle classes. On coming to power, Park initially sought to win the favor of students and Korea's middle classes by threatening to prosecute the *chaebol* and appropriate their property.[34] He quickly reversed this policy, determining that industrialization would require close collaboration with the *chaebol*, but he used the threat of prosecution to transform them from rent-seekers into world-class manufacturers.[35]

A second policy initiative provides an even starker contrast with the developmental state. Park initially promised a new deal for Korean agriculture, including new infrastructural and research projects, debt relief, increased credit, and, most significantly, improvement of the agricultural terms of trade through lowering prices for fertilizer and paying higher prices for foodgrains.[36] This was a significant policy reversal. The Japa-

---

[31] David C. Cole and Princeton N. Lyman, *Korean Development: The Interplay of Politics and Economics* (Cambridge: Harvard University Press, 1971), 93.

[32] Opposition parties polled 53 percent of the presidential votes and 66 percent of the Assembly votes in the 1963 election but lost both elections due to their fragmentation.

[33] *Pathways from the Periphery*, 74.

[34] Mark Clifford, *Troubled Tiger: Businessmen, Bureaucrats, and Generals in South Korea* (Armonk, N.Y.: M. E. Sharpe, 1994), 36–40.

[35] Kyoung-Dong, "Political Factors in the Formation of the South Korean Entrepreneurial Elite," 470–77.

[36] Larry Burmeister, "State, Industrialization and Agricultural Policy in Korea," *Development and Change* 21 (1990), 205. Haggard, *Pathways from the Periphery*, 67, writes that the

nese had begun intervening in the grain market in 1939, paying below-market prices to farmers, a policy that was briefly continued by U.S. military authorities. A new Grain Purchase Law was enacted by the new government of the Republic of Korea in November 1948, and grain prices paid to farmers were below market prices through the 1950s.[37] Park's promise to farmers, then, represents a decisive shift in policy compared to the previous twenty years.

Park sought peasant support during a time when his own rule was far from consolidated, running for election in 1963 with the slogan "Agriculture First." By the end of 1964, however, Park had established his dominance within the regime, centralized power within the executive, and successfully confronted demonstrations protesting his negotiations with Japan. It was thus from a relatively powerful position that Park elected to cease purchasing rural support by cutting back on liberal credit policies and ending subsidies for fertilizer.[38] Significantly, Park made this decision because he feared that ongoing subsidies for farmers would spur inflation and thus undermine the currency devaluation that was central to boosting exports.[39] Indeed, the expansionary macroeconomic policies associated with Park's early flirtation with populism had undermined initial steps toward boosting exports instituted in the period 1961–1963.[40] Consequently, by 1964, agri-

---

regime was influenced by populist economic advice, but it seems more likely that the regime was responding to political unrest and threats to its incumbency.

[37] Pal-Yong Moon and Bong-Soon Kan, "The Republic of Korea," in *The Political Economy of Agricultural Pricing Policy: Asia,* ed. Anne O. Krueger, et al. (Baltimore: Johns Hopkins University Press for the World Bank, 1991), 24–26. After 1955, American grain provided through the Public Law 480 program helped the government keep domestic grain prices low.

[38] Haggard, *Pathways from the Periphery,* 69, argues that the demands of economic stabilization dictated the retreat from populism. Yet when faced with a similar economic crisis, the Turkish leadership adamantly refused to succumb to American pressure to cut agricultural subsidies, even though "Agricultural policy was the fundamental locus of U.S.–Turkish conflict." [Sylvia Maxfield and James Nolt, "Protectionism and the Internationalization of Capital: U.S. Sponsorship of Import Substitution Industrialization in the Philippines, Turkey, and Argentina," *International Studies Quarterly* 34 (1990), 69]. Turkish insistence on subsidizing farmers in the face of economic crisis and American pressure supports the counterfactual that had elite conflict in Korea been more intense, Park would not have ended agricultural support. Haggard's position, on the other hand, is supported by the proposition that resource-poor countries such as Korea have little choice but to develop non-traditional exports. Turkey's comparatively well-endowed agricultural sector, in other words, made ISI a more viable strategy.

[39] Cole and Lyman, *Korean Development,* 95. The regime allowed exchange rates to float freely, beginning in the spring of 1965, essentially decoupling domestic inflation from currency value. But by 1965, Park had no reason to return to subsidizing peasants, which he would do only after political unrest reemerged in 1972. Subsidizing peasants would have raised wages, cutting into Korea's international competitiveness.

[40] These measures included a 1961 currency devaluation that brought the official exchange rate close to the free-market rate and various export subsidies. By 1963, inflation had largely eliminated these incentives to export. See Dani Rodrik, "Getting Interventions Right: How South Korea and Taiwan Grew Rich," *Economic Policy* 20 (April 1995), 61.

cultural terms of trade which had risen through 1963, began to turn heavily against farmers and remained so until the 1970s.[41] Whether Korea's move toward ELG was the crucial factor accounting for subsequent development remains a contentious question, explored further in Chapter 7.[42] Without political conditions permitting the reversal of Park's populist policies, however, ELG reforms would have had no effect at all.

Taken together, the campaign to prosecute the *chaebol* and the initial move to raise agricultural incomes make Park Chung Hee resemble more closely Syria under the Ba`th party than the founder of a developmental state.[43] But Park and his collaborators differed from their Syrian counterparts in that they did not belong to antioligarchic movements in the 1960s, precisely because land reform had removed the structural prerequisites of an oligarchic state; thus, unlike the Ba`th party, Park did not have to mobilize the peasantry to oppose rural elites. Park's flirtation with populism, however brief, cautions us against presuming that the creation of a developmental state in Korea was a simple matter of reimposing the Japanese system. Similarly, there is no evidence that Park's initial populist orientation was a response to the demands of powerful classes; Korean peasants, after all, had not mobilized in the early 1960s.

Indeed, although I have stressed the presence of elite conflict in Korea, we must not exaggerate its intensity. I defined elite conflict as intense when it arose due to threats to an elites' immediate material interests and its long-term control over the sources of elite status. By this definition, elite conflict in Korea was less intense than in Syria and Turkey. Although the Korean elite was divided, the opposition to Park Chung Hee was extremely factionalized, reducing the potency of its political challenge to

[41] Data collected by Edward Mason and his colleagues indicate that the index of prices received by farmers to prices they paid for manufactured goods increased from 85.2 in 1962 to 113.6 in 1963, from where it began to decline again, remaining below 100 from 1966 to 1970 (1970 = 100). The index reached the 1963 level again only in 1973. See their *The Economic and Social Modernization of the Republic of Korea* (Cambridge: Harvard University Press, 1980), 236. According to Clive Hamilton, the terms of trade substantially increased between 1962 and 1964 but still remained below 100 until 1973. He gives the numbers 70 for 1962, 93 for 1963, and 92 for 1964. For the rest of the decade, the index fluctuated between the low 80s and high 70s. Clive Hamilton, *Capitalist Industrialization in Korea* (Boulder, Colo.: Westview Press, 1986), 40. All authors agree that for most of the decade, a surplus was extracted from agriculture to keep urban wages low.

[42] Rodrik, "Getting Interventions Right," argues that export-oriented policy reforms were not critical to Korea's economic growth.

[43] Without pushing the parallel to the Ba`th too far, we can note that Park, like the Syrian military officers who made the 1963 coup, came from a lower-class rural background and was influenced by socialist ideas. See Lee-Jay Cho and Yoon Hyung Kim, "Major Economic Policies of the Park Administration," in *Economic Development in the Republic of Korea: A Policy Perspective,* ed. Lee-Jay Cho and Yoon Hyung Kim (Honolulu: University of Hawaii Press, 1991), 18; and Jon Huer, *Marching Orders: The Role of the Military in South Korea's "Economic Miracle," 1961–1971* (New York: Greenwood Press, 1989), 59–62. Other populist policies included expanded public works, pay increases for state employees, and rejection of budgetary and monetary discipline. Haggard, *Pathways from the Periphery,* 67–68.

the Park government. The disunity of the Korean opposition indicates that personalistic competition more than ideological divisions or threats to elite status drove its leaders into opposition.[44]

That factionalism and not polarization into competing camps characterized elite conflict was in turn a function of the nature of economic discontent. Economic grievances increasingly fueled opposition beginning in the late 1950s, but these grievances stemmed from the corruption endemic in Rhee's patronage system and the economic stagnation it engendered more than they stemmed from competing political-economic visions. Given the heterogeneous nature of their grievances, opposition leaders faced tremendous obstacles in forging a social coalition and thus consistently appealed not to the economic interests of specific groups, but "more to values and to generalized conditions."[45] The point is not simply that class actors were powerless to impose their preferences on the state; rather, in the absence of intense and polarizing conflicts over fundamental political-economic projects that threatened the status of existing elites, there were limited possibilities or incentives for opposition elites to build a mass coalition. Thus incentives were limited for the Park government to engage in its own project of coalition building. Had opposition leaders indicated the willingness and the capacity to mobilize a powerful mass coalition, Park undoubtedly would have maintained his own populist policies. In the absence of this threat to his rule, Park reached accommodation with large businessmen and with the opposition and quickly ended his own nascent populist project. Indeed, by 1965, with the conclusion of treaty negotiations with Japan, the government had reached a compromise with its opponents over permitted forms of political protest and activity, and there was emerging consensus over the new economic strategy.[46]

Conservative Coalitions in Korea and Tawain

Bolstered by elite cohesion, the governments of Korea and Taiwan consolidated their rule and established unmediated relations with popular classes without popular incorporation. In contrast to the broad, cross-

---

[44] Cole and Lyman, *Korean Development,* 52–53, write that the principal opposition came from the leaders of the Democratic party of the 1950s who lacked a specific program motivating their opposition.

[45] Ibid., 54. The authors are emphatic on this point, writing "[T]here were no firm labor, business, or farm interests to give substance or direction to the opposition's economic outlook or even to provide a solid base of support should the opposition attain power. As for developing such groupings, the existing opposition leaders had no feel for labor support in the urban strongholds, were by background and disposition unsuited to be real champions of the small farmers, and were too far from the seats of power to be able to command strong business backing."

[46] Ibid., 74 and 94.

class coalitions characteristic of precocious Keynesian states, East Asian developmental states rest on what Pempel called "conservative coalitions."[47] Conservative coalitions are narrowly based coalitions supporting collaboration between the state and large business; significant sectors of the population are excluded from these coalitions, and deliberate efforts are made to minimize side-payments to popular classes.[48] The exclusionary character of these societal coalitions, expressed as the absence of side-payments to lower classes, distinguishes Korea and Taiwan from Syria and Turkey. Moreover, as I have argued, a necessary though not sufficient condition for the construction of the developmental state is the absence of state commitments to popular sectors.

In both Korea and Taiwan, strict control over labor has been critical to the success of ELG based initially on labor-intensive industries. State elites in both countries afforded priority to replacing independent labor organizations with state-controlled ones, while keeping wages low. When the KMT elite emigrated to Taiwan, they carried with them repressive labor legislation that had been enacted during the civil war on the mainland. In addition, KMT cadres dominated local unions, while the state established controls over personnel practices at the enterprise level. Because Taiwanese industrialization has been realized through the proliferation of small enterprises, this form of control at the level of the shop floor has been more important to maintaining labor discipline than direct state management of industrial conflict.[49] In Korea, the Park regime confronted a more active labor movement. Park responded by prohibiting strikes, arresting labor leaders, deregistering all existing unions, and establishing a state-controlled, peak labor confederation, the Federation of Korean Trade Unions.[50]

Both the Syrian and Turkish states established, with more or less success, strict controls over labor organizations and activities. But in these cases, a bargain was struck with labor that provided relatively high levels of material compensation for political marginalization. In Korea and Taiwan, on the other hand, controls over labor have not been the price labor

[47] T. J. Pempel, *Policy and Politics in Japan: Creative Conservatism* (Philadelphia: Temple University Press, 1982), 24–32.

[48] Note that Pempel traces the incorporation of agriculture into the Japanese conservative coalition to the 1940s. For the next fifteen years, however, rural support for the state was not based on extensive side-payments; producer prices for rice, the primary agricultural commodity, exceeded world market prices only in the 1960s, well after the institutions of the developmental state were reestablished and the Japanese economic miracle was well under way. See Michael W. Donnelly, "Setting the Price of Rice: A Study in Political Decision-making," in *Policymaking in Contemporary Japan,* ed. T. J. Pempel (Ithaca: Cornell University Press, 1977), 143–200.

[49] Frederic C. Deyo, "State and Labor: Modes of Political Exclusion in East Asian Development," in *Political Economy of the New Asian Industrialism,* 184–85.

[50] Ibid., 185–86.

pays for material benefits; they have been the means by which the state has denied labor material benefits, creating the low-wage labor force needed to make ELG successful. In Taiwan, for example, wages during the 1960s were among the lowest in the world, particularly for workers in export-processing zones, where workers' earnings were below subsistence level. Through the mid-1970s, the official minimum wage remained constant, and wage increases lagged well behind productivity gains.[51] In Korea in the early 1960s, wages were deliberately pushed below their 1959 peak, a policy that provided significant benefits to entrepreneurs.[52] Even as labor markets tightened toward the end of the 1960s, rapid wage increases through 1975 remained below rates of productivity growth. Yet in light industrial sectors such as textiles, wages never rose above subsistence levels.[53] In addition, in both countries, government welfare expenditures lagged well behind those of other developing countries, even into the 1980s.[54]

Similarly, in contrast to the precocious Keynesianism of Syria and Turkey, both East Asian states successfully exploited their unmediated relations with rural producers to extract resources from agriculture to help fund industrialization. In Taiwan, for example, as the state siphoned agricultural surplus, per capita rural consumption throughout the 1950s remained at its 1930s level. One important mechanism for transferring surplus was the state-controlled compulsory system of bartering fertilizer for rice at terms highly favorable to the state; hence, in 1964–1965, Taiwanese rural producers paid prices for fertilizer that were 40 percent higher than the price paid by American, Dutch, Belgian, Japanese, and Indian farmers. This rice tax mobilized more revenue for the government than income taxes for every year through 1963, and rural households paid much higher tax burdens than urban households.[55] Similarly, the terms of trade between agricultural and industrial goods remained sharply biased against agriculture, and imports of foodstuffs at concessionary prices further pushed down food prices. Through these and

[51] Frederic C. Deyo, "Economic Policy and the Popular Sector," in *Manufacturing Miracles*, 183. Recall that in Turkey, and perhaps in Syria as well, wage increases outpaced productivity gains.

[52] Haggard, *Pathways from the Periphery*, 63.

[53] Alice H. Amsden, *Asia's Next Giant: South Korea and Late Industrialization* (New York: Oxford University Press, 1989), 189-202; Frederic C. Deyo, *Beneath the Miracle: Labor Subordination in the New Asian Industrialism* (Berkeley: University of California Press, 1989), 90–94.

[54] The percentage of total government expenditures for health, social security, and welfare were 15 percent for Taiwan (1984) and only 8 percent for Korea (1985), whereas it attained 40 percent for both Brazil and Argentina in the early 1980s, although only 13 percent for Mexico. Deyo, "Economic Policy and the Popular Sector," 183.

[55] Alice Amsden, "Taiwan's Economic History: A Case of Etatisme and a Challenge to Dependency Theory," *Modern China* 5 (July 1979), 357–58.

other mechanisms such as low interest rates on forced savings, Taiwanese agriculture transferred surplus amounting to 34 percent of gross domestic investment between 1952 and 1960.[56] Antirural policies continued into the 1970s. Between 1962 and 1972, most gains in farm household income came from nonfarm sources.[57] Although the state embarked on a "New Deal" for agriculture in 1969, these antirural policies were only slowly dismantled; not until 1977 did the official price for rice rise above the market price.[58] As Robert Wade notes, by depressing food prices, these policies also depressed wages, "allowing industry to have more internationally competitive costs than otherwise."[59] Note, however, that some of the funds transferred out of agriculture were reinvested in schemes to modernize the agricultural sector, so that subsequent measures to subsidize Taiwanese farmers "were therefore less of a potential drain on state finances."[60]

As we saw above, in the early 1960s, when the Park regime in Korea had not yet stabilized its rule, higher prices were paid to farmers. After 1963, however, terms of trade turned sharply against agriculture, and the index remained below its 1963 level until the early 1970s.[61] Despite these policies, the widespread distribution of lands to peasant farmers in the 1950s created a reservoir of support that was sufficient for the regime at a time when it did not face serious challenges.[62] When such challenges did emerge, the state moved with alacrity to shore up its rural base of support. This occurred following the elections of 1971, when opposition candidate Kim Dae Jung mobilized rural support by emphasizing the lack of attention paid to farmers, resulting in rural incomes that averaged only one-third of urban incomes. In response, Park Chung Hee declared mar-

---

[56] Chih-Ming Ka and Mark Selden, "Original Accumulation, Equity and Late Industrialization: The Cases of Socialist China and Capitalist Taiwan," *World Development* 14 (October-November 1986): 1293–1310.

[57] Amsden, "Taiwan's Economic History," 359–60.

[58] Mick Moore, "Agriculture in Taiwan and South Korea: The Minimalist State," *IDS Bulletin* 15 (April 1984), 59. Moreover, between 1965 and 1969, the weighted average of agricultural protection was only 2 percent in Taiwan, rising only to 17 percent between 1970 and 1974. Kym Anderson et al., "The Growth of Agricultural Protection," in Kym Anderson et al., *The Political Economy of Agricultural Protection: East Asia in International Perspective* (Sydney: Allen & Unwin, 1986), 22.

[59] Robert Wade, *Governing the Market: Economic Theory and the Role of Government in East Asian Industrialization* (Princeton: Princeton University Press, 1990), 77.

[60] Bullock, "Agricultural Development in Korea and Taiwan," 63.

[61] The state deliberately drove down prices for agricultural goods by denying the sector protection while importing food at concessionary terms. Moore, "Agriculture in Taiwan and South Korea," 58. For figures on agricultural terms of trade, see footnote 41 above.

[62] As Larry Burmeister writes, "After the military coup, the state was able to deploy its resources in the countryside effectively because the political problem of the Korean peasantry had been resolved *before* the state systematically harnessed agriculture to support the national industrialization project." See his "State, Industrialization, and Agricultural Policy in Korea," 203–4.

tial law, codified in the 1972 Yushin Constitution. In addition to beefing up the institutions of authoritarian rule, Park also implemented a set of policies in the winter of 1971–1972, known as the New Community Movement (*Saemaul Undong*), to shore up rural political support by raising the rural standard of living. Prices paid for agricultural products were increased, and government loans and investment in agriculture were almost twice as high in the period 1972–1975 (1,460,000 million won) as they had been during 1967–1971 (769,800 million won).[63] In the 1970s, the producer prices for rice finally rose above market prices. Nominal rates of protection on agricultural products rose faster in Korea than in Taiwan, from a weighted average of 9 percent between 1965 and 1969, to an average of 55 percent between 1970 and 1974.[64] By the mid-1970s, the Korean state was supporting farmer incomes. By this point, however, Korea was already beginning to shift into more capital-intensive industries and could thus afford to subsidize peasant incomes, which in turn expanded the domestic market.

The Institutional Profile of Developmental States

I argued in Chapter 2 that low levels of elite conflict were a necessary but not sufficient condition for the construction of developmental states; it allowed their construction but did not dictate that elites would embark on the project. Here, I can demonstrate only that levels of elite conflict yielded state structures different from precocious Keynesian states. Due to space constraints, the following brief sketch of the institutional expression of developmental states does not incorporate the voluminous and detailed literature on the institutional preconditions for East Asian development, and references have been limited to the major texts. Chapter 7 discusses the counterarguments made by neoliberal economists, however this chapter omits references to authors who have called for substantial modification of the developmental state approach, or even its replacement; although important, many of these criticisms, almost exclusively made with reference to Japan, acquire their analytic bite only by assaulting claims never made by developmental state theorists, for example, that bureaucrats are omniscient and omnipotent and intervene uniformly in every economic and industrial sector.[65] We need demonstrate only that

---

[63] Mason et al., *Economic and Social Modernization of the Republic of Korea*, 230–31. In terms of a real index, the rate of increase in government expenditures lagged behind the GNP growth rate until 1974.

[64] Anderson, "The Growth of Agricultural Protection," 22.

[65] That said, much can be learned from this excellent body of literature. See David Friedman, *The Misunderstood Miracle: Industrial Development and Political Change in Japan* (Ithaca: Cornell University Press, 1988); Daniel Okimoto, *Between MITI and the Market: Japanese In-*

East Asian political economies are organized differently from precocious Keynesian ones with demonstrable consequences for economic performance and not that they represent the ideal political-economic arrangement. Note also that the following discussion underemphasizes the fluidity of state-society relations in East Asia; as many scholars have noted, developmental states' links to the private sector became increasingly unstable in the 1980s as large firms reduced their dependence on state assistance.[66] The analysis parallels that of Syria and Turkey by ending with the onset of economic liberalization in the early 1980s.

Chalmers Johnson proposes the concept of the developmental state to explain successful industrial strategy in Japan. He argues that all states intervene in their economies; what is important is *how* they intervene. In plan-ideological states like the Soviet Union, the state perceived bureaucratic planning as a value in itself, and state control over the economy almost completely supplanted the market. In contrast, a market-rational state like the United States concerns itself with regulatory matters—the rules of economic activity—without intervening in substantive matters. The plan-rational or developmental state in Japan combines features of both: it coexists with the market, as in market-rational states, but it intervenes in substantive affairs, like plan-ideological states. State intervention in the market is goal oriented and speaks to the exigencies of late development, resulting in a specific set of state economic priorities: "In the plan-rational state, the government will give greatest precedence to industrial policy; that is, to a concern with the structure of domestic industry and with promoting the structure that enhances the nation's international competitiveness."[67]

The generic elements of the developmental state reside in the following institutional innovations characteristic of the fast-growth East Asian economies. First, in contrast to the precocious Keynesian regime of constituency clientelism, they possess a political regime that allows relatively depoliticized economic policy making. Labor and agriculture have little

---

dustrial Policy for High Technology (Stanford: Stanford University Press, 1989); Richard Samuels, *The Business of the Japanese State: Energy Markets in Comparative and Historical Perspective* (Ithaca: Cornell University Press, 1987); and Robert M. Uriu, *Troubled Industries: Confronting Economic Change in Japan* (Ithaca: Cornell University Press, 1996).

66 Scott Callon, *Divided Sun: MITI and the Breakdown of Japanese High-Tech Industrial Policy, 1975–1993* (Stanford: Stanford University Press, 1995), examines the unravelling of the state-business alliance in Japan after 1975, stressing the growing financial independence of high-tech firms and the declining capacity of MITI to foster technological development once Japan reached the technological frontier. See also Chung-In Moon, "The Demise of the Developmentalist State? Neoconservative Reforms and Political Consequences in South Korea," *Journal of Developing Societies* 4 (January 1988): 67–84; and Eun Mee Kim, "Contradictions and Limits of a Developmental State: With Illustrations from the South Korean Case," *Social Problems* 40 (May 1993): 228–49.

67 Chalmers Johnson, *MITI and the Japanese Miracle: The Growth of Industrial Policy, 1925–1975* (Stanford: Stanford University Press, 1982), 18–19.

influence to derail production by making distributional demands, and, because of the narrow base of the conservative coalition, efforts to placate popular constituencies do not constrain economic decision making.[68] Relations with lower classes may be based on the provision of public goods as in constituency clientelism; an example of this is Korean agricultural policy after 1972. The net payoffs to constituencies are relatively low, however, and these payoffs do not require the wholesale redefinition of other institutional properties. Furthermore, these payoffs begin only after the country has successfully penetrated export markets with labor-intensive manufactures and has begun to shift into more capital-intensive industries.

Second, in contrast to the politicized bureaucracies of precocious Keynesian states, the political executive is organized so that politicians reign and bureaucrats rule, permitting the formulation of long-term development strategy.[69] The bureaucracy is characterized by "embedded autonomy," welding together formal norms of organization and informal norms of coherence and esprit de corps, permitting the sustained immersion with social groups necessary for the state to promote development without succumbing to corruption or loss of coherence.[70] To be sure, corruption, patronage appointments, and bureaucratic inefficiency are not wholly absent from developmental states. As David Kang argues, for example, Park Chung Hee staffed Korean domestic service ministries (Construction, Agriculture, and Home Affairs) with political appointees and permitted some corruption and inefficiency to reign unchecked. The central ministries supervising the economy (Trade and Industry, Economic Planning Board, and Finance), however, were held to far stricter standards.[71] Strict meritocratic norms govern recruitment into these pilot agencies of the bureaucracy. Moreover, relieved of the need to dedicate public policy to satisfying lower-class coalition members, political leaders secure in their rule delegate tremendous authority to bureaucrats and provide them with the organizational resources they need to formulate and implement coherent and comprehensive policy.[72]

---

[68] As Ziya Onis, "The Logic of the Developmental State," *Comparative Politics,* 24 (October 1991), 113, writes, "the welfare state function has been virtually absent. The state has assumed no responsibilities outside the domains of production and capital accumulation."

[69] Chalmers Johnson, "Political Institutions and Economic Performance: The Government-Business Relationship in Japan, South Korea, and Taiwan," in *The Political Economy of the New Asian Industrialism,* 151–56.

[70] Peter Evans, *Embedded Autonomy: States and Industrial Transformation* (Princeton: Princeton University Press, 1995).

[71] "South Korean and Taiwanese Development," 573–75. The same pattern may exist in Taiwan and Japan; see, for example, Brian Woodall's analysis of the construction industry's ties to the Japanese Ministry of Construction, "The Logic of Collusive Action: The Political Roots of Japan's *Dango* System," *Comparative Politics* 25 (April 1993), esp. 307–8.

[72] With reference to corruption, Mason et al., *Economic and Social Modernization of the Republic of Korea,* 265, note that bureaucratic supervision of firm behavior "could well be sub-

Third, in contrast to the distributive fiscal practices of precocious Keynesian states, fiscal policy is controlled by a state elite that is singularly devoted to economic development and that uses state resources only for production and capital accumulation. Investment in human capital is largely limited to higher education to create a recruitment pool for the bureaucracy and entrepreneurial elite, and efforts to create an educated workforce. State control over the financial system is thus relatively unencumbered by the burden of financing government deficits and can be used almost exclusively for developmental tasks. The necessary condition for this pattern of fiscal policy is the presence of a conservative coalition, which minimizes the redistributive aspects of fiscal policy.[73]

Finally, deliberate efforts to blend efficaciously public authority and firm-level decision making define the character of state economic intervention. State intervention is limited largely to measures that will either guide the economy into targeted sectors or assist firms in given sectors to become internationally competitive. Every effort is made to restrict modes of intervention that allow entrepreneurs to gain excess profits without corresponding private measures to increase productivity and competitiveness.[74] This blend of command and demand is expressed structurally as the juxtaposition of the soft-authoritarian state over a market system and institutionally as strategic industrial policy. States control markets by getting the prices "wrong" and inducing private-sector entrepreneurs to strive to achieve competitive advantage, while markets discipline states to prevent or at least delimit the scope of corrupt administrations.[75] Of course, as we have seen, other dimensions of state intervention are designed to direct benefits in a discriminate manner to targeted groups to maintain political stability; this form of intervention is kept within manageable boundaries, however, and becomes important only after substantial industrial development and transformation, accompanied by the acquisition of international competitiveness in a range of industries.

---

ject to corruption . . . but again it must be emphasized that there is very little evidence that such corruption as exists interferes in any serious way with production processes."

[73] Kent Calder, for example, argues that redistributive public policies in Japan, made possible by its high-growth economy, were responses to episodic political crisis and not due to the "routine lobbying of corporatist interest groups (either business federations or labor unions) or even the strategic planning of the state." Over time, however, these episodic policies accumulated into substantial redistribution. See his *Crisis and Compensation: Public Policy and Political Stability in Japan* (Princeton: Princeton University Press, 1988), 20.

[74] On this point, Johnson observes that the developmental elite in East Asia "appreciates that the socialist displacement of the market threatens its goals by generating bureaucratism, corruption, loss of incentives, and an inefficient allociation of resources . . . [therefore] its primary leadership task is to discover how, organizationally, to make its own developmental goals compatible with the market mechanism." "Political Institutions and Economic Performance," 140.

[75] The strategy of getting prices wrong, a central theme in Amsden's *Asia's Next Giant*, is discussed further in Chapter 8.

Successful state intervention works through two institutions: state control over the financial system and administrative guidance. State control over the financial system is a distinguishing characteristic of the developmental state, for it allows planners to manipulate entrepreneurs' calculations of profitability and risk and thereby to guide economic activity into targeted sectors.[76] Jung-En Woo argues that the nationalization of the Korean banking sector in 1963 was the most important of the reforms that launched Korea into rapid development.[77] In Taiwan as well, the state dominated the financial system, deploying its influence to implement industrial policy and foster development, although less directly and comprehensively than in Korea.[78]

East Asian states do more than just manipulate macroeconomic variables and target investments; discretionary, micro-level intervention by state planners is also prevalent in Japan, Korea, and Taiwan. State officials influence decision making at the level of economic sectors, industrial sectors, and individual enterprises. As one study characterized administrative guidance in Korea, "A firm that does not respond as expected to particular incentives may find that its tax returns are subject to careful examination, or that its application for bank credit is studiously ignored, or that its outstanding bank loans are not renewed. If incentive procedures do not work, government agencies show no hesitation in resorting to command backed by compulsion. In general, it does not take a Korean firm long to learn that it will 'get along' best by 'going along.'"[79] Similarly, Taiwanese officials approach individual firms with suggestions about appropriate products or technologies. As Taiwanese planners bargain with firms, they offer various incentives to solicit cooperation, but "the firms know that the government has a variety of more or less subtle ways to make life awkward if they do not respond."[80]

---

[76] Johnson, "Political Institutions and Economic Performance," 147–49.

[77] Jung-En Woo, *Race to the Swift: State and Finance in Korean Industrialization* (New York: Columbia University Press, 1991), 84. See also Hagen Koo and Eun Mee Kim, "The Developmental State and Capital Accumulation in South Korea," in *States and Development in the Asian Pacific Rim*, ed. Richard P. Appelbaum and Jeffrey Henderson (Newbury Park, Calif.: Sage Publications, 1992), 121–49; and Mason et al., *The Economic and Social Modernization of Korea*, 326–37, esp. 330, where the authors discuss an early financial innovation, state guarantees for foreign loans. For a complete list of the financial incentives employed by the Korean state, see Youngil Lim, *Government Policy and Private Enterprise: Korean Enterprise in Industrialization*, Korean Research Monograph No. 6. (Berkeley: Institute of East Asian Studies, 1981), 19–20.

[78] Wade, *Governing the Market*, 159–72; and Tun-jen Cheng, "Guarding the Commanding Heights: The State as Banker in Taiwan," in *The Politics of Finance in Developing Countries*, ed. Stephan Haggard, Chung H. Lee, and Sylvia Maxfield (Ithaca: Cornell University Press, 1993), 55–92. Cheng stresses the political rationale motivating the Taiwanese state to restrict public finance to the state-owned sector at the expense of the small- and medium-sized private sector.

[79] Mason, et al., *The Economic and Social Modernization of the Republic of Korea*, 265.

[80] Wade, *Governing the Market*, 284–85.

As these citations about administrative guidance make clear, the Korean and Taiwanese states do bargain with private capitalists. The nature of this bargain is clearly illustrated by Woo's description of the "historical compromise" in Korea: "General Park summoned the ten major business leaders and struck a deal with them. In exchange for exempting businessmen from criminal prosecution and respecting their properties . . . business 'paid' fines levied on them by establishing industrial firms and then donating shares to the government. In retrospect, this deal had the quality of an historical compromise; in any case, it occasioned the launching of 'Korea Inc.' Henceforth, state and big business would share the same destiny; prosper or perish."[81] Because popular classes were excluded from coalitions in Korea and Taiwan, bargaining took place between only two actors: the state and business. Bargaining was a relatively simple process of determining the contribution of each party to development. In Syria and Turkey, on the other hand, the inclusion of popular classes made the bargaining process more complex and produced different economic outcomes. These differing bargaining dynamics and their developmental consequences are explored further in Chapter 8.

Explaining Levels of Elite Conflict

I have demonstrated that high levels of elite conflict impelled Syrian and Turkish elites to incorporate workers and peasants into cross-class coalitions, whereas low levels of elite conflict permitted Korean and Taiwanese elites to exclude lower classes and build conservative coalitions. Incentive structures produced by levels of elite conflict, in other words, governed coalition strategies, and not the power of subaltern groups to demand incorporation. These different coalition-building strategies in turn produced precocious Keynesian states in Syria and Turkey and made possible the construction of developmental states in Korea and Taiwan.

Before turning to the economic implications of these institutional frameworks, we can use the comparisons of the two sets of cases to explore the sources of differing levels of elite conflict. Conflict over the proper relationship of the state to economy and society existed in all four cases. But the nature of that conflict and its resolution differed markedly across the two sets of cases. Specifically, we are interested in discovering the circumstances under which conflict over state economic intervention produces polarizing and destabilizing conflict that is resolved through popular incorporation. The following discussion extracts some general conclusions and hypotheses about why the level of inter-elite conflict dif-

---

[81] Woo, *Race to the Swift*, 84.

fered across the two sets of cases, while recognizing that more cases need to be analyzed before more definitive answers can be supplied.

Elite conflict over the alternative relationships between political authority and economic activity entails opposition to current arrangements and the articulation and implementation of new ones. Elites must calculate the costs of political-economic transformation relative to the gains promised by new arrangements. To the extent that this transformation is predicated on the decisive acquisition of political power that can be realized only through popular incorporation, the costs of imposing new political-economic visions is potentially quite high, for it reduces elite monopoly over power resources.[82] From this perspective, as I argued in Chapter 2, conflict will be most polarizing when current or proposed political-economic arrangements disadvantage not only the economic interests of elite groups, but also their future political privileges and prerogatives and hence their future capacity to advance or defend their interests. When elite conflict reaches this level, current or expected changes in modes of state economic intervention threaten not only immediate material interests, but also the capacity of elites to reproduce their elite status, making the costs of popular incorporation more tolerable.

The most significant variable governing the degree of elite conflict is the degree of sociological homogeneity of the political elite. Elites from relatively homogeneous backgrounds share common experiences, interests, and values, and intense conflicts are less likely to erupt. "Tolerance and mutual security," Robert Dahl posits, "are more likely to develop among a small elite sharing similar perspectives than among a large and heterogeneous collection of leaders representing social strata with widely varying goals, interests, and outlooks."[83] When the elite is composed of diverse groups drawn from different class and status backgrounds, elites are more likely to divide, because their different and often competing interests in maintaining or transforming the status quo lead to different projections of the costs and benefits of state building and economic development. Homogeneity is maximized when core members of the political elite owe their status to organizational affiliation, especially membership in dominant single parties. The potential for conflict is further dampened when this elite effectively rules without the collaboration of powerful socioeconomic elites. In this case, even divisive conflicts may

---

[82] The direct costs to elites of popular incorporation, in terms of restrictions on their power and privileges, surely varies cross-nationally. As we saw in Chapter 4, for example, property-owning elites in Turkey incurred few costs in cultivating a mass base. The costs of incorporation were much higher for Syrian elites, so that it was an antioligarchic movement that created a mass base.

[83] Robert A. Dahl, *Polyarchy: Participation and Opposition* (New Haven: Yale University Press, 1971), 37.

not provide sufficient incentives to embark on popular incorporation, which would threaten the organization's monopoly of political power and its core value commitments.[84] Furthermore, conflict over political-economic issues is likely to be framed in terms of economic efficiency and to be confined to technocratic agencies. Because efficiency issues are resolvable according to pragmatic considerations and through reference to intellectual arguments amenable to empirical confirmation or disconfirmation, they are often less divisive.[85] Moreover, shifts in policy related to efficiency can often be accomplished without altering the existing organization of power, and thus pose less of a threat to elite political privileges. Efficiency issues are therefore unlikely to result in polarizing elite conflict that prompts mass incorporation.[86]

In contrast, elite conflict is most intense when state-led industrialization entails the extension of state capacity to the detriment of previously autonomous elites who are the local agents of mediated states. In this case, conflict pits central state elites against social elites, especially landlords, who possess politically relevant resources autonomous from state control, which they use to mediate between state and society.[87] The latter must fear immediate material losses as well as reductions in their political power that would undermine their future capacity to defend their material interests. The threat of economic and political losses may in turn motivate them to defect from a dominant coalition and mobilize popular-sector support. Alternatively, socioeconomic elites who fear that popular incorporation will encroach on their privileges may enjoy sufficient political power to block projects of state building or state-led industrialization, compelling their rivals to mobilize popular-sector support to overthrow them.

---

[84] Writing about the crisis of de-Stalinization in East Central Europe, Grzegorz Ekiert argues that it "did not undermine political, economic, and ideological foundations of Soviet-type regimes because the challengers did not question the principal tenets of state socialism, such as the political monopoly of the communist party, state ownership of the means of production, central planning in the economy, or the alliance with the Soviet Union. It was diffused by a removal of the Stalinist power elite and a change in the state's economic and political practices without any significant modifications of the institutional architecture of the party-state." See his *The State Against Society: Political Crises and Their Aftermath in East Central Europe* (Princeton: Princeton University Press, 1996), 6.

[85] Judgments about the relative efficiency of markets versus political authority, however, are often intertwined with normative assessments of the legitimacy of particular arrangements or their implications for protecting liberty from political despots. My comments here refer solely to the efficiency aspects of state economic intervention.

[86] Individual bureaucrats or even entire ministries might oppose new policies or arrangements, but they are unlikely to lead reform movements.

[87] This proposition reformulates Theda Skocpol's necessary condition for political crises that, when combined with the conditions permitting peasant insurrections, results in social revolutions. See her *States and Social Revolutions: A Comparative Analysis of France, Russia, & China* (Cambridge: Cambridge University Press, 1979).

Korea and Taiwan represent relative elite homogeneity. The greater degree of elite homogeneity in East Asia did not preclude the emergence of elite conflict, but it tempered the intensity of that conflict. Taiwanese leaders all owed their status to their organizational position within the KMT, and had no incentive to challenge the status quo. Moreover, the political elite did not embrace actors whose status was based on the autonomous control of social resources. Conflict over political-economic policies was confined to the KMT elite, primarily located in economic bureaucracies, and was largely resolved with reference to pragmatic considerations. The importance of landlords in the Korean elite in the immediate postwar period distinguishes Korea from Taiwan; it is thus not surprising that politics were especially polarized prior to the American-sponsored land reform, and that Rhee viewed land reform as an important instrument for enhancing his power. Significantly, however, after the land reform, most members of the Korean elite were cut off from their social bases of power, while businessmen were not prominent members of the political elite. In the late 1950s, although many opponents of the Rhee regime were former landlords, members of the Korean political elite for the most part owed their elite status to positions in political organizations. When Park came to power in the early 1960s, despite initial steps to prosecute businessmen, he was not compelled to assault elite socioeconomic privileges to consolidate his rule and was able to reverse the drift toward Syrian-style precocious Keynesianism. Moreover, his elite rivals contested his autocratic rule, but not his political-economic project, and they were thus unable to articulate a competing vision that could attract mass support. Peter Evans has forcefully argued that the absence of large landlords in Korea and Taiwan made the state more autonomous in development policy making.[88] Equally important is that the absence of landlords rendered the political elite more homogeneous and fostered relative elite cohesion, removing incentives for elements in the elite to offer side-payments to popular classes. Before the question of who makes policy is whether elites make side-payments.

In contrast, Syria and Turkey were characterized by elite heterogeneity. In both cases, representatives of property-owning classes were key members of the elite. In Syria, landlords and their bourgeois cousins had succeeded in establishing an oligarchic state, in which inequalities in property ownership and in political power reinforced each other. Oligarchic states rest on shaky social foundations. The relatively liberal economic policies typically pursued by oligarchic states provoke demands for state intervention to ameliorate inequalities or to spur more widespread devel-

---

[88] "Class, State, and Dependence in East Asia: Lessons for Latin Americanists," in *Political Economy of the New Asian Industrialism*, 214–15.

opment, demands to which oligarchs will be loathe to respond for fear of undermining their monopoly of power, privilege, and prestige.[89] In this sense, political elites ruling oligarchic states are not capable of sustained state-building projects or of promoting economic development because these projects threaten to erode the bases of their social power.[90] The traditional Syrian elite first divided between reformers and conservative defenders of the status quo, blocking reform projects. The clear link between property and political power, combined with an inequitable economic system incapable of sustained development, provoked widespread resentment and polarizing conflict, which in turn elicited rival state-building projects. As bureaucrats and military officers recruited from non-elite classes reached high-ranking positions within the state, they constituted a counter-elite who envisioned an alternative state-building project.

In Turkey, on the other hand, the political elite was formed by an alliance between property owners and high-ranking administrative officials. As long as the Kemalist state-building project did not impinge on the position of social elites, the two groups were able to collaborate. Over time, however, the state's expanding economic power alarmed the state's elite allies, who saw state power as a threat to their property. In response, they came to view the state as despotic and arbitrary, creating a zero-sum game in which they had to capture control over the state to protect their interests. In this context, mobilizing popular support was clearly the lesser of two evils, particularly because popular incorporation did not require property redistribution, reducing its costs. Thus, in both Syria and Turkey, the division of the elite into two camps, one composed of property owners and the other composed of high-ranking state officials, created a potential for intense conflict over political-economic priorities that was absent in both Korea and Taiwan. There were strong incentives for insurgent groups to mobilize mass support, for this was the only means available for breaking the existing monopoly of power by other segments of the elite.

Scholars of East Asian development have suggested that external security threats motivate the construction of developmental states.[91] Military officers convinced that existing political-economic arrangements weaken

[89] Distributive issues were relatively unimportant in East Asia, where the devastation of World War II produced relative income equality that persisted until after the developmental state was established.

[90] On this point, see the insightful comments of A. F. K. Organski, *The Stages of Political Development* (New York: Alfred A. Knopf, 1965), 122–56.

[91] Winckler, "Mass Political Incorporation," 64, argues that for Taiwan, "external circumstances strongly condition internal development." See also Kang, "South Korean and Taiwanese Development," 582–87.

the military power of the state are likely to move into the opposition and seek to capture state power to implement what Richard Sklar has termed an "organizational revolution." Organizational revolutions are revolutions whose goal is to reorganize authority to "facilitate the effective exercise of social control."[92] But the pre-1963 Syrian elite was also concerned with external threats: Syria fought and lost a war with Israel in 1948, had numerous skirmishes with the Israeli army throughout the 1950s and early 1960s, and watched the Israeli army destroy the Egyptian army in 1956. This high level of external threat produced neither a unified elite nor development. Instead, high-ranking military officers became convinced that the civilian elite was incapable of developing the economy in order to confront Israel. However, they could capture and retain power only by way of popular incorporation, in contrast to Park's coup in Korea. Thus, while security threats may indeed prompt state-building projects, the degree of elite homogeneity and hence elite unity intervenes to produce divergent outcomes.

In short, political stability is a function of the level of consensus about the proper economic role of the state, which in turn is strongly influenced by the degree of elite homogeneity. Elites can resolve relatively technical questions about efficiency within the parameters of existing political arrangements, and even conflict about distributive concerns may be peacefully resolved through compromise. When debate erupts about the legitimacy of economic outcomes or about the threats to property posed by state control over the economy, however, it is unlikely that people will act in the predictable, routine ways that constitute institutionalized polities. Furthermore, when positions on the political economy are more polarized, outcomes tend to be zero-sum. Advocates of contending positions over the interest rate are likely to submit their dispute to established political channels; advocates of contending positions about property ownership are not. When positions predicated on basic, deeply held value commitments are polarized, political stability is jeopardized.

Of course, these observations only assist us in analyzing different levels of elite conflict; they do not directly dictate how conflicts will be resolved. In some cases, such as organizational revolutions against an oligarchic state, the outcome seems to be highly determined; it seems unlikely that a new elite dedicated to rapid development can coexist with an oligarchic elite. But the case of Turkey sensitizes us to the possible importance of

[92] Richard Sklar, "Postimperialism: A Class Analysis of Multinational Corporation Expansion," *Comparative Politics* 9 (October 1976), 82. Samuel Huntington referred to the same phenomenon as a breakthrough coup, in which military officers from middle-class backgrounds overthrow oligarchic states to implement a program of socioeconomic reform and national development. See his *Political Order in Changing Societies* (New Haven: Yale University Press, 1968), 198–208.

contingent factors. It would have been conceivable for the military-bureaucratic wing of the elite to reconcile itself to the need of property owners to have secure control over the means of production. The Kemalist elite, after all, was ideologically committed to private property and threatened that property only in response to the exigencies of development and wartime mobilization. Had President Inonu not made the decision to liberalize the political system, furthermore, the defecting members of the elite would not have had the opportunity to mobilize popular support for their contending developmental project. On the other hand, the decision to democratize was in part a response to elite conflict. Once the decision to allow free elections was made, however, precocious Keynesianism was an inescapable outcome, for the defecting elite had little to offer potential supporters other than the promise of material benefits on gaining office.

Chapters 3 through 6 have presented the independent and intervening variables of this study. I have demonstrated that the intensity of elite conflict distinguished the Syrian and Turkish cases from the Korean and Taiwanese cases. Furthermore, I have argued that given the dynamics of conflict resolution in Syria and Turkey, the institutional profile of a precocious Keynesian state—constituency clientelism, distributive fiscal policies, politicized bureaucracies, and patterns of state intervention that protect constituencies from market forces—were necessary outcomes. I argued that the institutional configuration of developmental states, however, are not necessary outcomes of lower levels of elite conflict in Korea and Taiwan; I argued only that low levels of conflict are a necessary but not sufficient condition for constructing developmental states. While high levels of elite outcomes are constraining conditions, in other words, low levels of elite conflict are permissive conditions. What is clear is that the set of institutions constituting the political economies of the two sets of cases differ starkly from each other. The next two chapters link these institutions to different economic outcomes.

CHAPTER SEVEN

The Collective Dilemmas
of Late Development

Chapters 2 through 6 advanced propositions accounting for the institutional configurations of precocious Keynesian and developmental states. This chapter and the next explore the causal links between institutions and observed outcomes of economic development. Briefly, I argue that manifold collective dilemmas are inherent in the process of economic development. Collective dilemmas, which include collective action problems, coordination problems, and distributive conflicts, arise when "choices made by rational individuals lead to outcomes that no one prefers."[1] Because collective dilemmas create gaps between individual and collective rationality, the actions of utility-maximizing individuals produce socially suboptimal outcomes. Some institutions present potential solutions to collective dilemmas, whereas other institutions leave them unresolved. Two countries confronting the same set of collective dilemmas, but possessing different institutional capacities to resolve them, should then reach divergent economic outcomes. Chapter 8 completes the argument by exploring how the institutional frameworks of precocious Keynesian and developmental states either resolve or exacerbate collective dilemmas.

The chapter begins with a critique of neoliberal growth theory, which unequivocally condemns state economic intervention for producing outcomes inferior to those produced by free markets.[2] Although I accept that state intervention often creates suboptimal outcomes, I argue that the neoliberal case neglects the diverse ways states intervene in their

[1] Robert H. Bates, "Contra Contractarianism: Some Reflections on the New Institutionalism," *Politics & Society* 16 (1988): 387–401.

[2] I distinguish neoliberal growth theory from its neoclassical predecessor. Whereas neoclassical economics emphasizes allocative efficiency associated with free markets, neoliberal growth theory supplements this emphasis by analyzing the unproductive rent-seeking behavior associated with state intervention, as discussed below.

economies and the different institutional bases of that intervention; it thus leaves unexplored and unexplained the different outcomes resulting from state economic intervention. In the second section, I propose a semantic and four-part operational definition of the concept of development. The final section discusses the collective dilemmas entailed in each of the four constituent elements of economic development. Here, I distinguish between Gerschenkronian collective dilemmas and Kaldorian collective dilemmas. Gerschenkronian collective dilemmas refer to problems of capital accumulation; their resolution leads to new investments and the expansion of industrial production, or extensive growth. Kaldorian collective dilemmas refer to problems of enhancing efficiency and achieving international competitiveness; their resolution results in intensive growth.[3] The distinction is crucial; in Chapter 8, I argue that whereas developmental states resolve both types of collective dilemmas, precocious Keynesian states partially resolve Gerschenkronian collective dilemmas but only at the expense of exacerbating Kaldorian collective dilemmas. By demonstrating this claim and tracing the differential capacity to resolve collective dilemmas back to the institutional profiles whose origins were explained in preceding chapters, I account for divergent developmental trajectories.

Neoliberal Growth Theory

The orthodox account of economic development rests on the core tenet of neoclassical economics: market determination of prices allows entrepreneurs to equate price to marginal cost, yielding optimal resource allocation. The removal of all barriers to free trade, which results in "getting the prices right," then, is "both a necessary and a nearly sufficient condition for maximizing the rate of long-term growth."[4] More recently, mainstream economists bolster their critique of state economic interven-

---

[3] By Gerschenkronian collective dilemmas I refer to the work of the economic historian Alexander Gerschenkron, especially the title essay in his *Economic Backwardness in Historical Perspective* (Cambridge: Harvard University Press, 1962). By Kaldorian collective dilemmas, I refer to the work of the development economist Nicholas Kaldor. A compilation of his work has been published as *The Essential Kaldor*, ed. F. Targetti and A. P. Thirwall (London: Gerald Duckworth, 1989). See in particular two essays contained in this volume, "Causes of the Slow Rate of Growth of the United Kingdom" and "The Role of Increasing Returns, Technical Progress and Cumulative Causation in the Theory of International Trade and Economic Growth."

[4] Robert Wade, "East Asia's Economic Success: Conflicting Perspectives, Partial Insights, Shaky Evidence," *World Politics* 44 (January 1992), 271. Wade cites (273) James Riedel, who draws from East Asia the lesson that "neo-classical economic principles are alive and well, and working particularly effectively in the East Asian countries. Once public goods are provided for, and the most obvious distortions corrected, markets seem to do the job of allocating resources reasonably well, and certainly better than centralized decision-making. That is evident in East Asia . . . and is after all the main tenet of neo-classical economics."

tion through analysis of its effect on entrepreneurial behavior. They argue that by misallocating resources, state intervention produces above-normal profits, or rents, that is, payments to factors of production that exceed their opportunity costs. To capture rents, economic actors waste additional resources as political entrepreneurs. Moreover, by guaranteeing profits and socializing risks while reducing competition faced by domestic firms, protection-induced rents encourage the proliferation of firms and overcapacity, reward rather than penalize inefficient production practices, and discourage innovation. In short, state intervention removes the incentive for firms to become internationally competitive.[5] Consequently, state intervention to address market failures produces only greater welfare losses.[6] Cross-national studies that associate faster rates of growth with export-led growth (ELG) and slower rates of growth with import-substituting industrialization (ISI) seem, at first glance, to support these theoretical propositions.[7]

All aspects of the orthodox account have been subject to critique, eroding the agreement that had only recently been codified as the "Washington Consensus."[8] After distilling the ten-part Washington Consensus down to two broad categories, free markets and sound money, Krugman observes that neither of these policies pack the analytic punch attributed to them. He notes that the complete reduction of protectionist barriers in a highly protected economy would yield only a one-time, 5 percent boost to gross domestic product (GDP), while, according to standard estimates, the costs of inflation are even lower, so that a reduction in the inflation rate from 20 percent to 2 percent would yield negligible gains and, given the draconian measures frequently employed to combat inflation, may incur sizable costs.[9] More fundamentally, Alice Amsden argues that the exclusive emphasis on efficient resource allocation neglects production-related issues, leaving unexplored the problematic processes by which firms acquire the capability to produce goods competitive in world markets.[10]

[5] Anne Kreuger, "The Political Economy of the Rent-Seeking Society," *American Economic Review* 64 (1974): 291–303; Jagdish N. Bhagwati, "Directly Unproductive, Profit-seeking (DUP) Activities," *Journal of Political Economy* 90 (October 1982): 988–1002.

[6] See Deepak Lal, *The Poverty of "Development Economics"* (London: The Institute of Economic Affairs, 1983).

[7] For a taste of this large literature, see Ian Little, Tibor Scitovsky, and Maurice Scott, *Industry and Trade in Some Developing Countries: A Comparative Study* (London: Oxford University Press, 1970), and Bela Belassa, *The Newly Industrializing Countries in the World Economy* (New York: Pergamon, 1981).

[8] For the ten-part Washington Consensus, see John Williamson, "What Washington Means by Policy Reform," in *Latin American Adjustment: How Much Has Happened?* ed. John Williamson (Washington, D.C.: Institute for International Economics, 1990), 7–20.

[9] Paul Krugman, "Dutch Tulips and Emerging Markets," *Foreign Affairs* 74 (July/August 1995), 28–34.

[10] See her "Bringing Production Back In: Understanding Government's Economic Role in Late Industrialization," *World Development* 25 (April 1997): 469–80.

Amsden's point is underscored by critical scrutiny of the correlation linking growth rates to trade strategy, raising doubts about the direction of the causal link connecting exports and growth in developing countries. Santo Dodaro concludes, for example, that the benefits of export promotion become significant only in countries that have already achieved "some degree of economic development and internal productive efficiency enabling them to be competitive in manufactures and processed goods on the world market."[11] More provocatively, Dodaro argues in a later study that there is weak support for the contention that export growth promotes GDP growth, and slightly stronger, though still weak support, for the contention that GDP growth promotes growth in exports.[12] Most troubling for the standard account is Rodrik's recent analysis of Korean and Taiwanese development, which attributes no causal significance to outward-oriented policies or the growth of exports.[13] These studies attest to fundamental problems with the neoliberal account.

Indeed, the East Asian empirical record, on which the standard economic account stressing the role of relatively free trade rests, comports uneasily with the neoliberal critique of state intervention. Briefly, the economic reforms of the 1960s did not produce free markets. The Korean and Taiwanese governments, for example, consistently implemented selective trade policies that combined relatively free trade for internationally competitive industries with high tariffs and import quotas protecting industries that were not competitive. Robert Wade's conclusion about Taiwanese trade policy warrants our attention: "Putting together the evidence from 1969 with evidence from the subsequent period, we find that Taiwan has departed significantly from free trade. First, the regime of 1969 contained substantial amounts of industry and trade bias. Second, the rules of tariff rebate on import of capital equipment reflect the continuing importance of industry bias since 1969, the bias being derived from a wider industrial policy. Third, quantitative restrictions have been used extensively, right up to the mid 1980s and probably beyond. Fourth, these quantitative restrictions have been administered through highly discretionary procedures."[14]

---

[11] "Comparative Advantage, Trade and Growth: Export-led Growth Revisited," *World Development* 19 (1991), 1162. See also Michael Michaely, "Exports and Growth: An Empirical Investigation," *Journal of Development Economics* 4 (1977): 49–53.

[12] "Exports and Growth: A Reconsideration of Causality," *The Journal of Developing Areas* 27 (1993): 227–44. See also Albert Fishlow, "The Latin American State," *Journal of Economic Perspectives* 4 (1990): 61–74.

[13] Dani Rodrik, "Getting Interventions Right: How South Korea and Taiwan Grew Rich," *Economic Policy* 20 (April 1995), 60–75.

[14] Robert Wade, "Managing Trade: Taiwan and Korea as Challenges to Economics and Political Science," *Comparative Politics* 25 (January 1993), 149. See also his *Governing the Market: Economic Theory and the Role of Government in East Asian Industrialization* (Princeton: Princeton University Press, 1990), 52–72. For an analogous assessment of Korean trade

Similarly, although in the 1960s the Korean state altered real interest rates to encourage savings and discourage unproductive use of credit, measures meeting neoliberal approval, it did not liberalize the financial system. Instead, these reforms "greatly increased government controls over financial flows by attracting deposits into the banking system, away from a large number of highly active unregulated (or 'unorganized') financial institutions. The government has used its direct control over bank lending and its somewhat less pervasive control over foreign capital inflows to direct the allocation of sizable shares of both working capital and investment finance. Credit rationing has co-existed with a variety of selective preferential interest rate schemes."[15]

In light of this evidence, even neoliberal economists have modified their claim that East Asian development was based on free trade, arguing instead that an export-led strategy is one in which state protection of domestic industries is balanced by policies encouraging exports, creating a neutral regime. Bhagwati, for example, defines an export-led strategy not as a set of policy biases in favor of exports, but as a neutral policy that does not bias against exports, that is, the effective exchange rate of exports is equal to the effective exchange rate of imports. Bhagwati further recognizes that a "neutral" trade regime can conceal substantial intraindustry variation, such that "there may well be activities that are being import substituted."[16] But once we allow for variations in the pattern of protection, as clearly exist in Korea and Taiwan, the neoliberal case begins to lose its analytic bite: if state intervention creates a bias in favor of exports in some sectors and a bias against exports in other sectors, then state policy is violating the canons of standard trade theory, which calls for the complete absence of any biases. Indeed, any bias in favor of exports—in Korea, according to one estimate, there has been a net policy bias in favor of exports ranging from 16 to 30 percent—should result in the same dysfunctional behavior as protection. In the memorable phrase of Ronald Findlay, "right wing deviation" is no better than "left wing deviation": "In terms of the standard theory of trade and welfare, a bias in favor of exports is no better in principle than a bias against them. . . . It is therefore hard to see why an export-promotion strategy should produce such suc-

---

strategy, see Howard Pack and Larry E. Westphal, "Industrial Strategy and Technological Change: Theory Versus Reality," *Journal of Development Economics* 22 (1986): 87–128.

[15] Pack and Westphal, "Industrial Strategy and Technological Change," 95. Nor did Taiwan create a liberal financial system; see Tun-jen Cheng, "Guarding the Commanding Heights: The State as Banker in Taiwan." in *The Politics of Finance in Developing Countries*, ed. Stephan Haggard, Chung H. Lee, and Sylvia Maxfield (Ithaca: Cornell University Press, 1993), 55–92.

[16] Jagdish N. Bhagwati, "Rethinking Trade Strategy," in *Development Strategies Reconsidered*, ed. John P. Lewis and Valeriana Kallab (New Brunswick: Transaction Books, 1986), 92–93.

cessful results, since both types of bias are equally to be condemned from the standpoint of static allocative efficiency."[17]

These analytic critiques and East Asian empirics neither decisively establish that state intervention is necessary for rapid development nor deny that comprehensive state intervention yields developmental failures more often than successes.[18] With reference to East Asia, defenders of the standard economic account can select from many arguments: that government intervention in East Asia slowed down growth, that it neither hindered nor fostered growth, or that it only eased and accelerated a process that would have happened anyway.[19] The problem with this debate is that it lumps together distinct forms of state intervention and thus cannot account for varying outcomes. A more productive approach is to recognize that state intervention takes distinct forms and to demonstrate clear causal links between modes of state economic intervention and varying developmental outcomes.[20] In the following sections, I first present an operational definition of economic development that allows for more specific delineation of outcomes. Specifically, in accordance with Amsden's stress on production-related issues, I focus on the composition and processes of production. I then turn to the relationship of modes of state intervention and developmental trajectories.

Defining Development

Most orthodox economists adopt a purely quantitative definition of development, understanding it as an *outcome* measured by real increases in national income.[21] Recent discussions of economic change, however, em-

---

[17] Cited in Martin Fransman, "Explaining the Success of the East Asian NICs: Incentives and Technology," *IDS Bulletin* 15 (1984), 53.

[18] But note that some economists admit that their theory cannot capture the dynamic, process-oriented dimensions of development. See, for example, Lal, *The Poverty of 'Development Economics,'* 106, and Krugman, "Dutch Tulips and Emerging Markets," 44.

[19] These alternatives are articulated by Rodrik, "Getting Interventions Right," 96–97. For a decisive rebuttal of the argument that state intervention only accelerated a naturally occurring process, see Robert Wade, "Industrial Policy in East Asia: Does it Lead or Follow the Market?" in *Manufacturing Miracles: Paths of Industrialization in Latin America and East Asia,* ed. Gary Gereffi and Donald L. Wyman (Princeton: Princeton University Press, 1990), 231–66.

[20] Here, I follow the research strategy elaborated best in Peter Evans, *Embedded Autonomy: States and Industrial Transformation* (Princeton: Princeton University Press, 1995).

[21] One reason for the bias toward a quantitative definition of development may be that national income is a valid proxy for less tangible indicators of development. But this quantitative bias might also reflect the penchant of neoclassical economics to focus on mathematically elegant formulations to the exclusion of messy facts, a tendency often justified as necessary to comprehend underlying patterns. As Robert E. Lucas Jr., "On the Mechanics of Economic Development," *Journal of Monetary Economics* 22 (July 1988), 13, expressed it, "It seems to be universally agreed that the model I have just reviewed [the Solow-Dennison Growth Model] is not a theory of economic development. Indeed, I suppose this is why we think of 'growth' and 'development' as distinct fields, with growth theory defined as those

phasize not only how much is produced, but also what is produced and how it is produced. Eric Hobsbawm captured part of this distinction nicely when he noted, "It was not Birmingham, a city which produced a great deal more in 1850 than in 1750, but essentially in the old manner, that made contemporaries speak of an industrial revolution, but Manchester, a city which produced more in a more obviously revolutionary manner."[22] Studies of industrial adjustment in advanced industrial economies, for example, have emphasized that economic performance is highly sensitive to both shop-floor practices and sectoral organization, which condition efforts to enhance industrial productivity and international competitiveness.[23] Furthermore, there is growing evidence that a nation's future economic performance is deeply indebted to present production profiles and processes, which create path-dependent trajectories of economic change.[24] A more expansive, process-oriented notion of development distinguishes between a nation whose wealth is substantially derived solely from exports of raw materials, or even of labor-intensive manufactures, and one whose wealth accrues from the production of skill or knowledge-intensive goods. Santo Dodaro, for example, writes, "Normally, the lower the stage of processing, the lower the need for additional attributes and the greater the role of basic factors, such as natural resources, in the determination of comparative advantage. Conversely, the higher the level of product fabrication, the greater the degree of diversification and sophistication and the greater the need for a more varied array of skills, technology, knowledge, and other attributes normally associated with higher levels of development and per capita income."[25] Accordingly, I define development as changes in economic structures and processes that enhance the capacity to create value.[26] Development, then,

---

aspects of economic growth we have some understanding of, and development defined as those we don't." Of course, the quantitative bias of economics may also be another manifestation of the well-known observation of physicist, Max Planck: "That is real which can be measured," a statement that Heidegger viewed as the essence of modern science.

[22] *Industry and Empire* (Middlesex, England: Penguin Books, 1968), 34.

[23] Michael J. Piore and Charles F. Sable, *The Second Industrial Divide: Possibilities for Prosperity* (New York: Basic Books, 1984), and Michael H. Best, *The New Competition: Institutions of Industrial Restructuring* (Cambridge: Harvard University Press, 1990).

[24] See Michael Borrus and John Zysman, "Industrial Competitiveness and American National Security," in Wayne Sandholtz, et al., *The Highest Stakes: The Economic Foundations of the Next Security System* (Oxford: Oxford University Press, 1992), 19–35.

[25] See his "Exports and Growth," 230.

[26] Michael Porter argues that the principal economic goal of a nation is to produce a high and rising standard of living for its citizens. Because this is ultimately based on the productivity with which capital and labor are employed, value-added per worker or per unit of capital is the proper unit of measurement, not overall value-added. This claim holds for the analysis of the process of production of an established industry or industrial sector. It is silent, however, about two issues crucial for late development: the creation of linkages between economic or industrial sectors and the movement into new economic or industrial sectors. These two considerations essentially amount to creating new domains in which cap-

measures changes in the process of transforming inputs into finished products, and changes in the composition of production, based on the understanding that complex and sophisticated economies produce more value than economies based on more rudimentary forms of production.

Investments in new industrial plants producing finished light-industrial consumer goods based on borrowed product and process technology are perhaps the most fundamental way to increase the capacity to create value. These investments, which either introduce new products or expand production of existing products, are the standard starting point for late-developing economies in the twentieth century.[27] A second mechanism is to construct forward or backward linkages; an industry fosters linkages when it uses the outputs of other industries as its inputs or when its outputs are used by other industries as inputs. Albert Hirschman offers the simple example of Latin American bananas, which until the 1960s were shipped on the stem; as a result, there was minimal locally added post-harvest value. In the 1960s, local producers began packaging bananas before shipping, which meant more local processing of the product as well as reduced shipping costs. As a result, more of the final cost to consumers of bananas was captured by the producing country. As an added bonus, local packaging raised demand for the local paper and pulp mill industry.[28] Linkages, then, constitute steps in the transition from a series of unrelated enclave enterprises toward a tightly integrated dynamic economy capable of self-sustaining growth.

Other routes to enhanced capacity for creation of value are less closely tied to capital accumulation. As economic historians have regularly observed, "It is a great deal easier to find the capital for the construction of a modern industry than to run it. . . ."[29] Increased productivity is the third mechanism increasing the capacity to create value.[30] Productivity in-

---

ital or labor can be productively employed. Thus, value-added per worker remains only one element of my broader conceptualization of development. For Porter's argument, see his *The Competitive Advantage of Nations* (New York: Free Press, 1990), 6, esp. notes 5–6.

[27] Albert O. Hirschman, "The Political Economy of Import Substitution," in his *A Bias for Hope: Essays on Development and Latin America* (New Haven: Yale University Press, 1971).

[28] Albert O. Hirschman, "A Generalized Linkage Approach to Development with Special Reference to Staples," in *Essays in Trespassing: Economics to Politics and Beyond* (Cambridge: Cambridge University Press, 1981), 73.

[29] Hobsbawm, *Industry and Empire*, 61. See also Jan DeVries, *The Economy of Europe in an Age of Crisis, 1600–1750* (Cambridge: Cambridge University Press, 1976), 213–24; and David Landes, *The Unbound Prometheus: Technological Change and Industrial Development in Western Europe from 1750 to the Present* (Cambridge: Cambridge University Press, 1969), 77–80.

[30] Howard Pack estimates, for example, that raising the level of total industrial productivity in the Philippines to half that of the United States would result in a 100 percent increase in output without any change in the quantity of inputs. "Total Factor Productivity and Its Determinants: Some International Comparisons," in *Comparative Development Perspectives,* ed. Gustav Ranis, et al. (Boulder, Colo.: Westview Press, 1984), 17–35. By some accounts, increases in total factor productivity account for one-third of total growth in East Asia, with

creases are most commonly associated with upgrading process technology through new capital investments. But as we shall see in Chapter 8, purchasing new technology does not automatically translate into productivity increases; new technology embodied in capital equipment must be assimilated and effectively deployed. Specifically, more capital-intensive machinery must be embedded in efficient forms of work organization and shop-floor practices. These "soft" organizational innovations are distinct from the "hard" technological innovations constituted by machinery; consequently, the historical introduction of new technologies is closely linked to organizational innovations. As Herman Schwartz notes, "The sheer scale of investment needed to utilize new technologies mandated both new organizational forms and new work practices. Neither kind of innovation could stand alone: new work practices and management systems made little sense unless changes in machinery and power systems accompanied them; new machinery could not be used to its fullest potential without changes in work practices and the management of production."[31]

Changes in the organization of the production process are thus a necessary precondition for the deployment of more capital-intensive equipment; if the two are decoupled, as frequently happens among late developers, productivity may be reduced rather than augmented. As William Lazonick describes this relationship, "[A] firm that invests in capital-intensive technology will not automatically secure lower unit costs and competitive advantage. If the investing firm does not have the organizational capacities to utilize the fixed capital at its disposal—if it cannot create value by coordinating and controlling the efforts of its employees—then it might well find itself at a competitive disadvantage relative to a labor-intensive enterprise that is less burdened by fixed costs."[32]

Comprehensive and sustainable productivity increases, then, are tightly linked to alteration of the organization of production. Organizational innovations have historically yielded dramatic increases in productivity. Alfred Chandler identified fundamental changes in the organization of the production process as important stimulators of throughput, which refers to the speed and volume of the flow of materials through the production process: using existing technology, the greater speed of production asso-

---

capital accumulation accounting for the other two-thirds. See World Bank, *The East Asian Miracle: Economic Growth and Public Policy* (Oxford: Oxford University Press for the World Bank, 1993), 48.

[31] Herman Schwartz, *States versus Markets: History, Geography, and the Development of the International Political Economy* (New York: St. Martin's Press, 1994), 73. For further discussion, see William Lazonick, *Business Organization and the Myth of the Market Economy* (Cambridge: Cambridge University Press, 1991).

[32] *Competitive Advantage on the Shop Floor* (Cambridge: Harvard University Press, 1990), 73.

ciated with the shift to mass production yielded huge increases in productivity, as the innovations in Henry Ford's production system demonstrated. The shift to lean production resulted in a similarly discontinuous increase in productivity.[33]

Less dramatically, but often more important, learning-by-doing—incremental improvements in skills, shop-floor practices, and the organization of production—boost productivity. Because the knowledge and skill needed to produce high-quality goods at competitive prices are often tacit knowledge, they are obtained only through the actual experience of production, known as learning-by-doing.[34] Learning-by-doing entails assimilating the tacit knowledge embedded in technology and altering production processes to make best use of this knowledge. Greater accumulation and deployment of tacit knowledge result in more efficient production, as "workers produce more per unit of time with the same expenditure of effort."[35] Thus, while technological upgrading can increase productivity, its capacity to do so is a function of organizational innovation in management techniques and shop-floor practices, which, when efficient, also increase productivity independently of a level of technology. In short, technology can be treated neither as an exogenous variable nor as an endogenous variable that automatically and invariantly causes increased productivity.[36]

Productivity increases enhance the capacity to create value, even in industries producing long-established goods located at the end of the product cycle.[37] But because these are generally mature industries using sim-

---

[33] Alfred D. Chandler, *The Visible Hand: The Managerial Revolution in American Business* (Cambridge: Harvard University Press, 1977), esp. Chap. 8. On mass production in the automobile industry and its displacement by lean production, see James Womack, et al., *The Machine That Changed the World: The Story of Lean Production* (New York: Harper Perennial, 1990).

[34] For further discussion, see Martin Bell, "'Learning' and the Accumulation of Industrial Technological Capacity in Developing Countries," in *Technological Capability in the Third World*, ed. Martin Fransman and Kenneth King (London: MacMillan Press, Ltd., 1984), 187–209.

[35] Lazonick, *Competitive Advantage on the Shop Floor*, 61. Learning-by-doing is a critical component of productivity and competitiveness, even in light industries such as textiles, an industry in which skill requirements are wrongly considered to be minimal and quickly learned. See the discussion in Gavin Wright, *Old South, New South: Revolutions in the Southern Economy Since the Civil War* (Baton Rouge: Louisiana State University Press, 1986), 131–135.

[36] For a relatively nontechnical introduction to the literature on endogenous technical change, see Paul M. Romer, "The Origins of Endogenous Growth," *Journal of Economic Perspectives* 8 (Winter 1994): 3–22. For Romer's earlier, highly influential statement of the theory, see his "Increasing Returns and Long-Run Growth," *Journal of Political Economy* 94 (1986): 1002–37. But for a critical assessment of endogenous growth theory's explanatory power with reference to the East Asian NICs, see Howard Pack, "Endogenous Growth Theory: Intellectual Appeal and Empirical Shortcomings," *Journal of Economic Perspectives* 8 (Winter 1994): 55–72.

[37] On the product cycle, see Raymond Vernon, *Sovereignty at Bay: The Multinational Spread of U.S. Enterprises* (New York: Basic Books, 1971), and also his "International Investment and International Trade in the Product Cycle," *Quarterly Journal of Economics* 80 (May 1966): 190–207.

ple and widespread technologies and selling their products in markets in which demand has been substantially satisfied and expands slowly, they generally support only low average returns on investment. Moreover, because technology used in them is readily available and easily assimilated, there are few barriers to entry in these industries. The subsequent proliferation of competitors pushes down prices and wage rates in these industries. Of course, the productivity- and quality-enhancing measures discussed in the preceding paragraph protect firms in well-established industries from at least some of these pressures. But a final way to enhance the capacity to create value is through product innovation, or movement into the production of higher value-added goods based on large accumulations of technology, knowledge, and skills. Moving up the product cycle reduces the competition faced by innovating firms, allowing them to charge premium prices and support higher wages. As Gene Grossman and Elhanan Helpman argue, "When a new product is developed that substitutes imperfectly for existing brands, the innovator can establish a market niche and charge a price above marginal cost in the ensuing oligopolistic competition."[38]

Combining these considerations creates a four-part operationalization of development: new investments producing real increases in per capita national income; the creation of intersectoral and interindustry linkages; upgrading the productivity of the production process of any given industrial sector; and movement into the production of higher value-added goods.[39] The developmental trajectory of a country refers to the sum of changes along each of these dimensions. National economies that do not proceed along multiple tracks of development face daunting challenges to continued prosperity. As Michael Porter warns,

> Those industries in which labor costs or natural resources are important to competitive advantage also often have industry structures that support only low average returns on investment. . . . Developing nations are frequently trapped in such industries. Nearly all the exports of less developed nations tend to be tied to factor costs and to competing on price. . . . Nations in this situation will face a continual threat of losing competitive position and chronic problems in supporting attractive wages and returns to capital. Their ability to earn even modest profits is at the mercy of economic fluctuations.[40]

National prosperity thus hinges not only on capital accumulation and the creation of linkages, but also on enhancing productivity and product in-

[38] "Trade, Innovation, and Growth," *American Economic Review* 80 (May 1990), 87.

[39] Note that although these dimensions apply to all economic sectors, I restrict discussion to industrial development.

[40] *Competitive Advantage of Nations*, 15–16.

novation. Not all national economies successfully undertake these tasks, however. The reason for this is that all four of these processes are embedded in collective dilemmas.

Collective Dilemmas and Development

Adam Smith's famous formulation of the market as an invisible hand enshrined the idea that self-interested individuals spontaneously produce socially optimal outcomes with minimal state intervention. Smith's account, however, assumed that few collective dilemmas existed. Generically, collective dilemmas in their variant forms entail discrepancies between private and social rates of return. When collective dilemmas exist, utility-maximizing individuals seeking private interests produce suboptimal social outcomes; thus, Hardin provocatively refers to collective action problems as "the back of the visible hand."[41] In Mancur Olson's formulation, economic growth is continuously threatened by a serious collective action problem.[42] On the one hand, organizations desire economic efficiency, growth, and general prosperity, not out of altruism, but because making society more productive serves their members' interests. On the other hand, organizations can also serve their members' interests by redistributing wealth, obtaining for their members a larger share of society's production. But if sufficient numbers of organizations opt for redistribution over growth, the national economy stagnates. As I have argued, in precocious Keynesian states, it is elites who make side-payments for their own political goals and not redistributive-seeking groups that demand them, though subsequently they may defend them tenaciously. With this critical revision in mind, Olson's framework prompts the conclusion that in Syria and Turkey, intense elite conflict results in suboptimal economic development because it creates an intractable collective-action problem.[43]

[41] Russell Hardin, *Collective Action* (Baltimore: Johns Hopkins University Press, 1982), 6.

[42] Mancur Olson, *The Rise and Decline of Nations: Economic Growth, Stagflation, and Social Rigidities* (New Haven: Yale University Press, 1982). Olson accounts for cross-national variations in rates of growth by noting that for organizations to redistribute income, they must solve their internal collective action problems, that is, preventing their members from free riding.

[43] Insofar as opting for redistribution, or defection, is the dominant strategy of all players, yielding only one suboptimal equilibrium point, Olson's theory resembles a prisoner's dilemma game. But note that to draw this equivalence, the terms *cooperation* and *defection*, have to be redefined, as Olson has implicitly done, so that *cooperation* means engaging in activities supportive of the collective good and *defection* means engaging in activities detrimental to the collective good. Ironically, then, for Olson's groups to engage in rent-seeking behavior, or defect from the collective good, the members of the group must cooperate with each other. Below, I discuss several coordination problems, or "assurance games," in which interdependent decision-making yields multiple equilibria for which decentralized solutions are logically possible but, as we shall see, difficult to achieve. Strictly speaking, these are not collective action problems, which refer only to the prisoner's dilemma. For a brief

This conclusion is insufficient, for Olson's account reveals little about the causal mechanisms issuing in discrete outcomes; it plausibly explains different rates of growth but remains silent about the remaining elements of development discussed earlier.[44] Indeed, the story becomes more interesting when we focus on the development process itself, for each of its constituent elements is implicated in particular collective dilemmas. Moreover, these collective dilemmas involve not rent-seeking organizations, as in Olson's theory, but, more important, individual decision makers. In Michael Crichton's novel *Jurassic Park*, John Hammond, the late twentieth-century version of the mad scientist—actually, the mad entrepreneur who hires scientists—explains why he has used his prodigious entrepreneurial skills to establish a theme park rather than doing something that will actually help mankind: "Suppose you make a miracle drug for cancer or heart disease. . . . Suppose you now want to charge a thousand dollars or two thousand dollars a dose. You might imagine that is your privilege. After all, you invented the drug, you paid to develop and test it; you should be able to charge whatever you wish. No . . . *something* will force you to see reason—and to sell your drug at a lower cost. From a business standpoint, that makes helping mankind a very risky business. Personally, I would *never* help mankind."[45]

Hammond's defense of his individually rational but socially irrational behavior captures one of the central dilemmas of development: how to induce economic agents to engage in risky economic behavior where there is uncertainty about whether and to whom profits will accrue, such that individuals have incentives to "defect," to avoid risky but socially productive behavior, because others can profit from the results without bearing costs or exposing themselves to risks and perhaps profiting more than the individual who does bear risks and costs. More technically, economists call *externalities* those circumstances in which markets do not allocate to economic agents the full costs (negative externalities) or the full benefits (positive externalities) of an economic activity.[46] In this respect, externalities are like public goods: individuals will tend to free ride, or

---

introduction to assurance games, see Arthur Stein, "Coordination and Collaboration: Regimes in an Anarchic World," in Stephen Krasner, ed., *International Regimes* (Ithaca: Cornell University Press, 1982), 118–20.

[44] Olson's theory has generated a great deal of critical discussion. See, for example, David Cameron, "Distributional Coalitions and Other Sources of Economic Stagnation: On Olson's *Rise and Decline of Nations*," *International Organization* 42 (Autumn 1988): 561–603.

[45] Michael Crichton, *Jurassic Park* (New York: Alfred A. Knopf, 1990), 199, italics in original.

[46] In an early and important statement, Tibor Scitovosky defined externalities as situations of interdependence between producers that did not operate through the market mechanism. As a result, "The output of the individual producer may depend not only on his input of productive resources but also on the activities of other firms." "Two Concepts of External Economies," *Journal of Political Economy* 62 (1954), 144.

not contribute to the costs of providing them or remedying their negative effects. Consequently, markets undersupply positive externalities and fail to remedy fully negative externalities.[47]

If only a small subset of economic activities created externalities, they would be of intellectual interest but of little practical import. But, as North and Thomas make clear, achieving harmony between private and social benefits is the central dilemma plaguing economic change. They write, "The factors we have listed (innovation, economies of scale, education, capital accumulation, etc.) are not causes of growth; they *are* growth. . . . Growth will simply not occur unless the existing economic organization is efficient. Individuals must be lured by incentives to undertake the socially desirable activities. Some mechanism must be devised to bring social and private rates of return into closer parity."[48]

Recent research echoes and updates North and Thomas's emphasis on the detrimental developmental effects of positive externalities. As Paul Krugman summarizes, "What the new [strategic trade] theory tells us is that meaningful externalities occur not only when there are direct technological spillovers, but in any situation in which there are increasing returns and [where] market size matters. That means almost everywhere. In other words, the marginal social benefit of a dollar's worth of resources is not, as conventional theory would have it, equal in all activities except for a few exceptions. Divergences between social rates of return are pervasive. There are good industries and bad, good jobs and bad, and the optimal policy is to subsidize the good and tax the bad."[49]

Of course, positive externalities do not pose irresistible impediments to beneficial economic activities. In theory, problems posed by externalities are potentially resolvable by decentralized bargaining or by specialized, non-governmental institutions.[50] Moreover, as we shall see in Chapter 8, rather than resolving collective dilemmas, state intervention may exacerbate them, making suboptimal outcomes stable equilibria. The point is

---

[47] For lucid discussion, see Robert Heilbroner and Lester Thurow, *The Economic Problem,* 5th ed. (Englewood Cliffs, N.J.: Prentice-Hall, 1978), 227–35; and Heinz W. Arndt, "'Market Failure' and Underdevelopment," *World Development* 16 (February 1988): 219–29.

[48] Douglass C. North and Robert Paul Thomas, *The Rise of the Western World: A New Economic History* (Cambridge: Cambridge University Press, 1973), 2.

[49] As cited in Trevor Matthews and John Ravenhill, "Strategic Trade Policy: The Northeast Asian Experience," in *Business and Government in Industrialising Asia,* ed. Andrew C. Macintyre (Ithaca: Cornell University Press, 1994), 37.

[50] On decentralized bargains as coordinating solutions to problems raised by externalities, see Ronald Coase, "The Problem of Social Cost," *Journal of Law and Economics* 3 (1960): 1–44. In an important article, Richard Doner argues that in East Asia firms regularly contribute to solving collective action problems. His material suggests, however, that the Korean developmental state has also played a major role in their solution. See his "The Limits of State Strength: Toward an Institutionalist View of Economic Development," *World Politics* 44 (April 1992): 398–431.

simply that given the ubiquity of state intervention and its different modes, some types of state intervention are likely to resolve collective dilemmas and foster development, whereas other types are likely to exacerbate collective dilemmas and preclude development. By superimposing modes of state intervention over a map of collective dilemmas, we can account for divergent trajectories of economic development.

More specifically, the processes constituting economic development, such as capital accumulation, boosting productivity, and product and process innovation, are themselves embedded in collective dilemmas. As a first step in discussing them, we can divide the collective dilemmas inherent in development into two major categories: Gerschenkronian and Kaldorian collective dilemmas. Gerschenkronian collective dilemmas are obstacles to inducing capitalists to make investments in new industrial plant; their resolution produces extensive growth. Kaldorian collective dilemmas are obstacles jeopardizing efficient performance of these plants; their resolution yields intensive growth and innovation.

Gerschenkronian Collective Dilemmas

Gerschenkronian collective dilemmas render difficult capital accumulation and its subsequent socially productive investment in new industrial enterprises. Alexander Gerschenkron, for example, noted that while private investors amassed capital for relatively small-scale textile plants in England, private markets could not mobilize and supply the large-scale resources required in second-generation industrializing countries. Without institutional innovation, particularly direct state activity, latecomers would not be able to industrialize.[51] As Albert Hirschman observes, however, the problem of capital accumulation is not simply the relative scarcity of capital, but also the resistance of capitalists to deploy their assets in productive investments in the face of tremendous risks.[52] As George Stigler enumerated some of these risks, "Young industries are often strangers to the established economic system. They require new kinds of qualities of materials and hence make their own; they must overcome technical problems in the use of their products and cannot wait for potential users to overcome them; they must persuade customers to abandon other commodities and find specialized merchants to undertake the task. These young industries must design their specialized equipment

---

[51] Gerschenkron, "Economic Backwardness in Historical Perspective." The validity of Gerschenkron's thesis is assessed by the contributions to Richard Sylla and Gianni Toniolo, eds., *Patterns of European Industrialization: The Nineteenth Century* (London: Routledge, 1991).

[52] This argument is detailed in his *The Strategy of Economic Development* (Boulder, Colo.: Westview Press reprint, 1988).

and often manufacture it."[53] Similarly, Peter Evans considers the absence of institutions to spread risk across multiple capitalists to be the central problem plaguing late developers; drawing inspiration directly from Gerschenkron, Evans argues that this institutional void forces the state to act as a surrogate entrepreneur.[54] Economists appropriately argue that risk-bearing institutions should emerge to counteract this effect. But this functionalist approach to the origins of risk-bearing institutions lacks a supply-side theory of institutions and so ignores the collective dilemmas rendering problematic the development of these institutions and the role of institutional inertia in perpetuating suboptimal outcomes.

Hence, risk-averse behavior often yields suboptimal outcomes, even when capital is available. Furthermore, the problem of investments is not simply a function of risk-averse individuals, for there is a strategic dimension as well. In one of the earliest discussions of collective action problems, William Baumol explored how the strategic calculations of developing-country investors might produce suboptimal levels of investment:

> [T]he individual as a citizen, having his share of local pride, may desire an improvement in the future state of welfare in the community. If, however, he alone directs his activities in a manner conducive to it, the effects of his action may be quite negligible. It is true that in the process he may also be improving the value of his own assets, but his private return must be discounted by a risk factor which does not apply in the calculation of the expected gain to the community. Thus neither private interest nor altruism (except if he has grounds for assurance that others, too, will act in a manner designed to promote the future welfare of the community) can rationally lead him to invest for the future, and particularly the far distant future, to an extent appropriate from the point of view of the community as a whole. Taken as a commodity, improvement in the future state of the community as a whole is one that must serve a group demand and not just the demand of isolated individuals.[55]

Baumol's entrepreneur would prefer the cooperative outcome, but unsure of others' willingness to cooperate, defection is a rational strategy.

---

[53] "The Division of Labor Is Limited by the Extent of Market," *Journal of Political Economy* 59 (June 1951), 190. The level of risk and uncertainty involved in moving into new industrial activities explains why later developers would opt to industrialize on borrowed technology even after it becomes apparent that in doing so they risk becoming mired at the low end of the product cycle.

[54] Peter Evans, "The State as Problem and Solution: Predation, Embedded Autonomy, and Structural Change," in Stephan Haggard and Robert R. Kaufman, eds., *The Politics of Economic Adjustment* (Princeton: Princeton University Press, 1992), 147.

[55] William J. Baumol, *Welfare Economics and the Theory of the State* (Cambridge: Harvard University Press, 1952), as cited in Hardin, *Collective Action*, 21.

Note that by choosing not to invest—defection—the entrepreneur loses the opportunity to raise the value of her assets; without assurances that others will invest as well, she forgoes what was presumably the optimal return on her investments. Both the individual and society, then, receive suboptimal returns.[56]

Finally, note that even after entrepreneurs have built factories producing finished consumer goods, they face new reasons to oppose the construction of backward linkages. As Hirschman observes, resistance to the construction of linkages stems from fears on the part of finished-good producers that domestically produced inputs will be of inferior quality; fears of becoming dependent on a single domestic producer; and fears of increased domestic competition through the subsequent creation of forward linkages. "For all of these reasons, the interests of the converting, finishing, and mixing industries are often opposed to the establishment of domestic sources of supply for the products that they convert, finish, or mix."[57] One response to the reluctance of capitalists to make industrial investments is for the state to protect infant industries, offsetting investment-deterring risks with the promise of economic rents. This in turn creates a second-order collective dilemma that continues to militate against the construction of backward linkages. Hirschman notes that producers of finished goods under an ISI regime received rents from two sources: high tariff protection for the finished product and low or zero tariffs for inputs. Once backward linkages were created, that industrialist might continue to receive tariff protection for the finished product, but the cost of inputs would dramatically increase as the input-producing industry would itself receive protection and thus be in a position to charge higher profits and earn rents. Establishing backward linkages, then, meant the transfer of rents from the finished-goods producer to the intermediate-input producer.[58] Thus, in late developers with ISI regimes, the creation of backward linkages requires resolution of a distributive conflict, which is a type of collective dilemma.[59]

In sum, collective action and coordination problems constrain and render problematic investments in new industries, but they certainly do not preclude it. Various institutional solutions to these problems have been created. Still, accumulating capital and investing it in new plants is only the first, necessary stage of development. Since Solow's seminal 1957

---

[56] Depending on how we construct payoff schedules, Baumol could be read as describing a collective action problem or a coordination problem.

[57] "Political Economy of Import-Substituting Industrialization," 106–7.

[58] Ibid.

[59] As Hirschman makes clear, the clash between individual interests causes disjuncture between individual and collective interests. He writes, "While the resistances of the new industrialists are perfectly rational, one cannot but feel that they are based on a myopic, excessively short-run view of the development process." Ibid., 109.

analysis, economists have been aware that capital accumulation can account for only about half of growth in per capita income in this century. The gap between observed growth and that part of it attributable to increases in the capital-to-labor ratio, conventionally called the "Solow residual," is in more current theorizing attributed to accumulations of knowledge and skill (although current models still neglect the organization of production).[60] Once capital has been accumulated and invested, other factors forcing divergencies between private and social rates of return impede efforts to upgrade productivity or innovate in new products.

Kaldorian Collective Dilemmas

Kaldorian collective dilemmas refer to difficulties encountered in making existing factories more efficient and in moving up the product cycle. To be sure, many productivity-enhancing measures are not plagued by collective dilemmas 'and can be achieved without centralized coordination. Unilateral action by firms creates intrasectoral variations in levels of efficiency or propensities to innovate in new products within a national economy. But I argue that systemic constraints on enhancing productivity or innovating in new products tend to be resolved—or exacerbated—at the level of the national economy.[61] Therefore, even greater variations in efficiency and innovation distinguish almost all firms in an industrial sector of one national economy from almost all firms in another national economy.[62]

Consider first alterations of production processes and shop-floor practices underpinning productivity increases. In many important respects, these productivity-enhancing measures, particularly learning-by-doing,

---

[60] Robert M. Solow, "Technical Change and the Aggregate Production Function," *Review of Economics and Statistics* 39 (August 1957): 312–20. Briefly, because neoclassical growth models assume that increasing capital-intensity yields diminishing returns, poorer countries with growing capital stock should experience greater returns and ultimately converge with wealthier countries. That this has not happened has spurred the new growth theory to incorporate the accumulation of knowledge and skills that delay diminishing returns and permit increasing returns. See the citations in footnote 36. For a brief and lucid introduction, see "The Poor and the Rich," *The Economist*, May 25, 1996, 23–25.

[61] I follow here the arguments presented in, among many other works, Peter Katzenstein, ed., *Between Power and Plenty: Foreign Economic Policies of Advanced Industrial States* (Madison: University of Wisconsin Press, 1986); and Peter Hall, *Governing the Economy: The Politics of State Intervention in Britain and France* (New York: Oxford University Press, 1986). Note also that these works take the national economy as the unit of analysis and thus tend to neglect substantial intersectoral variation within national economies.

[62] For example, see David Morawetz, *Why the Emperor's New Clothes Are Not Made in Columbia: A Case Study in Latin American and East Asian Manufactured Exports* (New York: Oxford University Press, 1981), 147–49.

are linked to expanded output within individual factories.[63] In many industrial sectors, for example, economies of scales exist such that an increase in output causes long-run average costs to fall so that large-output volume can be produced at a lower cost per unit than small-output volumes.[64] But even in sectors not characterized by important scale economies, increased scale of output yields efficiency gains by fueling learning-by-doing. Nicholas Kaldor analyzed this relationship, concluding that increased output leads to a number of benefits, including "the development of skill and know-how; the opportunities for easy communication of ideas and experience; [and] the opportunity of ever-increasing differentiation of processes and of specialisation in human activities."[65] More succinctly, he argued that there is an "empirical relationship between the growth of productivity and the growth of production."[66] Thus, even firms expanding output but still producing at less than the threshold for technical economies of scale can benefit in other ways.

Increasing the scale of production and capturing the benefits of expanded output, however, are implicated in a potentially thorny problem stemming from strategic interdependence and large external economies. In an early exploration of this problem, Paul Rosenstein-Rodan argued that given a pre-industrial economy with surplus labor, shifting 20,000 previously unemployed workers into one shoe factory would produce insufficient demand for the product of that factory if it were to be built on scale sufficient to produce efficiently.[67] If, on the other hand, one million workers were hired by a range of factories, they would together constitute sufficient demand and permit industrial development. But while multiple investments of a large scale would allow pecuniary external economies to be internalized by firms as profits, no individual entrepreneur would make this investment without assurance that all other necessary investments would also be made, for the simple reason that uncoordinated investments would not earn profits. Analogously, W. Arthur Lewis argued that successful industrialization depends on the cultivation of a number of intraindustry externalities, stemming from collective learning curves

[63] Adam Smith was the first to identify this relationship, arguing that increasing the division of labor resulted in increasing efficiency and observing that "the division of labor is limited by the extent of the market." *The Wealth of Nations*, Book I, Chapter III.

[64] Economies of scale are seldom continuous and incremental, but begin to operate only after a fairly high threshold has been crossed. For elaboration, see Wilfred J. Ethier, "National and International Returns to Scale in the Modern Theory of International Trade," *The American Economic Review* 71 (June 1982): 389–405.

[65] See his "The Case for Regional Policies, in *The Essential Kaldor*, 314.

[66] Kaldor, "Causes of the Slow Rate of Growth in the United Kingdom," 288. Kaldor referred to this observation as the Verdoorn Law, after the exploratory work of P. J. Verdoorn in the 1940s.

[67] "Problems of Industrialisation of Eastern and South-Eastern Europe," *The Economic Journal* 53 (June-September 1943): 202–11.

and technological spillovers. Individual industrialists thus face a dilemma: their relatively small-scale investments would be plagued by suboptimal economic performance without guarantees that parallel investments in the same industry would take place. Lewis concluded that "the prospects of an area must be looked at as a whole; the standpoint of the individual industrialist is too narrow because he thinks only of one factory, and attaches more importance to immediate costliness than the community as a whole should."[68]

The arguments of Rosenstein-Rodan and Lewis can be generalized as coordination problems. A firm that expands its output creates beneficial external economies; it creates technological spillovers and, perhaps more important, enlarged markets, so that both its suppliers and other firms producing consumption goods can expand their output. But the original firm will expand its output only if its markets are also growing sufficiently to justify that expansion. As Paul Krugman neatly summarizes, "external economies arose from a circular relationship whereby the decision to invest in large-scale production depended on the size of the market, and in which the size of the market depended on the decision to invest."[69] Thus, it may often be the case that individual investments earn profits only if other investments are made simultaneously and at a similar scale; multiple equilibria exist, such that all firms would be better off if all of them expanded their output. But moving to more optimal levels of output is not painless; from the perspective of any individual firm, making costly investments without assurances that other firms will also invest in expanded output is tremendously risky, for if these other investments are not forthcoming, there will be insufficient demand for its expanded output. Indeed, each firm has an incentive to reduce risk by allowing other firms to move first; the temptation to defect looms large. But if all firms adopt this risk-averse strategy, output will remain at the suboptimal level. The prevalence of small-scale private-sector firms in Syria and Turkey before the precocious Keynesian period suggests the potency of this coordination problem.

Although his work was ignored for many years, apparently because of his assumptions of large external economies and increasing returns to scale and attendant imperfect markets, economists have recently rediscovered and confirmed Rosenstein-Rodan's analysis. Paul Krugman re-

[68] "An Economic Plan for Jamaica," November 1944, as cited by Gerald M. Meier, *Emerging from Poverty: The Economics That Really Matters* (New York: Oxford University Press, 1984), 143–44. Paul Krugman uses technological spillovers as part of his explanation of the geographical concentration of industrial sectors. See his *Geography and Trade* (Cambridge: MIT Press, 1991).

[69] "Toward a Counter-Counterrevolution in Development Theory," *Proceedings of the World Bank Annual Conference on Development Economics* (1992), 25.

cently rehabilitated what he called "high development theory," observing, "We can now see that whatever bad policies may have been implemented in the name of high development theory, the theory itself makes quite a lot of sense."[70] Indeed, a recent formal model of the "big push" into industrialization notes that "multiple equilibria arise naturally if an industrializing firm *raises* the size of other firms' markets even when it itself loses money." The authors also respond to an obvious objection—that if world trade is free and without cost, then an industry faces a world market, not a small domestic one—by citing extensive evidence of the dominant share of domestic demand in the growth of domestic industrial output.[71]

Exploiting increasing returns thus yields significant positive externalities but it also creates imperfect markets.[72] Therefore, the problem does not disappear once investment-prohibiting coordination problems have been solved. Under conditions of imperfect markets, market signals will not necessarily create the correct number of firms, particularly in the homogeneous product markets that characterize late developers. Instead, excess entry of firms typically results, restricting output for all firms and preventing any one of them from achieving scale economies. In other words, "marginal entry is more desirable to the entrant than it is to society because of the output reduction entry causes in other firms."[73] Moreover, market pressures alone may be insufficient to eliminate excess firms, because mass producers in imperfect markets have the option of acting strategically by reducing prices to maintain market share. The problem is that if all firms adopt this strategy, as we would predict, they will all lose money while continuing to produce at suboptimal levels. Firms in imperfect markets, in other words, confront "an environment analogous to that characterized by the tragedy of the commons. . . . While it may be privately rational to . . . drop prices, it is collectively irrational because of the effects it has on the actions of others."[74] Collective action

[70] Ibid., 29. Krugman suggests that Rosenstein-Rodan's work was ignored because it was not presented in the form of a mathematical model. But he also notes (20) that because mainstream economists rely on assumptions of constant returns to scale and hence perfect markets, they could not accept Rosenstein-Rodan's analysis and tended to ignore the role of external economies and attendant coordination problems.

[71] Kevin M. Murphy, Andrei Shleifer, and Robert W. Vishny, "Industrialization and the Big Push," *Journal of Political Economy* 97 (1989), 1005, italics in original. On the role of domestic demand in initial production of industrial goods, see also Vernon, "International Investment and International Trade."

[72] Briefly, the existence of increasing returns to scale rules out the possibility of perfect markets. This point underpins recent analyses of strategic trade theory. See Paul Krugman, ed., *Strategic Trade Theory and the New International Economics* (Cambridge: MIT Press, 1992).

[73] N. Gregory Mankiw and Michael D. Whinston, "Free Entry and Social Inefficiency," *Rand Journal of Economics* 17 (Spring 1986), 57.

[74] Best, *The New Competition*, 75. Best also notes that in late nineteenth-century America, one response to this collective action problem was "dominant-firm regulation": the largest firm in the market acted to constrain the behavior of subordinate firms. This is the domestic

problems thus intersect with coordination problems to impede efforts to promote productivity increases.

If the proliferation of plants prevents firms from achieving scale economies and exploiting their manifold external benefits, the logical solution is rationalization of the industry through consolidation.[75] This may occur through market processes: firms in fragmented markets with high costs and low production volumes should be driven out of the market by rising costs and declining sales. Firms seeking to maintain production to cover large fixed costs, however, possess multiple resources to circumvent these market pressures and thus "defect" by passing the burden of high cost structures on to their competitors. Among the resources used to pre-empt spontaneous rationalization are extensive financial reserves, deployed in the belief that long-term growth potential is high; the adaptability of new production processes to fragmented markets; and cross-financing, in which higher-volume/high-profit models subsidize losses from low-volume/low-profit models. Of course, the most potent resource is political: lobbying politicians to impose tariffs, making even fragmented markets profitable.[76] In short, increasing the scale of output within individual industrial plants potentially yields significant improvements in productivity and economic growth. But attaining and sustaining the proper volume and concentration of output requires first resolving coordination problems and then resolving collective action problems.

Finally, consider product innovations. In contrast to the inventions and innovations characteristic of nineteenth-century industrialization, late industrializers typically borrow technology, and those that achieve competitiveness do so through learning-by-doing; hence, the importance of expanded output to achieve scale economies and enhance learning-by-doing.[77] There are good reasons why little invention or innovation has occurred in late industrializing economies. As recent research indicates, innovative capacity is tightly linked to existing institutional frameworks at both the sectoral and the national levels.[78] Few late industrializing coun-

---

analogue to hegemonic stability theory. For evidence that contemporaries recognized that collective action problems plagued mass producers in imperfect markets, see the comments of nineteenth-century industrialist Andrew Carnegie, especially his critique of neoclassical economics, as cited in Richard Edwards, *Contested Terrain: The Transformation of the Workplace in the Twentieth Century* (New York: Basic Books, 1979), 40–41.

[75] This paragraph is drawn from Doner, "The Limits of State Strength," 410.

[76] In this case, tariffs are an example of institutional arrangements that exacerbate collective action problems. As we shall see, this is a characteristic outcome of precocious Keynesianism.

[77] Alice H. Amsden, *Asia's Next Giant: South Korea and Late Industrialization* (New York: Oxford University Press, 1989), 3.

[78] Herbert Kitschelt, "Industrial Governance Structures, Innovation Strategies, and the Case of Japan: Sectoral or Cross-National Comparative Analysis," *International Organization* 45 (Autumn 1991): 453–93.

tries possess institutional frameworks allowing even the successful exploitation of borrowed technologies, let alone the generation of new ones. Furthermore, by the early 1980s, the scale of skills and resources needed to generate new technologies has become so large that even leading firms in advanced industrial economies have been forced to pursue international corporate alliances.[79]

In part, the problem is that developing countries are mired in a vicious cycle: a country must accumulate technological capacity to innovate, but the initial acquisition of technological capacity is itself difficult and time-consuming. But more fundamentally, the problem of innovation stems from the existence of positive externalities.[80] One type of industrial innovation is product-specific information that can be protected by patents and other mechanisms; in principle, most of the benefits of product-specific information can be captured by the innovating firm. The second type of innovation comprises more general technical information related to products or to production processes. For a variety of reasons, it is economically infeasible, if not impossible, to appropriate many or even any of the benefits of these activities.[81] By creating externalities, technical innovation and unprotected generic product innovations reduce the cost of subsequent innovations and thus, by counteracting the tendency of returns to capital to fall through the capture of economic rents, make economic growth dynamic and sustainable.[82] Hence the dilemma of development: those features of economic activities that promote long-term growth also militate against their being supplied at optimal levels by the market alone.

There is some reason to believe that the suboptimal implications of externalities deter innovation more in developing countries that in devel-

---

[79] Peter F. Cowhey and Jonathan D. Aronson, *Managing the World Economy: The Consequences of Corporate Alliances* (New York: Council of Foreign Relations Press, 1993).

[80] Technological externalities are not a recent phenomenon; Krugman documents their importance for nineteenth-century American industrial history. See his *Geography and Trade*, 26.

[81] One recent example should illustrate this point. In November 1986, scientists at IBM Zurich discovered a new, potentially revolutionary form of low-temperature, electronic superconductors. Within days, skeptical researchers at Tokyo University had replicated the experiment; the cost of that and subsequent replications was almost zero, as IBM had demonstrated the proper direction, eliminating the need for costly trial and error. Within one month, the race to commercialize superconductivity had begun among a wide number of American and Japanese firms and research institutes. Within three years, the American firms had fallen far enough behind their Japanese rivals that they were forced to form partnerships with Japanese corporations. IBM research, in other words, acted as a massive subsidy for Japanese corporations. This story is used to preface Richard Florida and Martin Kenney's analysis of the failure of corporate America to capitalize on its own externalities. See their *The Breakthrough Illusion: Corporate America's Failure to Move from Innovation to Mass Production* (New York: Basic Books, 1990).

[82] Gene Grossman and Elhanan Helpman, *Innovation and Growth in the Global Economy* (Cambridge: MIT Press, 1991), 335–36.

oped countries. Whereas in developing countries, investment decisions entail allocating capital to establish new industries, in advanced industrial countries, firms facing competition must decide only whether to invest in marginal additions to existing sunk capital costs. Capitalists in advanced economies can also exploit prior accumulations of wealth, technology, skills, and learning, all of which reduce the risk of new investment in the development of new product or process technologies. Indeed, prior investment in industrial plant may act as an institutional constraint biasing decisions in favor of new investments. This bias stems from the interconnections between vested interests, sunk costs, and institutional rigidities. Vested interests originate in the interests of agents in the existing organization to prevent the reallocation of future resources. Sunk costs refer to the cost savings resulting from retaining existing institutional patterns rather than making expensive investments in new institutions. Refraining from investments in product or process technology, in other words, is analogous to a decision to forgo any returns from previous investments.[83] Finally, new investment may be allocated to existing enterprises because of the rigidities inherent in organizational routines. As Krasner argued, "institutions may persist because in a world of imperfect information altering established routines will be costly and time consuming, and the consequences of change cannot be fully predicted."[84] The result of vested interests, sunk costs, and institutional rigidities is that investment decisions are often path dependent; the initial decision to invest in an industry may direct future investments to that industry even if that is not the most efficient use of those resources. For the potential industrialist in the developing world, on the other hand, decisions to make initial investments are not institutionally constrained and, as we have seen, entail often daunting risks. The developing world capitalist, then, is likely to invest in new industrial plant only when existing technology can be borrowed.

Successful East Asian development entailed innovation in shop-floor practices, boosting efficiency and thus lowering costs, and improving product quality; only after several decades did Japan, Korea, or Taiwan begin to develop the capacity to innovate in product-specific technology.[85]

---

[83] This point is made by Arthur L. Stinchcombe, *Constructing Social Theories* (Chicago: University of Chicago Press, 1968), 121.

[84] Stephen D. Krasner, "Sovereignty: An Institutional Perspective," in *The Elusive State: International and Comparative Perspectives,* ed. James A. Caporaso (Newbury Park, Calif.: Sage Publications, 1989), 88.

[85] Amsden, *Asia's Next Giant.* Michael Borrus, James E. Millstein, and John Zysman, "Trade and Development in the Semiconductor Industry: Japanese Challenge and American Response," in *American Industry in International Competition: Government Policies and Corporate Strategies,* ed. John Zysman and Laura Tyson (Ithaca: Cornell University Press, 1983), 142–248, make the same point; Japanese competitive advantage was initially based on cost and quality improvements in standardized products developed in the United States. Only in

This gap between the capacity for product- and process-based innovation creates a huge disparity: advanced industrial economies can innovate in both product-specific and hence protected technology, where they can create and capture large economic rents, and general technology that might produce benefits for other firms. The rents earned from product-specific technology can then be used to subsidize process technology, compensating for the gains captured by other firms, sectors, or industries. Innovation in developing countries, on the other hand, will be solely in those areas with positive externalities.[86] Thus, while all industrial innovation is associated with positive externalities, the impact of these externalities is more damaging in developing countries because they cannot compensate by realizing rents that stem from product-specific technology.

This chapter makes three basic arguments: First, although neoliberal economists correctly observe that state economic intervention is frequently associated with economic failures, I argue that the standard economic account associating free markets with growth suffers from both theoretical and empirical deficiencies. Second, I argue that development is best understood as enhanced capacity to create value, realized through some combination of capital accumulation and investment; the creation of linkages; increasing productivity and international competitiveness; and product innovation. Progress along all four dimensions creates the greatest degree of sustainable economic growth. Third, I argue that systemic constraints create disjunctures between individual and collective interests, producing incentives for rational individuals to defect or to refrain from engaging in activities enhancing the capacity to create value.

The postwar field of development economics argued that collective dilemmas plagued developing countries, justifying state intervention.[87] Development economics, however, suffered from two defects that dissuaded most mainstream economists from accepting its arguments. First, although collective dilemmas, or market failures, could be identified in theory—as we have seen, even mainstream economists now recognize them—it was difficult to assess their practical importance. But there are good reasons why the arguments of development economists were more suggestive than definitive. First, it is always difficult to explain why some-

---

the 1970s did Japanese producers transcend a position of relative technological inferiority. This transformation in Japanese capacity for innovation is well captured in the title of Sheridan M. Tatsuno's book on the subject: *Created in Japan: From Imitators to World-Class Innovators* (New York: Harper Business, 1990).

[86] Hence, Japanese production innovations such as lean or flexible production, or just-in-time inventory, are now staples throughout the industrialized world.

[87] For an overview, see Christopher Colclough, "Structuralism versus Neo-liberalism: An Introduction," in *States or Markets: Neo-liberalism and the Development Policy Debate,* ed. Christopher Colclough and James Manor (Oxford: Clarendon Press, 1991), 1–25.

thing *did not* occur. Second, and related, the analysis of collective dilemmas explores the outcomes of perfectly free markets. But as Karl Polanyi made clear in his seminal work, and numerous subsequent works have corroborated, markets are never perfectly free but are always embedded in broader social and political institutions that affect their dynamics.[88] Our observations of entrepreneurial behavior thus always reflect the interaction of state institutions and market processes, producing a continuum ranging from complete resolution of all collective dilemmas to no resolution of any of them. Consequently, empirical discussions of the impact of collective dilemmas on specific cases remain inescapably inferential and circumstantial. The second defect of development economics was that it contained no theory of the state. Thus, while development economists presented a general brief for state intervention, they did not specify the circumstances allowing for successful state intervention. The accumulation of developmental problems associated with state intervention over the past five decades thus supplied economists skeptical of state intervention with abundant evidence to argue that even if collective dilemmas exist, the solution is more harmful than the disease.

Chapter 8 resolves these difficulties. By demonstrating that different forms of state economic intervention, rooted in divergent institutional profiles, produce different economic outcomes, I provide extensive evidence of the effect of collective dilemmas without assuming that state intervention always resolves them. To be sure, not all economic change is plagued by collective dilemmas, and market pressures undoubtedly resolve some of them. Thus, we should observe considerable interfirm variation within national economies. Moreover, I argue neither that state intervention is the only solution to collective dilemmas, nor that state intervention will always solve them. On the contrary, in the next chapter I argue that forms of state intervention characteristic of precocious Keynesian states exacerbate many collective dilemmas. In short, my argument is this: If patterns of state economic intervention associated with distinct institutional configurations have durable and distinct capacities or incapacities to resolve collective dilemmas, then we should be able to identify broad patterns of development distinguishing one national economy from another. We should expect this despite interfirm variations within each national economy. Mapping forms of state intervention over a grid of collective dilemmas, in other words, should account for divergent national developmental trajectories.

[88] See his *The Great Transformation: The Political and Economic Origins of Our Time* (Boston: Beacon Press, 1944).

CHAPTER EIGHT

The Developmental Consequences of Precocious Keynesianism

This chapter completes the argument linking institutional profiles to economic outcomes by analyzing the development outcomes of precocious Keynesianism in Syria (1963–1980) and Turkey (1950–1980), and contrasting them to the outcomes produced by developmental states in Korea and Taiwan between the early 1960s and 1980. To assess the degree of divergence of their outcomes requires the establishment of an initial base line. Taiwan had a larger industrial base at the beginning of the period analyzed here, whereas Korea started from a position roughly similar to that of Syria and Turkey. The share of manufacturing in gross domestic product (GDP) was 13 percent in Turkey, 15 percent in Syria, (although this figure includes mining), and about 14 percent in Korea.[1] In Taiwan, which inherited substantial heavy industry from the Japanese period, manufacturing output was 22 percent of GDP in 1960.[2] In all four countries, light industries, especially food products and textiles, were the largest industrial sector. These two sectors dominated the industrial landscape in Turkey and Syria, contributing 49 and 30 percent, respectively, to Turkish manufacturing output and almost all of Syrian manufacturing.[3] Korea was slightly more diversified in 1963, as all light industries added 63 percent to total manufacturing, intermediate inputs contributed another 30 percent, and machinery and transportation equip-

---

[1] Republic of Turkey, *Statistical Indicators, 1923-1990* (Ankara: State Institute of Statistics, 1991), 403; Yusuf Sayigh, *The Economies of the Arab World* (New York: St. Martin's Press, 1978), 230; and Edward S. Mason et al., *The Economic and Social Modernization of the Republic of Korea* (Cambridge: Harvard University Press, 1980), 100. The Korean figure is the average for 1960–1962.

[2] Robert Wade, *Governing the Market: Economic Theory and the Role of Government in East Asian Industrialization* (Princeton: Princeton University Press, 1990), 44.

[3] Republic of Turkey, *Statistical Indicators, 1923-1980*, 210-19.

ment chipped in for the remainder.[4] Taiwan was significantly more diversified than even Korea, with only 42 percent of 1961 manufacturing output coming from food and textiles, with chemical industries contributing 21 percent and metals, machinery, electrical machinery, and transportation equipment adding 13 percent.[5] Syrian and Turkish exports were almost exclusively primary products, and small quantities of manufactured exports were almost exclusively textiles.[6] Korean exports in 1960 were hardly more diversified, with primary products accounting for 83 percent and manufactured products only 12 percent, of which textiles accounted for more than half.[7] Here too, Taiwan had achieved more substantial industrial development, as manufactured products accounted for the bulk of its 1962 exports, with primary products accounting for only 10 percent, food products and textiles and leather and wood products, accounting for 41 percent and 30 percent, respectively, and chemical and metal products each adding 6 percentage points.[8]

Although the Syrian and Turkish economies grew at impressive rates during the precocious Keynesian period, with the rate of increase in manufacturing output outpacing that of overall economic growth, by 1980 the initial gap distinguishing their industrial development from that of Korea and Taiwan had expanded into an almost unbridgeable chasm. Korea and Taiwan surpassed Syria and Turkey in terms of manufacturing output and industrial diversification and deepening. Moreover, unlike Syria and Turkey, Korea and Taiwan substantially enhanced productivity and product quality, and even as they shifted into more capital- and skill-intensive industrial sectors, their goods remained competitive in international markets.

The following two sections detail outcomes of economic development in Turkey and Syria, respectively, illustrating the capacity to solve Gerschenkronian but not Kaldorian collective dilemmas. Indeed, I argue at the end of the chapter that the Turkish and Syrian states resolved Gerschenkronian collective dilemmas only at the expense of exacerbating Kaldorian collective dilemmas. The third section surveys state interven-

---

[4] Mason, *Economic and Social Modernization*, 144.

[5] Republic of China, *Statistical Yearbook of the Republic of China, 1984* (Taipei: Directorate-General of Budget, Accounting, and Statistics, 1984), 298.

[6] In 1963, about 91 percent of Syrian exports were agricultural products. Yahya Arudqi, *al-Iqtisad al-Suri al-Hadith*, vol. 1 (Damascus: Ministry of Culture, 1972), 221.

[7] Mason, *Economic and Social Modernization*, 137.

[8] Republic of China, *Statistical Yearbook of the Republic of China, 1975* (Taipei: Directorate-General of Budget, Accounting, and Statistics, 1975), 146. The figure for primary product exports seems unusually low; Gary Gereffi, "Paths of Industrialization: An Overview," in *Manufacturing Miracles: Paths of Industrialization in Latin America and East Asia*, ed. Gary Gereffi and Donald L. Wyman (Princeton: Princeton University Press, 1990), 13, reports that in 1965, primary commodities were 58 percent of all exports, which is still lower than the figures for the other three countries.

tion in East Asia, providing evidence of its resolution of both Ger-schenkronian and Kaldorian collective dilemmas. The fourth and final section argues that differences in state capacity to solve collective dilemmas best explain divergent economic outcomes.

Economic Transformation in Turkey

The Turkish economy experienced impressive growth and transformation between 1950 and 1980. The economy doubled in size during the 1950s, and annual growth rates averaged 6 percent between 1960 and 1970 and about 6.6 percent through 1979. By 1979, Turkey's per capita income had attained $1,330.[9] Manufacturing output grew even faster, averaging 10.9 percent during the 1960s before dipping to 7.7 percent between 1970 and 1979. Consequently, the share of agriculture in GDP plunged from 41 to 23 percent between 1960 and 1981, while the share of manufacturing increased from 13 to 23 percent over the same period.[10] Moreover, as Turkish planners emphasized industrial diversification after 1960, the share of consumer nondurables in total manufacturing output decreased from 62 percent in 1962 to 49 percent in 1977. Over the same period, the share of intermediate goods increased from 28 to 38 percent, and investment goods from 10 to 13 percent. The bulk of industrial diversification, however, occurred between 1962 and 1967.[11] Calculated as shares of manufacturing value-added in the period 1953–1978, food and textiles both played a diminishing role, dropping respectively from 34 to 20 percent and from 31 to 16 percent. Light intermediate goods such as wood, rubber and plastic, and paper products increased from 8 to 13 percent, while chemical and petroleum products, basic metals, cement, and glass increased from 15 to 22 percent and the machinery, metal products, and transportation equipment sectors increased their total share from 12 to 30 percent.[12] Finally, by 1980, 36 percent of Turkish exports, amounting to just under $3 billion, came from

[9] World Bank, *World Development Report, 1981* (New York: Oxford University Press, 1981), 135–37.

[10] World Bank, *World Development Report, 1983* (New York: Oxford University Press, 1983), 153.

[11] Yakup Kepenek, *Turkiye Ekonomisi: Gelisimi, Uretim Yapisi ve Sorunlariyla* (Ankara: Verso Yayincilik, 1990), 268. The consumer-goods sector is composed of food and beverage products, tobacco, textiles, and apparel. Intermediate goods include wood, paper and printing, rubber and plastic, chemical and petroleum products, basic metals, and nonmetallic products such as cement, glass, and ceramics. Investment goods include not only capital equipment, but also many consumer durables, such as automobiles, and electrical machinery, such as televisions, refrigerators, and washing machines.

[12] Merih Celasun, *Sources of Industrial Growth and Structural Change: The Case of Turkey* (Washington, D.C.: World Bank, 1983), 100.

the industrial sector. Textiles made up about 44 percent of manufactured exports in 1980, and processed food and beverages added 19 percent.[13]

The composition of Turkey's imports changed in step with the changing composition of manufacturing output. As a share of imports, consumer goods dropped from 21 to less than 3 percent between 1950 and 1980, indicating successful import substitution. Intermediate goods, on the other hand, increased from 33 to 61 percent, and capital goods decreased from only 46 to 37 percent, indicating limited import substitution in heavier industries.[14] Even these figures mask Turkey's relative inability to create linkages. Particular industries can be classified according to their contribution to import substitution and to creating linkages. Those sectors in which domestic production largely replaced imports, including vehicles, electrical machinery, machine tools, and petroleum, made only weak contributions to linkages. Conversely, those industries that constitute strong linkages, such as iron and steel, made the smallest contribution to import substitution. The greatest increases in production, in other words, took place in industries that remained highly dependent on imports of components and thus have correspondingly low potential for spurring further industrial development by stimulating demand or supplying inputs. Barkey concludes, "The accelerating growth of assembly industries is, in large measure, to blame for this development."[15] Vedat Milor reached a similar conclusion, arguing that, "Often the least essential imports were given the greatest incentive for domestic production and consequently what has been called the 'premature widening' of the productive structure (the production of high income durable consumer goods) took place, rather than the development of backward linkages towards intermediate and capital goods."[16]

Turkey's record at sustaining growth of productivity was similarly unimpressive. The most comprehensive analysis, that of Krueger and Tuncer, concluded that the average annual growth rate of total factor productivity in the period 1963–1976 was just over 2 percent, lower than the rate achieved by both developed and other developing countries: between 1960 and 1970, for example, the corresponding rates for Korea and Taiwan were 3.47 and 3.59, respectively.[17] Furthermore, most of Turkey's

[13] World Bank, *Turkey: Industrialization and Trade Strategy* (Washington, D.C.: World Bank, 1982), 414.

[14] Henri J. Barkey, *The State and the Industrialization Crisis in Turkey* (Boulder, Colo.: Westview Press, 1990), 65.

[15] Ibid., 86–88, citation from 86.

[16] Vedat Halit Milor, "A Comparative Study of Planning and Economic Development in Turkey and France: Bringing the State Back In," Ph.D. Dissertation, University of California, Berkeley, 1989, 285.

[17] Anne O. Krueger and Baran Tuncer, "Growth of Factor Productivity in Turkish Manufacturing Industries," *Journal of Development Economics* 11 (December 1982), 316–20.

productivity increase occurred during the subperiod 1963–1967, suggesting that productivity gains were due to initial investments in more capital-intensive plants, not incremental gains realized through learning-by-doing, reorganization of shop-floor practices and managerial routines, or technological assimilation. Indeed, between 1970 and 1979, while capital stock per worker increased by an average of 11 percent, value-added per worker increased by only 0.1 percent. Consequently, according to another study, between 1973 and 1979, while manufacturing output increased by an average of 6 percent, total factor productivity decreased by 2.8 percent.[18] Clearly, capital accumulation that is not complemented by efficient production practices and technological assimilation yields highly restricted benefits.

Analysis of individual industries supports and partially explains this conclusion. In Turkey's truck manufacturing industry, for example, the absence of entry restrictions permitted the excessive proliferation of small firms.[19] Consequently, whereas production volumes among 42 medium-sized firms worldwide ranged between 13,000 and 150,000 in the 1960s, in 1968, all of Turkey's plants combined to produce only 11,594 units, less than any single firm among global producers. A single plant operating at closer to the minimum economy of scale would have satisfied domestic demand. As a result, rates of capacity utilization averaged only 35 percent. Consequently, plants used general-purpose machinery rather than the dedicated machinery characteristic of mass production, driving up unit costs. Furthermore, domestic content regulations mandated the use of parts and components produced in relatively low-volume, small-scale plants employing outdated technology, contributing to high-cost, low-quality production. Note finally that rather than an example of excessive government intervention, the Turkish truck industry suffered from too little intervention of the type characteristic, as we shall see, of East Asia. As Ansal concludes, "The structure of the industry could have been controlled by restricting entry to the limited market so that economies of scale were gained and underutilization of capacity was eliminated. Furthermore, if the duration of protection had been determined *ex ante*, firms would have attempted to ensure that they had 'caught up' with the technological frontier by the end of this period."[20] Similar char-

[18] Korkut Boratav and Ergun Turkcan, *Turkiye'de Sanayilesmenin Yeni Boyutlari ve KIT'ler* (Istanbul: Turkiye Ekonomik ve Toplumsal Tarih Vakfi Yayindir, 1993), 30–32. Productivity fell in both the public and private sectors, but the decline was more precipitous in the public sector. According to their data, productivity increased by only 1.3 percent annually between 1963 and 1976, much lower than the estimate of Krueger and Tuncer.

[19] All information on the Turkish truck manufacturing industry is drawn from the excellent analysis of Hacer K. Ansal, "Technical Change and Industrial Policy: The Case of Truck Manufacturing In Turkey," *World Development* 18 (November 1990): 1513–28.

[20] Ibid., 1526.

acteristics mark the Turkish automobile industry, in which production reached over 67,000 units by the mid-1970s.[21] But even as production increased, the overall rate of capacity utilization remained quite low, driving up unit costs.[22] Furthermore, the industry suffered from insufficient technological capacity, and the quality of finished products was well below world standards.

Similar problems of underutilization of capacity, limited technological acquisition, and inefficient shop-floor practices plagued Turkey's steel industry.[23] Two of the three plants composing this sector averaged only 53 percent of capacity utilization in the late 1970s, whereas the third achieved 70 percent. Despite low production volumes, the plants remained massively overstaffed: whereas the Isdemir steel complex was designed to employ 8,000 workers while producing 1 million tons, in 1979 it employed 18,000 workers and produced only 250,000 tons.[24] The decoupling of employment levels from output levels resulted in extremely high ratios of labor hours to output: while 40 man-hours were needed to produce one ton of steel in the Turkish plants, American plants with similar levels of capital intensity required only eight man-hours per ton.[25] Consequently, according to one study, whereas annual output per worker in most industrialized countries was 200 tons, one Turkish plant produced only 86 tons, and a second only 24 tons.[26] As a result of low productivity and under-utilization of capacity, the industry was a tremendous drain on the state: between 1977 and 1982, the two plants with the lower level of capacity utilization lost 18,500 million Turkish lira. Finally, the Turkish iron and steel industry failed to complete the process of technology transfer. As Szyliowicz concluded, "All Turkish governments had adhered to a view of development that was quite simplistic; they believed

---

[21] Mine Sadiye Eder, "Crises of Late Industrialization: A Comparative Study of the Automotive Industry in Brazil, South Korea, and Turkey," Ph.D. Dissertation, University of Virginia, 1993, 146–54.

[22] After 1975, production plummeted, from 67,000 units in 1975 to 31,500 units in 1980. At this time, the minimum scale economy for producing passenger cars was estimated to be 200,000 units per plant.

[23] On Turkish steel, see Joseph S. Szyliowicz, *Politics, Technology, and Development: Decision-Making in the Turkish Iron and Steel Industry* (New York: St. Martin's Press, 1991). For a brief summary, see his "Technology Transfer and Development: The Case of the Turkish Iron and Steel Industry," in *The Middle East and North Africa: Essays in Honor of J.C. Hurewitz*, ed. Reeva S. Simon (New York: Columbia University Press, 1990), 262–75.

[24] John Waterbury, *Exposed to Innumerable Delusions: Public Enterprise and State Power in Egypt, India, Mexico, and Turkey* (Cambridge: Cambridge University Press, 1993), 126.

[25] Szyliowicz, *Politics, Technology, and Development*, xvi. By contrast, the Korean integrated steel mill at Pohang is one of the most efficient and profitable in the world and has captured a large share of the market for steel in both the United States and Japan. See Jung-En Woo, *Race to the Swift: State and Finance in Korean Industrialization* (New York: Columbia University Press, 1991), 134–35.

[26] World Bank, *Turkey: Industrialization and Trade Strategy*, 269.

that simply by increasing capacity, especially industrial capacity, the country would prosper."[27] Therefore, issues such as quality control, innovation, and international competitiveness were largely neglected; all three plants, for example, had maximum output levels insufficient to exploit economies of scale. Underlying this understanding of development, however, has been the subordination of economic rationality to political concerns. Many crucial decisions related to the establishment and operation of the plants were made by the political leadership, not a technocratic elite. As Szyliowicz put it,

> Turkish political leaders often made decisions that tended to ignore the economic and technological realities that are required if a project is to be successful. Hence, such decisions as plant location, pricing policy, hiring, and managerial appointments were often influenced by short-term political concerns of one kind or another. This situation, which characterized much of Turkish development in the 1950s, affected the steel plants directly in the 1970s, a period of weak coalition governments when a minor religious party, the National Salvation party, often secured the Ministry of Industry and used its power to advance the party's goals regardless of the impact of its decisions upon the functioning of the iron and steel works.[28]

The Turkish steel and vehicle industries have not been unmitigated failures. Domestic production has been established, local firms have gained experience, and local demand can be partially met without exhausting foreign exchange. But by 1980 neither industry had met global standards for price or quality, and they thus sold their product only in local markets. In both industrial sectors, minimal linkages were created, technological assimilation was limited, and most plants operated at well below minimum economies of scale. In sum, the Turkish state partially resolved Gerschenkronian collective dilemmas and so fostered new investments, but it did not resolve Kaldorian collective dilemmas, and so Turkish industry acquired only restricted capacity to create value.

Economic Transformation in Syria

Syrian GDP grew at an annual rate of 5.7 percent between 1960 and 1970, and at an impressive rate of 9 percent between 1970 and 1979. In 1979, per capita income was $1,030.[29] The annual growth rate of manu-

[27] Szyliowicz, "Technology Transfer and Development in Turkey," 268.
[28] Ibid., 268.
[29] World Bank, *World Development Report, 1981*, 134, 136.

facturing output was 5.6 percent between 1960 and 1970 and then 13.2 percent through 1979. Between 1963 and 1980, the share of agriculture in GDP declined from 27 to 20 percent, while the share of industry, which spans manufacturing, mining, and petroleum, also dropped, from 20 to 16 percent, although one year earlier, industry had contributed 20 percent, 2 percentage points higher than agriculture's share.[30] In absolute terms, manufacturing value-added increased from $575 million in 1970 to $1.3 billion in 1981.[31] In 1980, manufactured goods accounted for only 8 percent of all exports, one-half of which were textiles.[32] The sectoral composition of manufacturing output remained stable through 1970, as development plans devoted significant sums to basic infrastructural investment and to expanding production of light industries using local products as inputs. The third five-year plan initiated the production of heavier industrial products, such as consumer durables, engineering products, and chemicals; planners allocated over half of all public investments in the 1970s to these sectors. Consequently, by 1982, the chemicals and engineering sectors, which include iron and steel, fertilizers, cement, paper, consumer durables, and petroleum refining, were contributing about 25 percent of total manufacturing value added. Whereas food processing and textiles contributed more than 70 percent of value-added in manufacturing in 1970, by 1982 these two light industrial sectors had dropped below 30 percent of manufacturing value-added.[33]

The Syrian solution to Gerschenkronian collective dilemmas added industrial capacity but forged few linkages. In the most extensive survey of the Syrian public sector, Seurat and Hannoyer argue that due to the absence of careful studies preceding upstream investment, the creation of backward linkages bordered on the accidental.[34] Even projects designed to use agricultural products or natural resources as inputs confronted problems in welding together projected linkages, so that by 1980, despite massive investments, both sugar and pulp for the paper mill were still imported, as was much of the oil used in Syrian refineries. Even textile mills remained dependent on imports for all synthetic fibers, not to mention

---

[30] Syrian Arab Republic, *Statistical Abstract, 1989* (Damascus: Central Bureau of Statistics, 1989), 498. In contrast, the World Bank, *World Development Report, 1983,* (153) records the 1981 Syrian figures as 19 percent for agriculture; 31 percent for industry, of which 26 percent was manufacturing; and 50 percent for services.

[31] World Bank, *World Development Report, 1984* (New York: Oxford University Press, 1984), 231. Both figures are in 1975 dollars.

[32] World Bank, *World Development Report, 1983,* 167. These figures are skewed by the growth of petroleum exports, which accounted for 74 percent of all exports in 1980.

[33] Gunter Meyer, "Economic Development in Syria since 1970," in *Politics and the Economy in Syria,* ed. J. A. Allen (London: School of Oriental and African Studies, 1987), 50–52.

[34] Jean Hannoyer and Michel Seurat, *Etat et Secteur Public Industriel en Syrie* (Beirut: CERMOC, 1979), 76.

capital equipment. Indeed, most of the consumer durables industries were little more than assembly plants.[35] Only the cement and fertilizers industries produced inputs used by other economic sectors. Finally, the state missed a chance to build linkages by neglecting to establish factories producing spare parts for imported equipment, and Syria still produces almost no capital equipment. Consequently, during this period of import-substituting industrialization, the share of intermediate goods in all imports declined only from 58 percent to 48 percent.

Syrian industries neither achieved economies of scale nor produced at their technical level of capacity. To give only one of the more egregious examples, two separate refrigerator factories with combined capacity to produce 27,000 units annually produced together only 6,000 units in 1968, when domestic demand was estimated to be as high as 12,000 units.[36] As another example, a shoe factory in Damascus, built under contract by a French company to produce 3,500 pairs of shoes daily, actually produced only 1,500 pairs, or 42 percent of capacity.[37] By 1981, capacity utilization had hardly improved; food-processing industries produced at an average of 60 percent of capacity, porcelain at 40 percent, shoes at 35 percent, textiles at 65 percent, azotic fertilizers at 66 percent, and paints at 80 percent.[38] Indeed, the problem of underutilization of capacity was serious enough to prompt an article in *al-Ba`th*, the official newspaper of the Ba`th party, which stated, "If all productive capacity were being employed in each industry and economic sector. . . we could augment GNP by at least 45 percent. In other words, this would be as if we had realized new investment projects whose value was equivalent to 45 percent of current investments."[39] Consequently, the Prime Minister discussed this problem in the assembly, leading to the formation of a commission to investigate the overall level of capacity utilization. Apparently the results of their study were so disturbing that it was never published.

One important source of underutilization of capacity is the tendency of Syrian planners to establish redundant production facilities. Hannoyer and Seurat cite an article from *Tishrin*, an official newspaper, reporting cases in which new plants have been established when existing plants in

[35] Elisabeth Longuenesse, "L'Industrialisation et sa Signification Sociale," in *La Syrie d'Aujourd'hui*, ed. André Raymond (Paris: Centre National de la Recherche Scientifique, 1980), 341, 343.

[36] Nassouh Malass, "Coup d'Oeil sur les Principales Enterprises Industrielles," in L'Office Arabe de Presse et de Documentation, *Etudes sur le Secteur Public Industriel en République Arabe Syrienne* (Damascus, n.d.), 33–34. Malass's survey demonstrates striking levels of underutilization of capacity in almost every industrial sector.

[37] Hannoyer and Seurat, *Etat et Secteur Public Industriel*, 77–78.

[38] Huda Hawwa, "Linkages and Constraints of the Syrian Economy," in *State and Society in Syria and Lebanon*, ed. Youssef M. Choueri (New York: St. Martin's Press, 1993), 87, note 13.

[39] Cited in Hannoyer and Seurat, *Etat et Secteur Public Industriel*, 78. Author's translation.

the same industrial sector were operating at less than 50 percent of capacity.[40] Rather than an isolated example, the rush to establish new plants before existing plants in the same industrial sector had become efficient or begun to produce at capacity seems to have been the *modus operandi* of Syrian planners. As one analyst concluded, "We believe that the major reason for the stagnation in industry has been the diversion of resources to the new projects which have not yet come on stream, and the ensuing neglect to the established industries. Many replacement, refurbishing and even maintenance operations have accordingly been sacrificed to the detriment of production efficiency."[41]

Finally, Syria has suffered from its technological dependence on foreign suppliers of turnkey projects, many of which are built to specifications inappropriate for conditions in Syria. Both the paper and pulp mill and the fertilizer sector have suffered from design flaws that crippled their efficiency.[42] Technological problems can, of course, bedevil a project in an advanced industrial country. But when a country is both technologically dependent and making large, lumpy investments that cannot be sustained at high levels over time, the consequences of technological failure are devastating. At any rate, we can note that not only have the Syrians not made the transition from technological transfer to technological mastery, but technological transfer still causes manifold headaches. Indeed, the reliance on turnkey projects built by the supply company robbed Syrian technicians of the opportunity to assimilate technology while the plant was being built, reproducing Syria's technological dependence on suppliers.[43]

The result of these manifold deficiencies is that productivity growth in Syrian industry has been negligible. Between 1973 and 1980, when the bulk of new industrial investment took place and when industrial output nearly doubled, the index of value-added declined from 103 to 100. This figure rose in the 1980s, but much of that increase was accounted for by increased oil exploitation.[44] Thus, the best estimate of growth in value-added in industry between 1975 and 1983, excluding petroleum production, is roughly 1 percent annually.[45] Individual sectors fared even more poorly: taking 1970 as the base year of 100, productivity in 1974 in the

[40] Ibid., 77.

[41] David W. Carr, "Capital Flows and Development in Syria," *Middle East Journal* 34 (Autumn 1980), 464.

[42] See Elisabeth Tampier, "Syria: Trouble at Paper Mill," *Middle East Economic Digest (MEED)*, December 14, 1985, 70–71.

[43] Volker Perthes, *The Political Economy of Syria under As`ad* (London: I.B. Tauris, 1995), 43.

[44] Hawwa, "Linkages and Constraints of the Syrian Economy," 87–88.

[45] Eliahu Kanovsky, *What's Behind Syria's Current Economic Problems* (Tel Aviv: The Dayan Center for Middle Eastern and African Studies, Occasional Papers, 1985), 21.

textiles industry had reached only 102, whereas in the foods industry, it had declined to 89.[46]

In short, the Syrian state partially resolved Gerschenkronian collective dilemmas but did not resolve Kaldorian collective dilemmas; economic growth was extensive, based on new investments and growth in factor inputs, but not intensive, based on productivity increases. Massive investments multiplied industrial plant, but most of these suffered from problems militating against efficient production practices and few of them were linked to one another. State planners drew rough sketches of which industries they would like to establish, and allocated funds for those sectors to foreign contractors. Beyond these minimal functions, the state was incapable of inducing productivity increases. The Syrian state produced development projects, but it could not produce development.

Developmental States and Economic Transformation in Korea and Taiwan

Between 1965 and 1980, Korea and Taiwan recorded continuously high rates of growth, averaging 9.5 percent in Korea and 9.8 percent in Taiwan, about 50 percent higher than the Turkish rate and even higher than Syria's 9 percent growth rate in the 1970s.[47] Korean manufacturing grew at an annual rate of 17.6 percent in the 1960s (compared to 10.9 percent in Turkey and 5.6 percent in Syria) and 15.6 percent between 1970 and 1981 (compared to 7.7 percent in Turkey and 13.2 percent in Syria); manufacturing consequently doubled its share of GDP, from 14 percent in 1960 to 28 percent in 1981.[48] The share of manufacturing in Taiwanese GDP increased from 22 percent in 1960 to 38 percent in 1978, about twice as high as the corresponding figure for Syria and Turkey.[49] In Korea, as the chemicals, basic metals, and machinery and transportation equipment sectors grew, the share of light industry in total manufacturing output declined from 59.5 percent in 1971 to 43.7 percent in 1980.[50] In Taiwan, the share of light industry declined from 51.2 percent in 1965 to 43.4 percent in 1981.[51] Growth and industrial deep-

---

[46] Hannoyer and Seurat, *Etat et Secteur Public Industriel*, 74. See also Elisabeth Longuenesse, "Syrie, Secteur Public Industriel," *Maghreb-Machrek* #109 (July-September 1985), 12.

[47] Gereffi, "Paths of Industrialization," 11. The end date of 1980 corresponds to the end of the precocious Keynesian period in Syria and Turkey.

[48] World Bank, *World Development Report, 1983*, 151, 153.

[49] Thomas B. Gold, *State and Society in the Taiwan Miracle* (Armonk, N.Y.: M. E. Sharpe, Inc., 1986), 7.

[50] Alice H. Amsden, *Asia's Next Giant: South Korea and Late Industrialization* (New York: Oxford University Press, 1989), 58.

[51] Wade, *Governing the Market*, 45.

ening have been accompanied by the massive growth of manufactured exports. Korean exports grew from $200 million in 1965 to $47.2 billion in 1987; as a share of GDP, exports increased from 7 to 39 percent in the same period. Taiwanese exports grew from $500 million in 1965 to $50.8 billion in 1987; as a share of GDP, exports grew from 18 to 48 percent in the same period. The composition of exports underwent similarly dramatic change. In Korea, primary commodities declined from 40 percent to 7 percent of total exports between 1965 and 1987. During the same period, the share of textiles and clothing declined from 27 to 25 percent, while the share of machinery and transport equipment grew from 3 to 33 percent. In Taiwan, the share of primary commodities declined to 7 percent, the share of textiles and clothing grew from 5 to 17 percent, and the share of machinery and transport equipment grew from 4 to 30 percent.[52]

In comparison to Syria and Turkey, Korean and Taiwanese GDP grew at faster rates, their economies underwent more extensive industrial transformation, and they achieved international competitiveness in a range of manufactured products. This comprehensive development was based on extensive state economic intervention. In contrast to state intervention in Syria and Turkey that resolved Gerschenkronian but not Kaldorian collective dilemmas, abundant evidence strongly supports the claim that state economic intervention in East Asia successfully resolved *both* Gerschenkronian and Kaldorian collective dilemmas. As Robert Wade summarizes the literature on state-led development in East Asia, the state has taken as its objective the encouragement of investment

> on a scale sufficient to capture economies of scale where these are important; to coordinate the development of backwards and forwards linkages so that external economies from any one activity are captured *within* the national unit; and to encourage domestic producers to upgrade their technological capability by tying some of the incentives to such upgrading. If one accepts that external economies, economies of scale, and learning-curve economies are major sources of technological advance and productivity growth, the efforts of the state to make sure that market conditions do not obstruct their realization within the national unit take on great significance in explaining the superior economic performance of the East Asian three.[53]

[52] All figures on exports from Gereffi, "Paths of Industrialization," 13.
[53] Robert Wade, "The Role of Government in Overcoming Market Failure: Taiwan, Republic of Korea, and Japan," in *Achieving Industrialization in East Asia,* ed. Helen Hughes (Cambridge: Cambridge Universe Press, 1988), 154, italics in original.

Developmental states in East Asia resolved Gerschenkronian collective dilemmas by fostering the establishment of leading-edge industries through a variety of means, all of which have provided rents to industrialists. Risk-moderating tariffs and quotas protected noncompetitive industries into the 1980s, as I discussed in Chapter 7. Moreover, state control over credit and commercial policies subsidized new investments in targeted sectors. In Korea, the state promoted the growth of various export industries as well as the big push into heavy and chemical industries in the 1970s through control over investment finance.[54] Thus, the cost of capital for export industries was always cheaper than for industries producing for domestic markets, interest was lower for loans to heavy industries than to light industries, and smaller producers in all industries were forced to borrow on the high-interest, informal "curb markets."[55] In some cases, the state even socialized risk by implicitly assuring large industrial concerns that they would not be allowed to fail.[56] In Taiwan, despite tight state control over the financial system, the state made few industry-specific loans during the export period, and state loans were generally reserved for state-owned firms.[57] But while preferential bank lending has clearly been less important in Taiwan, evidence compiled by Wade suggests that "bank lending has corresponded fairly closely with government sectoral targets."[58] Moreover, in 1960, the state promulgated the Statute for the Encouragement of Investment, which granted a broad range of fiscal incentives, ranging from tax breaks to high depreciation allowances, to firms complying with overall state strategy. These measures allowed entrepreneurs to make long-term commitments of time and capital in products or activities whose final benefits were uncertain. Finally, in both countries, inducements to private investors have been comple-

[54] "In Korea, regulated finance has represented the most important source of economic rents since the mid-1960s, thus enabling the government to utilize it as the most powerful industrial policy instrument. In fact, it has been used as the fundamental tool with which Korean policy makers induced business cooperation and compliance in their efforts to promote exports and economic growth." Byung-Sun Choi, "Financial Policy and Big Business in Korea: The Perils of Financial Regulation," in *The Politics of Finance in Developing Countries,* ed. Stephan Haggard, Chung H. Lee, and Sylvia Maxfield (Ithaca: Cornell University Press, 1993), 23.

[55] Woo, *Race to the Swift,* 165-66. See Chapter 6, footnote 77 for additional citations on state control of Korean finance.

[56] Ibid., 170–75.

[57] Tun-jen Cheng, "Guarding the Commanding Heights: The State as Banker in Taiwan," in *The Politics of Finance in Developing Countires,* ed. Stephan Haggard, Chung H. Lee, and Sylvia Maxfield (Ithaca: Cornell University Press, 1993), 55-92; and Chalmers Johnson, "Political Institutions and Economic Performance: The Government-Business Relationship in Japan, South Korea, and Taiwan," in *The Political Economy of the New Asian Industrialism,* ed. Frederic C. Deyo (Ithaca: Cornell University Press, 1987), 149.

[58] Wade, *Governing the Market,* 171.

mented by public investment in state-owned firms. Korean state firms have pioneered a range of industries, such as fertilizers, petrochemicals, and steel. These firms have been managed as autonomous, profit-seeking agencies and have made net contributions to government revenue. Indeed, the Korean state-owned integrated steel mill at Pohang is considered one of the most efficient in the world.[59] State-owned firms are even more prominent in Taiwan than in Korea: in the former, four of the six largest firms are state-owned, whereas in Korea only one of the ten largest firms is state-owned.[60]

Inducements to investment were carefully crafted to create linkages. The Taiwanese Four-Year Plan of 1965, for example, stated that, "For further development, stress must be laid on basic heavy industries (such as chemical wood pulp, petrochemicals, and large-scale integrated steel production) instead of end product manufacturing or processing. . . . And around these products there should be development of both forward and backward industries, so that both specialization and complementarity may be achieved in the interest of Taiwan's economy."[61] The state then acted on this promise; one study, for example, concluded that "most of the DFI [direct foreign investment]-concentrated industries had high linkage indices, indicating that the public authorities in Taiwan gave some consideration to potential linkages in directing foreign investment activities."[62] The Korean state has also coordinated investments between sectors to allow each to achieve economies of scale. To cite just one example, the development of the steel industry was carefully synchronized with the development of the shipping industry to take advantage of economies of scale.[63] Furthermore, in the early 1970s, the Korean and Taiwanese governments initiated new development plans to diversify the economy and move into the production of more sophisticated goods. In Korea, the heavy industrialization plan entailed large investments in iron and steel, shipbuilding, chemicals, machines, and electronics. In Taiwan, the government guided new investments into steel, petrochemicals, computers, and telecommunications equipment.

East Asian states have also intervened to resolve Kaldorian collective dilemmas. Indeed, Rodrik argues that state coordination of investments was in response to the type of coordination problems I discussed in Chap-

---

[59] Woo, *Race to the Swift*, 134–35.

[60] Gary Gereffi, "Big Business and the State," in *Manufacturing Miracles*, 90–109.

[61] Cited in Wade, *Governing the Market*, 87. By the end of the 1960s, the creation of these linkages boosted demand for, and profits of, Taiwan's public-sector industries providing intermediate inputs. See Dani Rodrik, "Getting Interventions Right: How South Korea and Taiwan Grew Rich," *Economic Policy* 20 (April 1995), 83.

[62] Cited in Wade, *Governing the Market*, 156.

[63] Woo, *Race to the Swift*, 135.

ter 7. He argues that an "active government role helped remove the coordination failure that had blocked industrial growth. As private entrepreneurs responded to these measures, the resulting investments turned out to be profitable not only in financial terms, but in social terms as well."[64]

One method of intervention to resolve Kaldorian collective dilemmas was to encourage the growth of large firms. The Korean state, for example, favored helping larger firms capable of achieving economies of scale while ignoring smaller firms in the steel, shipbuilding, and machinery sectors.[65] In addition, the state encouraged large-scale production by restructuring and rationalizing industrial sectors, a highly interventionist strategy that, as we saw earlier, was strikingly absent in the Turkish automobile industry. Between 1979 and 1982, for example, the Korean state intervened to force restructuring of the shipbuilding, heavy electrical equipment, and fertilizer industries.[66] In the 1970s, the government carefully controlled entry into the automotive sector to facilitate achieving scale economies, allowing only three firms to begin production and stipulating the minimum size of plant. In 1980, the state imposed a new division of labor on the sector, forcing each firm to specialize in a particular segment, such as, for example, passenger cars and light trucks.[67] Similarly, Taiwanese government monopolies in upstream industries such as steel, shipbuilding, and petrochemicals have achieved scale economies. Moreover, in the late 1960s the Taiwanese state forced the merger of four private firms in the petrochemical industry with two public enterprises to create a single, more efficient producer.[68] Note finally that Alice Amsden identifies these efforts to achieve scale economies and stimulate learning-by-doing as the main dynamic of productivity growth in East Asia.[69]

State intervention to resolve Kaldorian collective dilemmas also entailed reconciling oligopolistic market structures with interfirm competition. As Johnson argued about Japanese development, "In implementing its industrial policy, the state must take care to preserve competition to as high a degree as is compatible with its priorities. This is necessary to avoid the deadening hand of state control and the inevitable inefficiency, loss

---

[64] Rodrik, "Getting Interventions Right," 78,

[65] Amsden, *Asia's Next Giant*, 73.

[66] Ibid., 132.

[67] Wade, "Industrial Policy in East Asia," 250–51. See also Howard Pack and Larry E. Westphal, "Industrial Strategy and Technological Change: Theory versus Reality," *Journal of Development Economics* 22 (1986), 96, and Richard Doner, *Driving a Bargain: Automobile Industrialization and Japanese Firms in Southeast Asia* (Berkeley: University of California Press, 1991).

[68] Wade, "Industrial Policy in East Asia," 240.

[69] *Asia's Next Giant*, 109–12.

of incentives, corruption, and bureaucratism that it generates."[70] Indeed, the Japanese pioneered measures to reconcile industrial concentration and interfirm competition.[71] Similar results have obtained in Korea. As a result of efforts to increase firm size to capture the efficiency gains accompanying large-scale production, the ten largest Korean business groups accounted for almost 70 percent of GNP by the mid-1980s. But the state prevented oligopolistic market structures from diluting efficiency gains induced by interfirm competition by creating a system Alice Amsden refers to as "oligopolist competition."[72]

Finally, whereas Korea and Taiwan began their export booms producing relatively low value-added goods, state intervention in East Asia has assisted local firms to move up the product cycle through large investments in education and training in science and technology; targeted fiscal and tax policies subsidizing access to foreign technology; and the creation of vehicles for the collection of technology, its dissemination throughout the national economy, and training firms in its use. As a result, in the 1970s, Korean and Taiwanese firms began to shift from producing relatively simple goods, such as calculators, transistor radios, and black-and-white televisions, in the Taiwanese electronics industry into the production of more sophisticated goods, such as computer peripherals and microelectronics. Efficient production techniques combined with low but rising wages kept unit costs low, allowing firms to capture large export shares in these products, while the incremental upgrading of product technology produced high-quality output, with product specifications often superior to original designs. By the late 1970s and into the 1980s, investment in research and development allowed Korean and Taiwanese firms in some sectors to reduce their dependence on external sources of technology for product and process knowledge and to begin product innovation.[73]

---

[70] Chalmers Johnson, *MITI and the Japanese Miracle: The Growth of Industrial Policy, 1925–1975* (Stanford: Stanford University Press, 1982), 317–18.

[71] Laura Tyson and John Zysman refer to this strategy as "controlled competition." They write, "Japanese government policy for development created an intense but controlled competition in a protected market. The logic of that competition provoked manufacturing innovation that established internationally competitive firms in a variety of industries." See their "Developmental Strategy and Product Innovation in Japan," in *Politics and Productivity: How Japan's Development Strategy Works*, ed. Chalmers Johnson, Laura D'Andrea Tyson, and John Zysman (New York: Harper Business, 1989), 63. For case studies, see Michael Borrus, James E. Millstein, and John Zysman, "Trade and Development in the Semiconductor Industry: Japanese Challenge and American Response," in *American Industry in International Competition*, ed. John Zysman and Laura Tyson (Ithaca: Cornell University Press, 1983), esp. 147. See also Marie Anchordoguy, "Mastering the Market: Japanese Government Targeting of the Computer Industry," *International Organization* 42 (Summer 1988): 509–39.

[72] Amsden, *Asia's Next Giant*, 129–30.

[73] For Taiwan, see Denis Fred Simon, "Taiwan's Strategy for Creating Competitive Advantage: The Role of the State in Managing Foreign Technology," in *Taiwan's Enterprises in*

East Asian states demonstrated their dedication to technological acquisition and diffusion by linking investment subsidies to firms' commitment to technological upgrading. In the Taiwanese machine tools industry, for example, firms that signed agreements with the state technology institute received almost guaranteed access to subsidized credit, along with assistance with training and design.[74] But state intervention extended beyond subsidies: in his study of the petrochemical industry, for example, Enos found that persistent and comprehensive state intervention accompanied the entire process of technology acquisition and assimilation beginning with ensuring access to technology on favorable terms and extending to the choice of suppliers of sophisticated technology, the specification of the conditions under which technology was to be provided, the construction and operation of plants, and the expansion of capacity.[75] Jacobsson found similar state intervention in the development of the Korean and Taiwanese machine tools industries and in the entry of firms into the production of computer numerically controlled machinery.[76]

The Taiwanese state has played an important but often more indirect role in promoting technology transfer and acquisition.[77] Government technology policy was expressed in the 1962 Statute for the Encouragement of Technological Cooperation. Other state initiatives include the establishment of the Industrial Technology Research Institute in 1973 and a series of "national strategic programs" launched in 1980 in the fields of energy, automation, information, materials, biotechnology, electro-optics, hepatitis B control, and food processing. There have also been a series of technology-upgrading projects, including programs to diffuse labor-saving automation equipment and to upgrade quality stan-

Global Perspective, ed. N. T. Wang (Armonk, N.Y.: M. E. Sharpe, 1992), 97–122. For Korea, see Larry E. Westphal, Yung W. Rhee, and Garry Pursell, "Sources of Technological Capability in South Korea," in *Technological Capability in the Third World*, ed. Martin Fransman and Kenneth King (London: Macmillan, 1984), 279–300; and Pack and Westphal, "Industrial Strategy and Technological Change," 87–128. Although Korea and Taiwan made significant advances in technological and product innovation relative to Syria and Turkey, they still remained substantially dependent on Japan for capital goods and technology into the 1990s. For discussion, see Mitchell Bernard and John Ravenhill, "Beyond Product Cycles and Flying Geese: Regionalization, Hierarchy, and the Industrialization of East Asia," *World Politics* 47 (January 1995): 171–209.

[74] Wade, *Governing the Market*, 100–101.

[75] John Enos, "Government Intervention in the Transfer of Technology: The Case of South Korea," *IDS Bulletin* 15 (1984): 26–31. As a result of technological acquisition and steady improvements in efficiency, the industry has surpassed design specification.

[76] Staffan Jacobsson, "Industrial Policy for the Machine Tool Industries of South Korea and Taiwan," *IDS Bulletin* 15 (1984): 44–49.

[77] For an overview, see Denis Fred Simon, "Technology Transfer and National Autonomy," in *Contending Approaches to the Political Economy of Taiwan*, ed. Edwin A. Winckler and Susan Greenhalgh (Armonk, N.Y.: M. E. Sharpe, 1988), 206–23.

dards.[78] The state has played an especially prominent role in building technical competence in advanced electronics.[79] The Taiwanese integrated-circuit industry, for example, "flourished only after the government became involved, establishing a demonstration factory, organizing manpower, transferring technology . . . providing . . . manufacturing services, [and] establishing [a] Common Design Service Center."[80] By the late 1970s, the state was beginning to shift its priorities toward developing local research and development capabilities, a commitment embodied in the decision to establish the Hsinchu Science and Industry Park and in various incentive schemes to attract high-tech foreign investment.

In summary, the Korean and Taiwanese states intervened to resolve both Kaldorian and Gerschenkronian collective dilemmas, producing a distinctive and impressive trajectory of economic development. Korea and Taiwan did so while pursuing an export-led growth (ELG) strategy, which distinguishes them from Syria and Turkey. But the character of state intervention—its goals and the instruments through which they are realized—also differed markedly across the two sets of cases. In the next section, I explore the causal connections between trade strategy, modes of state intervention, and development outcomes.

Explaining Development Outcomes

Syria and Turkey did not reach identical outcomes: the argument advanced here cannot explain all of the observed variance. In contrast to Korea and Taiwan, however, the similarities of the Syrian and Turkish outcomes become more prominent. Moreover, according to the criteria that I have argued are central to the conceptualization and process of development, Syria and Turkey in 1980 had reached outcomes that were remarkably similar, given all the factors that distinguish the two countries. Despite movement into the production of consumer durables and some intermediate goods, neither country had successfully established many linkages. Despite movement into more capital-intensive industries, neither country had experienced sustainable productivity increases: industrial plants had not attained economies of scale, most plants operated at well below capacity utilization, and shop-floor and managerial practices had not been transformed. Most production was thus high-cost and low-quality. Finally, despite industrial diversification, both countries remained

---

[78] Wade, *Governing the Economy*, 98–99.

[79] Ibid., 103. See also 99–108 for discussion of other industry-specific measures.

[80] Se-Hwa Wu, "The Dynamic Cooperation Between Government and Enterprise: The Development of Taiwan's Integrated Circuit Industry," in *Taiwan's Enterprises in Global Perspective*, 189.

low value-added producers, manufacturing basic commodities with borrowed, standardized technology that was not fully assimilated and relying heavily on imported components for assembly factories. Overall economic growth was steady, if not spectacular, and growth of industrial output generally outpaced overall growth. In that sense, Syrian and Turkey had industrialized by 1980. But almost all of that growth was simply a function of new investments; because the instruments needed to create value had not been put into place, self-sustaining growth was not possible. While Syria and Turkey had, to some extent, solved Gerschenkronian collective dilemmas, they had not addressed Kaldorian collective dilemmas.

This syndrome of economic practices, policies, and outcomes that has characterized the trajectory of economic development in Syria and Turkey is sufficiently similar to make it incumbent on us to seek a common explanation, one that simultaneously accounts for the superior economic performance of Korea and Taiwan. The most parsimonious explanation would attribute their developmental defects to the inevitably deleterious consequences of import-substituting industrialization (ISI), which, neoliberals argue, deviates from optimal allocative efficiency, leading to lower rates of growth, and of unnecessary state intervention, which induces pervasive, directly unproductive, rent-seeking behavior. Closer scrutiny of our cases, however, suggests that the economic effects of ISI and of state intervention are closely linked to the broader institutional context. Consider, for example, Stephan Haggard's summary of the modal consequences of ISI:

> Heavily protected ISI industries were oligopolistic in structure and characterized by excess capacity, inefficiency, high mark-up, and low-quality output. These internal distortions naturally had distributional consequences. Trade and exchange-rate policies raised the prices of manufactured goods relative to agricultural products, turning the terms of trade against the countryside. . . . As real resource transfers from the agricultural sector necessarily slowed, the temptation to subsidize industry from the central bank grew, exacerbating inflation. The emphasis on industry at the expense of agriculture limited the expansion of the domestic market. . . . Though ISI had been motivated by a desire to increase employment, the encouragement of capital-intensive production processes constrained the ability of the industrial sector to absorb labor.[81]

Haggard's description of ISI's pernicious consequences is only partially consistent with the Syrian and Turkish cases. ISI did not, as we have seen,

---

[81] Stephan Haggard, *Pathways From the Periphery: The Politics of Growth in the Newly Industrializing Countries* (Ithaca: Cornell University Press, 1990), 12.

lead to a deterioration of agricultural terms of trade. In the Turkish case, policy makers deliberately turned the terms of trade *in favor* of agriculture, a strategy mimicked in form, if not in intensity, by Syrian policy makers. Similarly, levels of employment were kept higher than was required by capital-intensive industries to absorb excess labor. Finally, it would be a mistake to assume that ISI always encourages oligopolistic market structures and that oligopoly always precludes competition, efficiency, and innovation, because East Asian developmental states in some cases deliberately created oligopolistic structures that were then rendered consistent with competition and innovation. Indeed, Korean firms in many sectors received substantial protection, which did not preclude their attaining efficiency and industrial competitiveness.

As I argued in Chapter 7, and as the evidence on East Asian development clearly demonstrates, we cannot equate East Asian export-led growth with the absence of state intervention and of rent-seeking behavior. East Asian states intervened heavily in their economies, both by protecting some industries and by altering prices to allow industrial firms to capture rents. In the Korean automobile industry, for example, beyond setting relatively high tariff levels that were only slowly reduced in the 1970s and enforcing domestic content regulations, the state also intervened at the level of the firm, making decisions about when to use subcontractors to supply high-quality parts and even which subcontractors to use, and requiring producers to cooperate in the production of standardized components. Finally, as we have seen, the Korean state restructured the industry to achieve economies of scale. These and other mechanisms of state intervention allowed firms to earn substantial rents.[82] As Byung-Sun Choi points out in his study of the Korean government's financial policy, government creation of rents "can be a source of a variety of evils, including political and bureaucratic corruption. But the creation of rents can also be a powerful policy instrument for eliciting business cooperation and support for government policies."[83] The prevalence of economic rents in East Asia raises a critical question: why has East Asian rent-seeking behavior been consistent with developmental imperatives, while in other cases, such as Syria and Turkey, rent-seeking behavior is unproductive and non-developmental?

Our answer must start with the understanding that not all rent-seeking behavior is unproductive. In his analysis of the dynamics of capitalism, Joseph Schumpeter argued that, like protection, innovation also restricted competition and thus earned rents for entrepreneurs: indeed, viewing innovation, or "creative gales of destruction," as the primary

[82] Wade, "Industrial Policy in East Asia," 250–51.
[83] Byung-Sun Choi, "Financial Policy and Big Business in Korea," 23.

source of progress in capitalism prompted Schumpeter to consider perfectly competitive markets inferior.[84] Rents earned by innovation, in other words, are productive and fuel long-run development. Indeed, neoliberal scholars have recently rediscovered Schumpeter and incorporated rent-driven technological innovations into their growth models,[85] while the recent elaboration of strategic trade theory by economists generally hostile to state intervention provides a rationale for state assistance that allows private capitalists to earn rents.[86] There remains a great deal of legitimate debate about whether state policy can successfully assist firms in earning rents and thus raising national income.[87] Yet, whether state economic intervention elicits directly unproductive, profit-seeking behavior or induces innovation, efficiency-inducing scale economies, and learning-by-doing, is an empirical question; depending on the broader institutional context, state economic intervention may either resolve or exacerbate collective dilemmas. Alice Amsden makes this point clearly in her study of Korean development: "In late-industrializing countries, *the state intervenes with subsidies to distort relative prices in order to stimulate economic activity.* This has been as true in Korea, Japan, and Taiwan, as it has been in Brazil, India, and Turkey. In Korea, Japan, and Taiwan, however, the state has exercised discipline over subsidy recipients. *In exchange for subsidies, the state has imposed performance standards on private firms.* Subsidies have not been giveaways, but instead have been dispensed on the principle of reciprocity."[88]

Discipline has two dimensions: (1) the establishment of a set of performance standards and their strict application, so that firms failing to meet performance standards are penalized and (2) the provision of rewards to firms meeting these standards. Consider, for example, Park Chung Hee's behavior toward one of Korea's largest steel companies in the mid-1960s, Yonhap Steel, which opposed the export drive because it was competitive

[84] Joseph A. Schumpeter, *Capitalism, Socialism, and Democracy* (New York: Harper Torchbooks, 1942), 87–106.

[85] In their *Innovation and Growth in the Global Economy* (Cambridge: MIT Press, 1991), 335, Gene Grossman and Elhanan Helpman write, "We take the view that technological progress results from the intentional actions of economic agents responding to perceived profit opportunities. Firms and entrepreneurs devote resources to R&D when they see prospects for reaping returns on their investments. Returns come often in the form of economic rents in imperfectly competitive product markets. Thus, monopoly profits provide the impetus for growth, just as in the Schumpeterian process of 'creative destruction.'"

[86] Paul Krugman writes, "If there are important rents in certain sectors, trade policy can raise national income by securing for a country a larger share of the rent-yielding industries." See his "Introduction: New Thinking about Trade Policy," in *Strategic Trade Policy and the New International Economics*, ed. Paul Krugman (Cambridge: MIT Press, 1986), 12–13.

[87] Laura D'Andrea Tyson makes the case for strategic trade policy in her *Who's Bashing Whom: Trade Conflict in High-Technology Industries* (Washington, D.C.: Institute for International Economics, 1992).

[88] Amsden, *Asia's Next Giant*, 8. Italics in original.

only in the protected local market due to its technological backwardness. "Yonhap refused to join with other companies to cooperate in the export drive because it was losing money on exports," company founder Kwon Chul Hyun said later. "That displeased President Park, who almost destroyed the company."[89] Through the provision of fiscal incentives and public investment, the state has promoted capital accumulation and development, resolving Gerschenkronian collective dilemmas. Through the application of discipline, coupled with measures to help firms achieve economies of scale, incorporate new technology, and innovate in production practices, developmental states in East Asia have successfully resolved Kaldorian collective dilemmas. The result has been development along all four of the dimensions I have discussed. But this answer to the question of why rent-seeking behavior produces divergent modes of economic activity with different developmental consequences, then, only reformulates our question: Why have only East Asian states been able to discipline capitalists?

To some extent, ELG spurs development independent of the institutional and microeconomic policy context accompanying it. International market forces provide incentives—and sanctions—for firms to become competitive, supplementing the direct role of the state in overcoming Kaldorian collective dilemmas and preventing the deterioration of Schumpeterian rent-seeking activities into directly unproductive activities. Moreover, participation in international markets directly helps firms become competitive by providing larger markets and thus greater potential for scale economies, as well as access to new technology and cutting-edge production practices, information indicating shifts in demand, and feedback from consumers.[90] Despite these potential benefits of ELG, however, an explanation based solely on trade policy remains insufficient. After all, the evidence of state intervention to boost competitiveness cannot be ignored. Furthermore, East Asian development states have frequently protected particular industrial sectors while making them more competitive; protection, then, can be accompanied by the resolution of Kaldorian collective dilemmas.[91] Finally, as we shall see in chapter 9, in

---

[89] Cited in Mark Clifford, *Troubled Tiger: Businessmen, Bureaucrats, and Generals in South Korea* (Armonk, N.Y.: M. E. Sharpe, 1994), 55. The Korean state penalized poorly performing firms by forcing the rationalization of industries weakened by overexpansion or by refusing to bail out large-scale but badly managed firms in otherwise healthy industries. See the examples cited in Amsden, *Asia's Next Giant*, 15, and Chapter 5.

[90] See Anne O. Krueger, "Comparative Advantage and Development Policy 20 Years Later," in *Economic Structure and Performance*, ed. Moshe Syrquin, Lance Taylor, and Larry E. Westphal (Orlando: Academic Press, 1984), 135–56, and Donald B. Keesing, "Linking Up to Distant Markets: South to North Exports of Manufactured Consumer Goods," *American Economic Review* 73 (May 1983): 338–42.

[91] Jaymin Lee's analysis of Korean "infant industries" and their performance behind protection concludes that contrary to most cases of protection, Korean protected industries

the absence of a developmental state, ELG in post-1980 Turkey produced export-induced rapid growth that did not entail the resolution of Kaldorian collective dilemmas. In short, macroeconomic policies designed to promote exports work best when combined with micro-level policies designed to assist firms to become competitive.

Still, there is no denying that while ISI is occasionally associated with positive developmental outcomes and ELG arguably did not work its magic in Turkey in the 1980s, ISI is more generally associated with developmental failure and ELG with success. For ISI to produce positive developmental outcomes, the state must check directly unproductive, rent-seeking activities. By deflecting market forces that would penalize inefficient producers, ISI makes requisite on the state an even greater capacity to resolve Kaldorian collective dilemmas than ELG does. Although ISI does not compel producers to be competitive, neither does it *necessarily* prevent them from doing so; as we have seen, the Korean state protected some industries and helped them become internationally competitive. The institutional context in which trade strategy is situated therefore determines the behavior of firms. In the postwar period, ISI has frequently been a consequence of coalition building through high levels of side-payments. High levels of side-payments, however, deny the state the institutional capacity to resolve Kaldorian collective dilemmas. Therefore, the same set of factors that result in ISI also typically result in low levels of state capacity to resolve Kaldorian collective dilemmas.

A simple bargaining model helps us to see clearly why precocious Keynesian states cannot discipline capitalists. Consider a bargain between the state and capital with no other participants. The state prefers that firms comply with performance standards such as increasing efficiency and achieving international competitiveness. In return, the state promises to provide resources benefiting recipients: subsidies, protective measures, large-scale infrastructural investments, absorption of the costs of externalities, and so forth. Because the state has not made side-payments to popular classes, it is not compelled to offer protection to industrialists as compensation for artificially high factor costs. Instead, the state promises subsidies and other sources of rents in exchange for specified economic performance. Export performance acts as a simple measure of compliance with the bargain and thus determines eligibility for future state assistance. Firms face incentives not only to invest in new factories but also, and more important, to collaborate with the state in continuous efforts to

---

dramatically improved their economic performance. Following Amsden, he attributes this in large part to the "effective contest" created by the Korean state, such that "Korean infant industries were not allowed to live complacently behind the wall of protection, but rather were driven to compete and improve performance." "The Maturation and Growth of Infant Industries: The Case of Korea," *World Development* 25 (August 1997), 1278.

produce more efficiently and to make output more competitive in international markets. Furthermore, because the state makes no side-payments to workers, firms in new, capital-intensive industries can more effectively bargain with workers possessing firm-specific skills, trading rising wages for cooperation with efforts to boost productivity and quality control.[92] This is the East Asian bargain, which resolved Gerschenkronian and Kaldorian collective dilemmas.

Now allow for third actors and side-payments. Once the state has made side-payments to third actors that raise the costs of production for industrialists, the latter must be compensated; they too must receive side-payments. Thus, the state provides subsidized credit or protection as compensation for increased factor costs. These payments are necessary to induce capitalists to make investments; in the absence of these side-payments, high factor costs will be prohibitive, and there will be limited private investment. Put differently, once a significant level of side-payments is made to third actors, the state must make side-payments to capitalists simply to resolve Gerschenkronian collective dilemmas. Moreover, the political determination of employment levels and wages reduces the incentives for workers to bargain with management, rendering it more difficult to refashion shop-floor practices in ways that enhance efficiency.

If the state makes payments to capital to resolve Gerschenkronian collective dilemmas, it exhausts the resources it might use to elicit cooperation on behalf of resolving Kaldorian collective dilemmas. Once compensatory payments consist of subsidies *and* protection simply on behalf of inducing investment in new plants, the state has given to capitalists all that they want. Consequently, the state no longer has leverage with which to discipline capitalists to raise productivity and enhance international competitiveness. Firms in protected markets that receive state support on behalf of encouraging investment in new plant face no incentives to undertake costly and risky efforts to improve productivity and boost export performance; their profits are guaranteed without these measures. Furthermore, as we saw in Chapter 5, as long as side-payments that raise factor costs are made to popular classes, states can neither reduce protection nor compel industrialists to export; high factor costs will continue to preclude competitiveness. In this case, the state solves the problem of capital accumulation and investment at the expense of reducing state capacity to intervene to solve the efficiency problem. Thus, when elites construct cross-class coalitions that require high levels of side-payments, states will lack the resources to discipline capitalists, and directly unproductive rent-seeking behavior with all of its negative consequences will be pervasive, at the expense of Schumpeterian rent-seeking behavior. In short, when

---

[92] Amsden, *Asia's Next Giant*, 208–09.

states make high levels of side-payments to third parties, *they resolve Ger-schenkronian collective dilemmas. This solution, however, makes it virtually impossible to resolve Kaldorian collective dilemmas.*

Although this model uses the language of state-capital bargaining, its logic also captures relations between the state and public-sector managers in Syria and Turkey: once high levels of side-payments have been made to workers and peasants, the state cannot discipline its own agents. John Waterbury's analysis of the performance of state-owned enterprises in Egypt, India, Mexico, and Turkey illustrates this point.[93] Public enterprises in these countries exhibit systemic deficiencies: their productivity levels are low and costs of production high, while their losses drain state finances. Principal-agent problems take center stage in Waterbury's analysis: public-sector managers, or agents, are trapped between the economic logic of their market position and the political logic of their political bosses, or principals. Because principals expect public-sector enterprises to respond to multiple, contradictory tasks, from advancing industrialization and earning profits to absorbing excess employment and supplying cheap goods to the population, agents are highly constrained to run their plants in inefficient ways. Waterbury argues that the pattern of incentives and control producing suboptimal performance is inherent in public-sector principal-agent relations. The passing reference he makes to the superior performance of public enterprises in Korea and Taiwan, however, casts doubt on this element of his interpretation; instead, as he briefly notes, it is coalitional dynamics and not factors inherent in public-sector enterprises that determine firm behavior.[94] Once cross-class coalitions are built through high levels of side-payments, states will be unable to discipline *either* private-sector capitalists or public-sector managers.

To be sure, by the 1980s, East Asian developmental states were making side-payments to popular classes, although they were of a smaller magnitude than side-payments in Syria and Turkey. Furthermore, over time, as East Asian capitalists accumulated sufficient capital to finance further investments, they correspondingly reduced their dependence on the state. Finally, East Asian economies shifted into new industrial sectors in which state intervention was less effective. But in the critical years of East Asian development that saw Japan, Korea, and Taiwan become industrial powerhouses (1950–1975 in Japan, 1965–1980 in Korea and Taiwan), state capacity to resolve collective dilemmas rested on the nexus of three institutional arrangements: an insulated and highly competent set of agencies within the bureaucratic apparatus that formulated and implemented long-term industrial strategy; a high degree of control over the financial

---

[93] *Exposed to Innumerable Delusions,* Chapter 4.

[94] Waterbury writes, ibid., 119, "Outside of Korea and Taiwan, policy makers have perpetuated regimes that sustain political coalitions but damage productivity."

system that afforded state executives tremendous leverage over the investment and production decisions of public-sector managers and private businessmen; and discriminate state economic intervention that guided industrial activity into targeted industrial sectors and assisted firms in those industries in becoming competitive in international markets. These three institutions in turn rested on a political base forged into a conservative coalition; constructing and maintaining this coalition did not entail burdening the state with financial obligations, meaning that state control over the financial system was not used to underwrite state budgets. Furthermore, providing benefits to the members of this coalition did not conflict in any major way with the dictates of late development.

In stark contrast, Syrian and Turkish state elites constructed large-scale, cross-class coalitions embracing such large segments of the populace that not only were state resources burdened with huge obligations, but a whole set of institutions that play critical roles in development had to be reoriented toward eliciting and reproducing coalitional support. Thus, state agencies left exposed to political pressures could not formulate or implement long-term development strategy. State control over the financial system siphoned resources to underwrite state budgets and thus afforded minimal leverage over private entrepreneurs. State economic intervention protected the interests of constituents at the expense of building competitive advantage. Consequently, precocious Keynesian states had only limited capacity to overcome collective dilemmas. Burdened with impaired planning capacity and a marked proclivity to avoid any measures that might corrode coalitional support, the Syrian and Turkish states, despite their massive involvement in the economy, had only attenuated capacity to foster comprehensive economic development other than by encouraging new investments. It was the institutional incapacities of the Syrian and Turkish states that led their governments to emphasize new capital investments without showing parallel concern for enhancing the efficiency of these plants or more tightly linking them to the rest of the economy.[95] Their only effective policy instruments were investment-inducing subsidies and profit-boosting protection that granted rents to even highly inefficient firms.

A brief comparison of postwar Turkish development with its experiment with state-led development in the 1930s further demonstrates the impact of the broader institutional context on the outcomes of ISI. As we saw in Chapter 3, in the early 1930s, Turkey embarked on a state-led development project behind protectionist barriers. Development was financed by turning the terms of trade against the agricultural sector, keep-

---

[95] In contrast, many analysts attribute dysfunctional behavior to bad planning or deficient understanding of the requisites of development. For examples, Victor Lavy and Eliezer Sheffer, *Foreign Aid and Economic Development in the Middle East: Egypt, Syria, and Jordan,* (New York: Praeger, 1990), 1; Szyliowicz, "Technology Transfer and Development in Turkey," 268.

ing wages low, and selling goods at artificially high prices, so that farmers, workers, and urban middle classes paid the costs of development.[96] Most of the rents derived from artificially high prices accrued directly to the state, financing further development, although private industrialists also benefited from higher prices.[97] During the etatist period, manufacturing increased its share of GDP from about 8 percent in the late 1920s to over 13 percent at the end of the decade.[98] Along with increased output of consumer goods was significant vertical integration into the production of cement, iron, and steel; capital-intensive industries increased their share of manufacturing output from 18 to 27 percent.[99] Hansen estimates that as a result of growing capital intensity, between 1927 and 1938 labor productivity increased about 6 percent annually.[100] Finally, throughout the 1930s, Turkey enjoyed a modest balance of trade surplus, despite the inflow of foreign loans.

Why was ISI more successful in the 1930s than in the postwar period? Because state-society relations were not based on constituency clientelism, the state was able to pin the costs of development on popular sectors and avoid budget deficits, macroeconomic instability, and trade deficits. Furthermore, Turkey's elite bureaucracy was not constrained by political calculations and was thus able to channel those resources directly into projects targeted by long-term industrial planning. Finally, state intervention was not governed by the need to protect constituencies from market pressures or to enhance their welfare. In summary, the relative lack of success of postwar Syrian and Turkish ISI cannot be accounted for in isolation from other crucial dimensions of the political economy, such as state-society relations and the politicization of the bureaucratic apparatus. This proposition is supported by evidence from other cases demonstrating the success of ISI policies within specific institutional contexts.[101]

---

[96] Two additional sources of finance were external loans and domestic borrowing. Foreign loans were quite limited in scope and were generally tied to specific projects, while domestic borrowing—issuing Treasury Bills, direct loans from the public, and Central Bank emissions—amounted to between 10 and 12 percent of total government revenues. See Z. Y. Hershlag, *Turkey: The Challenge of Growth*, (Leiden: E. J. Brill, 1968), 87, 93–94.

[97] Korkut Boratav, *Turkiye Iktisat Tarihi, 1908–1985* (Istanbul: Gercek Yayinevi, 1988), 53–54.

[98] Bent Hansen, *The Political Economy of Poverty, Equity, and Growth: Egypt and Turkey*, (Oxford: Oxford University Press, 1991), 330.

[99] Hershlag, *Turkey: The Challenge of Growth*, 100–103; Hansen, *Political Economy of Poverty, Equity, and Growth*, 325.

[100] At constant 1948 prices, GDP derived from industry increased at about 8.8 percent annually, whereas the industrial labor force grew at an annual rate of about 2.9 percent. Hansen, *Political Economy of Poverty, Equity, and Growth*, 330–31.

[101] See Barbara Geddes, "Building 'State' Autonomy in Brazil, 1930–1964." *Comparative Politics* 22 (January 1990): 217–35, and Peter Evans, *Embedded Autonomy: States and Industrial Transformation* (Princeton: Princeton University Press, 1995), for examples.

The Fiscal Crisis of Precocious Keynesian States

By the late 1970s, fiscal constraints severely limited the capacity of the Turkish and Syrian states to resolve even Gerschenkronian collective dilemmas. The economic crisis that emerged in Turkey in the late 1970s was the third in a series of "state intervention cycles" that had occurred in approximately ten-year intervals dating back to 1958. But the third crisis hit especially hard, coupled as it was with a sharp reduction in access to foreign currency. Particularly hard hit was the manufacturing sector: whereas the average annual increase in manufacturing output between 1960 and 1973 had reached 10.3 percent, between 1973 and 1976 it declined to 8.3 percent, a relatively minor glitch compared to the descent to 2.1 percent annual growth between 1976 and 1979. The stagnation in manufacturing was due to both the systemic production inefficiencies discussed earlier, and, more directly, a shortage in foreign exchange, as the oil price increase of the mid-1970s exacerbated a foreign exchange crisis precipitated by decreased worker remittances and official transfers from the United States.[102]

As the late 1970s were a period of fragile coalition governments and increasing street violence, it surprised no one that successive governments responded with shortsighted palliatives. During the mid-1970s, the recirculation of petrodollars made it easy for Turkey to resort to short-term credit at high interest rates, leading to a crushing debt burden. During Bulent Ecevit's short-lived government in 1978, he attempted to gain control over scarce foreign exchange by imposing a wide array of controls over the allocation of imports. This resulted only in widespread shortages and an increase in contraband trade; many industrialists had to double as smugglers merely to survive. At the same time, the application of precocious Keynesianism became completely uncontrolled: between 1974 and 1978, real public sector wages rose by 58 percent and total employment increased by 28 percent. During the same period, value-added *fell* by 20 percent, whereas wages, as a share of value-added, increased from 27 to 38 percent.[103] In the 1950s and 1960s, precocious Keynesianism in Turkey was marked by a failure to enhance the productivity of an expanding industrial base; by the end of the 1970s, it was resulting in diminishing capacity to mobilize the resources to expand industrial capacity.

---

[102] Remittances declined from $1.4 billion in 1974 to an average of 980 million dollars between 1976 and 1978. When added to the import bills inflated by increased oil prices, the ratio of imports paid for by worker remittances slid from 38 percent in 1974 to 17 percent in 1977. Caglar Keyder, *State and Class in Turkey: A Study in Capitalist Development*, (London: Verso, 1987), 185.

[103] John Waterbury, "Export-Led Growth and the Center-Right Coalition in Turkey," *Comparative Politics* 24 (January 1992), 139.

By the late 1970s, Syrian state officials were voicing serious concerns about the lack of efficiency of public-sector industries. The decline in oil prices beginning in the early 1980s exacerbated the impending crisis of the Syrian economy in three ways. First, state revenues from the export of oil from Syrian fields began to slide. Second, the oil-producing countries of the Gulf began to scale back their transfers to Syria, both in response to their own declining revenues and as a function of regional politics. Arab financial assistance to Syria decreased from about $1.6 billion in 1980 to around $500 million in 1982, and by 1988 it was estimated that Syria was sending more money back to other Arab states than it received from them. Finally, Syrian migrant workers in the Gulf states remitted fewer funds as host countries facing budgetary constraints began to cut back on their public spending. By May 1980, foreign exchange reserves were as low as 385 million pounds sterling, and foreign exchange shortages would hamper the Syrian economy for most of the 1980s. Consequently, the fourth five-year plan issued in 1980 slashed spending and suspended all new projects.[104] Gross domestic investment declined from its peak of almost 29 percent of GDP in 1977 to 20 percent in 1981. After rising by 10 percent in 1981, GDP growth slowed to only 3 percent in 1982 and 1983, although even these modest figures may stem from underestimation of inflation.[105]

Consequently, in the 1980s, Syrian and Turkish governments devised new political-economic arrangements that departed from precocious Keynesianism, significantly in Turkey and more incrementally in Syria. I discuss these experiments in Chapter 9.

---

[104] In addition, beginning in 1977, Syria embarked on a massive campaign to achieve strategic parity with Israel through expanding the size of the armed forces and equipping them with the newest weaponry. Budgeted spending on operating expenses—salaries, food, housing, operations, and maintenance—increased from about 900 million U.S. dollars in 1976 to about 1.9 billion U.S. dollars in 1983. Off-budget expenditures for arms imports, primarily from the Soviet Union, reached a peak of 5.8 billion dollars in 1980–1981. Financing for this arms buildup came from Arab oil-exporting states. This spending, however, did not constitute the diversion of resources from economic uses; almost all Arab assistance was specifically earmarked to finance military spending. See Patrick Clawson, *Unaffordable Ambitions: Syria's Military Build-Up and Economic Crisis*, (Washington, D.C.: The Washington Institute for Near East Policy, 1989), 7–10, 31.

[105] Kanovsky, *What's Behind Syria's Current Economic Problems*, 8.

CHAPTER NINE

Pathways from
Precocious Keynesianism

By the end of the 1970s, the convergence of inefficient domestic economies incapable of financing new rounds of investment with changes in the international economy that slashed capital inflows generated economic crisis that rendered unreconstructed precocious Keynesianism unsustainable. By eroding the capacity to maintain coalitional support, economic crisis threatened political crisis, triggering new debates over the proper relationship of state and economy. Often raucous, this debate did not spark intense and escalating inter-elite conflict as it had in the earlier period that produced precocious Keynesianism. Although Syrian and Turkish elites divided over how to rebalance public authority and private economic activity, this conflict did not threaten the short-term economic and long-term political interests of powerful elite groups. Moreover, major social actors in both countries agreed that the state would continue to play a central role in the economy. Absent threats to private property or to the political power of elites, no major political actors sought to break the hold of the current state elite over the economy as a means of reducing arbitrary state power or of breaking the political power of an agrarian oligarchy. Indeed, in both cases, governing elites assessed alternative visions of the political economy according to technical criteria: what combination of centralized authority and decentralized decision making was most conducive to producing sustainable economic growth. These pragmatic considerations yield less intense elite conflict.

Consequently, despite the existence of often heated debate among political and economic actors, the elite remained relatively unified in both Turkey and Syria. At the same time, state agents were concerned with distributional issues, which defined the capacity to maintain coalitional stability. New policies, then, were never purely technocratic in nature, but were always tightly enmeshed in coalitional politics. But policy makers recognized and worked to minimize the serious conflict between growth-oriented policy making and coalition politics. Rather than formulating economic policies that supported coalition strategies, political elites first selected economic reform policies and then, to the extent possible, reconciled coalitional imperatives to them.

This chapter surveys the course of economic reform in Syria and Turkey in the 1980s. I do not present detailed information on policy reforms themselves, because this topic is well covered in the existing literature. Instead, discussion here is restricted to five themes. First, I advance propositions explaining why Syrian officials elected incremental economic reform without drastic reformulation of their political coalition, whereas Turkish officials experimented with more radical and comprehensive reforms, including wholesale reconstruction of their political coalition. The next three sections deal exclusively with Turkey. In the second section, I discuss the efforts of Turkish Prime Minister Turgut Ozal to build a new coalition that would support his vision of a newly liberalized Turkish economy fully integrated into the international economy. In the third section, I explore how the construction of a new coalition gave Ozal the opportunity to refashion Turkish state institutions, as well as the limits of his institutional project. In the fourth section, I look at the consequences of economic reform for Turkish economic performance, and conclude that despite the impressive growth of exports following the transition to export-led growth (ELG), Turkey still has not matched the level of economic performance and transformation the East Asian newly industrializing countries had achieved by 1980 (approximately 15 years after their transition to ELG). The divergence in economic performance suggests that ELG is at most a necessary condition for rapid growth and industrial transformation, but it is not a sufficient condition. The combination of ELG with a restructured but still non-developmental Turkish state continued to yield suboptimal economic performance.

The last section of this chapter looks at Syria's program of incremental economic reform. As in Turkey, Syria's leaders partially subordinated coalitional considerations to the dictates of renewed growth. Briefly, I argue that Syria's leaders struck a new balance between political stability and economic performance, securing political stability by retaining their coalitional base but minimizing the deleterious economic consequences by reducing payoffs to their constituencies. At the same time, they enacted macroeconomic reforms needed to improve performance without eroding the capacity of the state to intervene in ways consolidating its coalition base.

Explaining Structural Adjustment Strategies

In his cross-national study of economic reform, John Waterbury suggests a useful distinction between system-maintaining reforms and system-transforming reforms.[1] Reforms oriented toward system maintenance tinker with the public sector without making fundamental changes in the property regime. These reforms restructure principal-agent relations in the hopes of making the public sector more efficient and profitable and are typically accompanied by efforts to adjust the distribution of costs and benefits within the existing coalition to reduce the burdens of welfare-enhancing policies on the public sector. Although they include elements of economic stabilization and liberalization, these reforms preserve a substantial economic role for the state and thus do not constitute a decisive transformation of the political economy. System-transforming reforms, on the other hand, make more radical adjustments to the property regime through privatization or liquidation of the public sector. These reforms of the public sector are typically accompanied by a shift in development strategy from import-substituting industrialization (ISI) to ELG and from state-led development to market-oriented strategies based on the private sector. Finally, system-transforming reforms are built on new coalition arrangements, deliberately crafted to support the new market-oriented strategy.

Syrian policy makers pursued a system-maintaining strategy, whereas their Turkish counterparts implemented a system-transforming strategy. Put differently, Turkish state elites attempted a cleaner break with precocious Keynesianism than did Syrian state elites. In Syria, the Asad regime introduced liberalizing reforms incrementally; not until 1990 did the contours of the Syrian political economy even begin to resemble a more "liberal" economy, and even then, direct state control over the economy remained comprehensive. Indeed, through the mid-1990s, there had been no measures to privatize the public sector. In terms of coalition politics, the regime retained its existing social support base, while altering the level of payoffs sustaining support. In contrast, Turkish liberalization reached down to the roots of the political economy, entailing a decisive shift from ISI to ELG, a greater role for market forces in determining prices, and sustained efforts toward privatization. Furthermore, with the return to democracy in 1983, Turkish elites deliberately tied their reform programs to the transformation of the coalition underlying state rule.

In both cases, then, economic reform strategies intersected with coalition politics. At several important junctures, the specifics of reform were

---

[1] John Waterbury, *Exposed to Innumerable Delusions: Public Enterprise and State Power in Egypt, India, Mexico, and Turkey* (Cambridge: Cambridge University Press, 1993), Chapter 5.

altered to make them consistent with the logic of coalition maintenance. In general, however, state elites enjoyed a great deal of latitude in devising economic reform strategies in insulation from coalition politics. This does not mean that coalition considerations were absent from their calculations, nor that their choice of strategy was completely unconstrained by other factors, but only that elites first devised a development strategy and then worked to render their political coalitions consistent with it. This is because, as I argued above, inter-elite conflict did not lead competing elites to bid for social support. When this happened in the earlier period, development strategies were a by-product of coalition strategies. In the 1980s, the more stable political environment permitted reforming elites to reverse the relationship between coalition and developmental strategies, affording priority to the latter.

Why, then, did relatively autonomous elites in the two countries pursue such different strategies? My account starts from the assumption that incumbent elites prefer system-maintaining reforms over system-transforming reforms. Because system-maintaining reforms rest on the existing social coalition, they pose less of a threat to regime incumbency. The status quo, after all, had supported state elites for three decades in Turkey, albeit with bouts of instability, and for almost 20 years in Syria. By definition, creating a new coalition would inject a high degree of uncertainty into regime calculations. Given the capacity to sustain system-maintaining reforms in the short to medium term, then, an elite concerned with its tenure in office will select the risk-averse strategy. Only when system-maintaining reforms are precluded by the previous path of development will an elite select system-transforming reforms as the initial response to economic crisis.

The cases of Syria and Turkey suggest that the choice of reform strategy is sharply constrained by the earlier configuration of the political economy. In particular, the relative share of the public industrial sector in total manufacturing output seems to have been critical. In Syria, the bulk of industrial development had taken place in the public sector, and private businessmen were limited to small-scale industrial enterprises while concentrating their activities in the nontradables sector. Consequently, the regime had the option of making incremental reforms designed to mobilize private capital for the next round of industrial development. As the Syrian Minister of Foreign Trade and Economy Muhammad al-Imadi observed, the goal of economic liberalization was to mobilize "private sector money for investment in the productive sectors, for its own interest and in the interest of society."[2]

---

[2] Quoted in Volker Perthes, "The Syrian Economy in the 1980s," *Middle East Journal* 46 (Winter 1992), 49. From a more analytic perspective, Stephen Heydemann argues that economic reform in Syria "has taken the form of mobilizing the economic participation of sectors previously excluded from the regime's ruling coalition, notably the private commercial,

This option was not available to the Turkish elite. Turkish private businessmen had played a significant role in economic development through 1980. The participation of private capital had been dependent on high levels of state expenditure and subsidization. By 1980, not only had this arrangement produced unsatisfactory results, but also it was no longer sustainable. Therefore, economic reform had to be more fundamental than in Syria; it was not a matter of bringing private capital in, but of changing the terms on which private capital contributed to development, while reducing the burdens on the state.

Of course, the propensity toward risk aversion may in turn be tempered by other factors. An elite that is cognitively committed to orthodox economic policies, for example, may believe that system-maintaining reforms are simply not viable in even the short term and will therefore have no choice but to opt for the riskier strategy.[3] One could argue, for example, that Turgut Ozal, the chief architect of Turkish economic reform, was motivated by the understanding of neoliberal economics that he acquired during his tenure at the World Bank in the 1970s. This explanation, however, would have difficulty accounting for Ozal's shift toward more heterodox policies later in the decade in response to his declining electoral support, suggesting that ideas lose their causal powers when they clash with political exigencies.

Regime type more significantly affects risk aversion. As Adam Przeworski posits, the institutions of electoral competition lengthen the time horizons of political actors; in a democratic setting, political actors might more willingly assume the risks inherent in system-transforming reforms knowing that if they lose in the present, "the institutional framework that organizes the democratic competition will permit them to advance their interests in the future."[4] Turkey's return to democracy in 1983, following the military coup of September 1980, gave Ozal some latitude to experiment with more radical reforms demanded by the structure of the Turkish industrial sector. The Asad regime in Syria did not enjoy this luxury:

---

agricultural, and light manufacturing sectors, in order to generate the resources needed to satisfy the demands of politically important coalition members." See his "The Political Logic of Economic Rationality: Selective Stabilization in Syria," in *The Politics of Economic Reform in the Middle East*, ed. Henri Barkey (New York: St. Martin's Press, 1992), 19.

[3] In this example, beliefs take the form of what Goldstein and Keohane call causal beliefs, or "beliefs about cause-effect relationships which derive authority from the shared consensus of recognized elites. . . . Such causal beliefs provide guides for individuals on how to achieve their objectives." See Judith Goldstein and Robert O. Keohane, "Ideas and Foreign Policy: An Analytical Framework," in *Ideas and Foreign Policy: Beliefs, Institutions, and Political Change*, ed. Judith Goldstein and Robert O. Keohane (Ithaca: Cornell University Press, 1993), 10.

[4] Adam Przeworski, *Democracy and the Market: Political and Economic Reforms in Eastern Europe and Latin America* (Cambridge: Cambridge University Press, 1991), 19.

loss of coalition support threatened the stability of the regime, and the rules of the political game offered little hope of regaining office in a subsequent round of political competition. Furthermore, given the tight connection between state officials, party cadres, and regime incumbents, a far greater number of people were staking their political position, if not their physical well-being, on a less disruptive departure from the status quo. Thus, regime-level factors heightened a propensity to risk aversion that could be accommodated because a system-maintaining option was available.

Economic and Political Reforms in Turkey

In response to widespread political instability and polarization that derailed economic reform in early 1980, the Turkish military deposed the civilian government and established an authoritarian regime in September 1980. Under authoritarian rule, economic reform proceeded rapidly. The main architect of economic reform was Turgut Ozal, who served the military government as deputy prime minister in charge of economic affairs from September 1980 until mid-1982, returning to power as prime minister following the November 1983 general elections. Ozal promptly devalued the Turkish lira; unified multiple exchange rates; introduced export subsidies; and unleashed domestic market forces by raising the prices charged by Turkey's public sector, permitting individual public enterprises to set their own prices and prohibiting them from financing losses from government budgets. By ending an era of subsidized prices, these latter reforms removed a central pillar of patronage politics in Turkey. Post-1983 reforms continued the devaluation of the Turkish lira and began to dismantle the protectionist trade regime, reducing tariffs by an average of 20 percent while shrinking the list of goods requiring import licenses. Furthermore, new reforms reduced state control over the financial system by lowering legal reserve requirements and liquidity ratios, creating an interbank money market, authorizing the reopening of the Istanbul stock exchange, permitting banks to set interests rates, and allowing foreign banks to enter Turkish financial markets. By the end of the decade, Turkey had a relatively liberal financial system and had decisively shifted to ELG.[5]

---

[5] One study of Turkish reforms, for example, concluded that "the achievements of the Turkish program of trade liberalization and switching to an outer-oriented trade regime are remarkable by any standard. The Turkish economy has been restructured from being inward looking and insulated to an outward orientation. Exports have been a major engine of growth." Anne Krueger and Okan H. Aktan, *Swimming Against the Tide: Turkish Trade Reform in the 1980s* (San Francisco: Institute for Contemporary Studies, 1992), 2.

In 1984, the government turned to privatization of state economic enterprises, offering to the public revenue-sharing certificates in several
large infrastructural projects, which were quickly oversubscribed. In 1988,
in the first case of actual divestiture of state assets, the government sold
about half of its 40 percent holdings in a telecommunications company
to the general public. More than 40,000 local investors became shareholders. But the value of these stocks declined precipitously in the course
of 1988, dulling enthusiasm for further sales to the general public, and
privatization was largely postponed until the mid-1990s.[6] Liberalization
and structural adjustment were thus not unmitigated successes. In particular, the failure to either privatize or reform the public sector resulted in
continued deficits that were financed from government budgets, subject-
ing the economy to a large degree of macroeconomic instability.[7] Still, by
the end of the decade, liberalization had substantially transformed the
Turkish political economy, opening it to world markets and encouraging
exports. Turkey's effective exchange rate following the first devaluation
of 1980 was still 1.95, meaning that exchange rate bias favored import-
competing producers who earned on average 1.95 times the number of
liras per dollar as did exporters. By mid-decade, this bias had declined to
1.33, and by the end of the decade it approached parity at 1.08.[8]

The shift to ELG and other reforms constituted a decisive assault on
the privileges enjoyed by members of the old coalition. By 1986, the index of manufacturing wages, 100 in 1977, had declined to 74, while the
index of all wages declined to 54. The ratio of wages to value-added in
private-sector industry declined from 34 to 18 percent by 1986. As state
support for agricultural incomes was withdrawn, the index of agricultural
terms of trade plummeted from 100 in 1977 to under 47 by 1986. Prices
paid to farmers were cut and prices for basic food prices rose as the state
lifted price controls and ended subsidies that had compensated urban
consumers for prorural policies.[9] These dual cuts in the costs of inputs
made exporting more viable, particularly for textile firms.

[6] Ziya Onis "Privatization and the Logic of Coalition Building: A Comparative Analysis of
State Divestiture in Turkey and the United Kingdom," *Comparative Political Studies* 24 (July
1991), 246.
[7] As a share of GNP, public-sector borrowing had declined from a high of 10.5 percent
in 1980 to only 4.6 percent by mid-decade, but then reached a new high of 12.6 percent in
1991. Although the annual inflation rate did not return to its 1980 high of 107 percent, it
reached 68 percent by 1990. Ziya Onis, "The Political Economy of Export-Oriented Industrialization in Turkey," in *Turkey: Political, Social, and Economic Challenges in the 1990s*, ed. Cig-
dem Balim, et al. (Leiden: E. J. Brill, 1995), 119.
[8] Krueger and Aktan, *Swimming Against the Tide*, 91.
[9] Korkut Boratav, "Contradictions of 'Structural Adjustment': Capital and the State in
Post-1980 Turkey," in *Developmentalism and Beyond: Society and Politics in Egypt and Turkey*, ed.
Ayse Oncu, Caglar Keyder, and Saad Eddin Ibrahim (Cairo: American University in Cairo
Press, 1994), 162.

The return to electoral politics in 1983, however, pressed on Ozal the need to build a new coalition, albeit one that would not impinge on economic liberalization.[10] Ozal envisioned a new coalition in which urban middle classes supportive of his strategy of tighter integration into the global economy would supplant workers and farmers. At the same time, however, he could not secure the loyalty of new coalition members through patronage policies that might debilitate economic performance, for this would undermine the capacity of ELG trade policies to produce an export boom. Privatization appeared to provide an appropriate coalition-building formula: the state would shed public-sector firms draining the treasury and channel funds into state coffers by selling state assets to middle-class supporters. Moreover, because returns on private purchases of state assets rested on improved economic performance, new shareholders would support efforts to make newly privatized enterprises internationally competitive, including sustained repression of wages and rural incomes. Therefore, privatization promised to be the cornerstone of a new electoral coalition, while acting as a mechanism for reducing fiscal crises and macroeconomic instability and for creating public pressure on firms to enhance productivity.[11]

Between 1983 and 1987, however, electoral support for Ozal's Motherland Party declined. As the 1987 general elections approached, Ozal grasped that his electoral strategy, even when based on a broad notion of middle-class constituents, was simply incompatible with Turkish demographics. Realizing that garnering sufficient electoral support required the renewal of overtures to rural voters, the government transferred almost $2 billion to rural voters in the form of input subsidies and increased purchase prices in the months leading up to the 1987 elections. At the same time, price caps were placed on the output of state enterprises to win the support of middle-class voters. After the election, however, state enterprises were permitted large price increases, leading to a new burst of inflation in 1988.[12] Austerity measures taken to combat inflation led to a massive decline of share prices on the Istanbul stock exchange, particularly shares of the telecommunications firm that had been partially privatized early in 1988.[13] Ozal's inability to reconcile coalitional

---

[10] For an overview of Turkish democratization, see Ziya Onis and Steven B. Webb, "Turkey: Democratization and Adjustment from Above," in *Voting for Reform: Democracy, Political Liberalization, and Economic Adjustment*, ed. Stephan Haggard and Steven B. Webb (Oxford: Oxford University Press, 1994), 132–35.

[11] The best analysis of Ozal's electoral strategy is John Waterbury, "Export-led Growth and the Center-Right Coalition in Turkey," *Comparative Politics* 24 (January 1992): 127–145. See also Onis, "Privatization and the Logic of Coalition Building."

[12] Waterbury, "Export-Led Growth and the Center-Right Coalition in Turkey," 130–32.

[13] Onis "Privatization and the Logic of Coalition Building," 246–47.

logic with economic strategy did not signal the reversal of reform, but it did indicate that elements of precocious Keynesianism would have to be reincorporated. This had two implications. First, state spending increased through direct payoffs to constituents and through underwriting the deficits of state enterprises, both of which helped fuel inflation.[14] Second, privatization was removed from the political agenda for several years. Thus, the two most noticeable failures of Turkish economic reform resulted from the sacrifice of long-term economic goals to the imperatives of incumbency.

Institutional Reform in the 1980s

I have argued that the formation of large, cross-class coalitions precludes the construction of a developmental state. Moments of coalition reformulation, conversely, are potential windows of opportunity for state builders to reconfigure the institutions linking the state to economy and society. The destruction of the precocious Keynesian coalition, along with other measures introduced by the military regime that enhanced state autonomy, provided an opportunity for Ozal to emulate East Asian state institutions. Scholars such as John Waterbury have suggested that successful economic reform is predicated on the creation of one element of a developmental state: an autonomous bureaucracy, populated by technocrat "change teams" that are sufficiently insulated from political pressures to allow them to formulate and implement technically feasible reform programs.[15] Seizing the opportunity provided by altered political circumstances, Ozal created new bureaucratic agencies by recruiting a select group of technocrats from outside the ranks of the traditional bureaucracy. These new bureaucratic agencies were made responsible directly to the president or the prime minister to insulate them from pressures emanating from society, the traditional bureaucracy, or parliament.[16] Consequently, in the period 1980–1987, economic decision making in Turkey was largely depoliticized.[17] Furthermore, transformation of the logic of coalitional politics diluted incentives to substitute politically motivated

[14] Both public-sector borrowing and the rate of inflation accelerated after 1987. For figures, see footnote 7, above.

[15] John Waterbury, "The Heart of the Matter?: Public Enterprise and the Adjustment Process," in *The Politics of Economic Adjustment,* ed. Stephan Haggard and Robert R. Kaufman (Princeton: Princeton University Press, 1992), 191–92.

[16] Boratav, "Contradictions of 'Structural Adjustment'," 168; and Onis and Webb, "Turkey: Democratization and Adjustment from Above," 147–51.

[17] Sabri Sayari, "Politics and Economic Policy-Making in Turkey, 1980–1988," in *Economics and Politics of Turkish Liberalization,* ed. Tevfik F. Nas and Mehmet Odekon (Bethlehem, Pa.: Lehigh University Press, 1992), 32.

policies for economically efficient policies, and thus enhanced the potential for formulating long-term development policy. But this creation of an economic general staff within the political agencies of the state rather than in the bureaucratic apparatus constituted only a second-best solution to the task of creating an effective policy-making apparatus. The autonomy of the new technocrats rested precariously on Ozal's political fortunes, and effective policy making was possible only as long as the president and prime minister protected and supported the technocrats.[18] As soon as political exigencies dictated a return to patronage politics, technocrats had no institutional means of protecting their autonomy and exercising control over public policy.[19]

Transferring administrative guidance from East Asia to Turkey proved even more difficult.[20] In place of the tight collaboration between the state and the private sector characteristic of East Asian developmental states, Ozal's relations with the private sector were hostile and often antagonistic, despite his pro-business orientation. As early as 1982, leading businessmen mobilized to oppose policies they believed placed an unfair burden on their balance sheets, forcing the military leadership to remove Ozal from office. Antagonistic relations continued after Ozal was elected prime minister in 1983, and over the remainder of the decade Ozal regularly expressed his frustration at his inability to induce industrialists to give priority to exporting. Businessmen, for their part, continued to demand state protection and policies to ease the costs of adjustment.[21]

As I discussed in Chapters 5 and 8, recent contributions to the study of East Asian dynamism have presented strong evidence that at the core of administrative guidance lies state control over the financial system, which furnishes state elites with leverage over the investment decisions of economic actors. The failure of the Turkish state to achieve similar leverage in the 1980s was a function of its continued infirm control over financial markets. That control had been weak throughout the pre-1980 period; measures liberalizing financial markets in the 1980s gave the private sector even further control over the allocation of capital, permitting businessmen to ignore the wishes of state elites. Indeed, deregulation of credit markets, when combined with macroeconomic instability and heavy public sector borrowing, made traditional banking—deposit taking

---

[18] For a similar observation about bureaucratic autonomy in Brazil, see Barbara Geddes, "Building 'State' Autonomy in Brazil, 1930–1964." *Comparative Politics* 22 (January 1990), 233.

[19] Onis and Webb, "Turkey: Democratization and Adjustment from Above," 177.

[20] Ziya Onis, "Redemocratization and Economic Liberalization in Turkey: The Limits of State Autonomy," *Studies in Comparative International Development* 27 (1992), 16–18.

[21] Marcie Patton, "Constraints to Privatization in Turkey," in *Privatization and Liberalization in the Middle East*, ed. Iliya Harik and Denis J. Sullivan (Bloomington: Indiana University Press, 1992), 118–20.

and credit issuing—extremely risky and unprofitable. In response, banks turned to foreign exchange markets, where profits are high, and to purchasing government bonds.[22] Liberalization thus made the banking system even less amenable to development than it had been previously. An evocative illustration of the relative incapacity of the Turkish state to orient private economic activity through its control over the financial system emerged from an infamous meeting between Ozal and leading businessmen in which Ozal was urging businessmen to increase their investments. When asked where the resources for investment were to come from, he could do little more than respond "Sell your villas!"[23]

In summary, despite efforts to recast the Turkish state in the image of the East Asian developmental state, important elements of the model did not survive the journey to Ankara. Technocratic policy making remains elusive, as politicians continue to address their coalitional concerns by intervening in policy making, and the state has only minimal influence over the investment decisions of private entrepreneurs. Turkish state elites made great strides toward achieving ELG trade policies in the 1980s, but they failed to construct a developmental state.

The Developmental Outcome of Turkish Liberalization

Despite the shortcomings of Turkish economic reform detailed above, the increase in exports that followed liberalization fueled economic recovery from the stagnation of the late 1970s. Averaging about 6 percent of gross national product (GNP) in the 1970s, exports increased to 21.5 percent of GNP in 1985.[24] In real terms, exports increased from just under $3 billion in 1980 to well over $11 billion in 1989. Furthermore, the

---

[22] As Ayse Oncu and Deniz Gokce explain, "This strategy of frequent re-adjustments in fixed rates has dramatically narrowed the profit margins of traditional commercial banks in credit operations. Higher deposit rates have increased the cost of loanable funds. So banks have found that unless they sacrificed their profit margins, or took on the risk of non-performing loans, they had to remain confined to a very narrow base of sound credit customers. Inevitably, commercial banks have been squeezed at both ends, and they have had to reduce their profit margins. Nonetheless, their potential pool of sound interest customers, that is, enterprises able to bear the high credit costs without the risk of non-performing loans, has been steadily decreasing in number." See their "Macro-Politics of De-Regulation and Micro-Politics of Banks," in *Strong State and Economic Interest Groups: The Post-1980 Turkish Experience*, ed. Metin Heper (Berlin: Walter de Gruyter, 1991), 114–15.

[23] Osman Ulugay, *Kim Kazandi Kim Kaybetti Ozal Ekonomisinde Paramiz Pul Olurken* (Ankara: Bilgi Yayinevi, 1987), 181. Onis, "Redemocratization and Economic Liberalization in Turkey," 18, also points to Turkey's ongoing budget deficits and financial weakness as rendering state-business relations more antagonistic.

[24] Dani Rodrik, "External Debt and Economic Performance in Turkey," in *Liberalization and the Turkish Economy*, ed. Tevfik F. Nas and Mehmet Odekon (New York: Greenwood Press, 1988), 168.

share of industrial goods in total exports increased from 36 percent in 1980 to 79 percent in 1989, while the share of agricultural products in total exports decreased from 57 to 18 percent during the same period.[25] While textiles and clothing continued to be the largest manufactured export item, making up over 40 percent of all exports in 1989, the chemicals industry, which increased its exports from $76 million in 1980 to $774 million in 1989, and the iron and steel industry, whose exports grew from $34 million to $1.3 billion during the same period, both recorded significant increases.[26] As Dani Rodrik writes, "The export boom in this period has been rather miraculous for a country long steeped in the traditions of export pessimism."[27] Consequently, annual growth in gross domestic product (GDP) averaged 4.9 percent for the period 1981–1991.

By some accounts, these numbers conceal more than they reveal. Critics of Turkish economic policy underscore two factors accounting for the rise in exports: fictitious exports, designed to capture rents from export subsidies, and the Iran-Iraq war, which allowed Turkish manufacturers to dump surplus capacity in regional markets cut off from global trade, or to reexport European goods after minimal processing.[28] Indeed, one econometric analysis of the period 1979–1984 found that fictitious exports accounted for 21 percent of total exports while the special circumstances of the Iran-Iraq war accounted for 42 percent of real exports. But an additional 35 percent of real exports stemmed from real currency depreciation, and 10 percent of exports met the increased demand of industrial countries for Turkish goods.[29] Furthermore, the export boom outlasted the Iran-Iraq war, rising to $13.6 billion in 1991 with little evidence of continued fictitious exports.

Although Turkey improved its export performance, it measures less well on other dimensions of development: the creation of linkages, changes in production processes enhancing productivity and quality, and movement up the product cycle into higher value-added activities. In contrast to ELG in East Asia, which entailed movement into capital intensive and high-tech industries, steady efficiency gains through changes in shop-floor practices, successful assimilation of new technology, and some prod-

[25] Anne O. Krueger and Ilter Turan, "The Politics and Economics of Turkish Policy Reforms in the 1980s," in *Political and Economic Interactions in Economic Policy Reform*, ed. Robert Bates and Anne O. Krueger (London: Basil Blackwell, 1993), 371.

[26] Krueger and Aktan, *Swimming Against the Tide*, 152.

[27] Rodrik, "External Debt and Economic Performance in Turkey," 175.

[28] Rodrik, "External Debt and Economic Performance in Turkey," 176–79; Henri J. Barkey, "The Silent Victor: Turkey's Role in the Gulf War," in *The Iran-Iraq War: Impact and Implications*, ed. Efraim Karsh (New York: St. Martin's Press, 1988), 133–53; and Halis Akder, "Turkey's Export Expansion in the Middle East, 1980–1985," *Middle East Journal* 41 (1987): 553–67.

[29] Rodrik, "External Debt and Economic Performance in Turkey," 178–80.

uct innovation, Turkey's boom has been based on the production for export of goods that were produced before 1980, using the same level of technology and without major reorganization of the production process. Turkish industrialists are aware that their competitive advantage cannot rest indefinitely on cheap labor and existing plants and that new technologies must be incorporated into the production process. But few firms have made a full commitment to technological upgrading, relying instead on what Duruiz and Yenturk call "selective automation."[30] Here, introduction of new technologies is largely a piecemeal process of replacing obsolete machinery and not an effort to completely overhaul the production process to create systematic improvements in productivity and quality.[31] Turkish textile firms, for example, have increased exports by relying on cheap labor, not by upgrading their increasingly obsolete technological capacity.[32] Even when new technologies are selectively introduced, they are not fully exploited due to critical shortfalls in engineering and management skills. Few Turkish firms have recognized the need for "soft" organizational innovations to accompany the introduction of "hard" technologies. Thus, shop-floor innovations that rendered East Asian firms world-class producers are conspicuous by their absence in Turkey.

To be sure, part of the problem is the effect of macroeconomic instability on investment. As a share of GNP, investment dropped from an annual average of 31 percent between 1975 and 1980, to an annual average of 24 percent between 1981 and 1988. The annual average of private investment dropped at an even faster rate, from 14.2 percent between 1975 and 1980 to 10 percent in the period 1981–1988.[33] These trends in levels of investment suggest that macroeconomic instability remains the Achilles' heel of Turkish development, deterring businessmen from making investments. Note, however, that public and private investment reached their lowest levels in the early 1980s, when the rate of inflation slowed from 104 percent in 1980 to 28 percent in 1983; in the latter half of the decade, investment levels rose along with the rate of inflation, albeit at a slower pace. Note furthermore that despite reduced levels of investment, Turkey's average annual investment rate in the 1980s was only marginally inferior to that of Korea and Taiwan in the 15 years following their transition to ELG. In Taiwan, while inflation averaged only 8 per-

---

[30] Lale Duruiz and Nurhan Yenturk, *Facing the Challenge: Turkish Automobile, Steel, and Clothing Industries' Responses to the Post-Fordist Restructuring* (Istanbul: n.p., 1992), draw on firm-level studies of the clothing, iron and steel, and automobile industries to reach this conclusion.

[31] Korkut Boratav and Ergun Turkcan, *Turkiye'de Sanayilesmenin Yeni Boyutlari ve KIT'ler* (Istanbul: Tarih Vakfi Yurt Yayinlari, 1993).

[32] Ibid., 129–30.

[33] Krueger and Aktan, *Swimming Against the Tide*, 188.

cent between 1965 and 1980, investment averaged 28 percent of GNP.[34] In Korea, the rate of investment averaged 23 percent of GNP between 1965 and 1977, a level lower than that of Turkey in the 1980s. Korean investment jumped in the last three years of the 1970s to over 30 percent annually, yielding a 15-year annual average of 25 percent, only slightly higher than the Turkish level in the 1980s.[35] Interestingly, Korean investment at the end of the 1970s increased as the rate of inflation was also increasing, from an annual average of 17 percent between 1967 and 1977 to an annual average of 23 percent between 1978 and 1980.[36] Thus, if inflation and its inhibiting effect on investment were necessary and sufficient explanatory factors, Korean investment should have declined rather than increased as inflation rose, should have been markedly lower than Taiwanese investment, and should have been markedly higher than Turkish investment. Indeed, by all accounts, the decline in Turkish investment levels in the 1980s was accompanied by economic performance far superior to that of the higher-investment 1970s. Neither decreased investment nor increased inflation—whatever their relationship to one another—fully explain Turkish economic performance in the 1980s.

Still, a further problem is that Turkish investors altered the sectoral composition of their investments from traded to nontraded sectors, perhaps in response to macroeconomic instability. While investment in manufacturing increased by an annual average of only 2.6 percent between 1980 and 1989, the growth rates of investment in tourism and housing in the same period were 34 and 9.9 percent, respectively. Consequently, the share of manufacturing in total investment dropped from 14.6 to 12.1 percent in this period, while tourism increased from 0.3 to 3.6 percent and housing from 16.2 to 28.6 percent.[37] But again, relatively high rates of inflation in Korea did not impede concentrated investments in manufacturing. Instead, a comparison of the politics of finance in Korea, Taiwan, and Turkey strongly supports the position that it is not inflation levels but the nature of the financial system, especially the role of the state, that critically determines the level and allocation of investment.

As I have argued, other aspects of development are less sensitive to investment levels. One benefit of the Turkish export boom is that it has allowed Turkish firms to operate at higher levels of capacity utilization. Thus, one analysis argues that the Turkish export boom is largely based

[34] Robert Wade, *Governing the Market: Economic Theory and the Role of Government in East Asian Industrialization* (Princeton: Princeton University Press, 1990), 42, 47.

[35] Alice H. Amsden, *Asia's Next Giant: South Korea and Late Industrialization* (New York: Oxford University Press, 1989), 75.

[36] Ibid., 56.

[37] Krueger and Aktan, *Swimming Against the Tide,* 182.

on increased capacity utilization, which, as we have seen, was quite low throughout the 1970s.[38] But even as Turkish firms produce at closer to installed capacity, they are often unable to achieve technical economies of scale due to prevailing market structures. As discussed in Chapter 8, in the Turkish automobile sector, 15 plants were in operation in 1976, with average output remaining under 10,000 units, well below minimum economies of scale. By 1990, the number of plants had decreased to 11, but the average production of each firm was under 22,000 units, still well below minimum economies of scale.[39] In contrast, between 1976 and 1990, the average output of five Korean plants increased from under 10,000 cars to over 264,000 units. Between 1975 and 1990, when Korean average capacity utilization was increasing from 18 to almost 60 percent, Turkish capacity utilization was decreasing from 68 to 48 percent. Consequently, as Korean automobiles penetrate global markets, Turkish automobiles sell in domestic markets at almost three times the price of an equivalent car in European markets.[40] Indeed, the absence of scale economies is one main reason automobile firms give for the failure to upgrade their technological base.[41] Not only equipment, but also products remain outdated; Turkey remains mired at the bottom end of the product cycle, producing goods such as the Renault models 12 and 21, which are obsolete in Europe.[42] Moreover, the recent burst of foreign direct investment in the Turkish automobile industry is not designed to incorporate Turkish firms into global commodity chains producing finished goods for European markets. Instead, transnational corporations began to invest in Turkish automobile production to gain a foothold in less competitive markets in Central Asia and the Middle East, not to reexport to markets in advanced industrial economies.

Turkish economic performance can be taken to confirm neoliberal analysis that regards market liberalization and exporting as the main determinants of growth. This conclusion, however, is linked to our measurement of success. Neoliberals measure success by growth in GDP. But our understanding of development must stretch to include other critical

---

[38] Duruiz and Yenturk, *Facing the Challenge*, 44. Krueger and Aktan, *Swimming Against the Tide*, 174, claim that increased output in the absence of new investments "attests to the increases in economic efficiency that *may* have resulted from the policy reforms of the early 1980s." Italics added. In the absence of any evidence of increased efficiency, it seems clear that increased output was instead a function of increased capacity utilization.

[39] Consequently, the annual unit output of Turkish workers was less than 25 percent of that of German workers and less than 20 percent of that of Japanese workers. Boratav and Turkcan, *Turkiye'de Sanayilesmenin Yeni Boyutlari*, 160.

[40] Mine Sadiye Eder, "Crises of Late Industrialization: A Comparative Study of the Automotive Industry in Brazil, South Korea, and Turkey," Ph.D. Dissertation, University of Virginia, 1993, 161, 305.

[41] Ibid., 306.

[42] Ibid., 307.

changes in the economic structure. This more expansive conceptualization of development forces us to downgrade our assessment of Turkish economic performance and to revise our evaluation of neoliberal prescriptions. Indeed, the Turkish case suggests that, at best, ELG is a necessary but not sufficient condition for rapid development. In the absence of a developmental state, Turkish economic performance improved but did not match East Asian development. To be sure, the persistence of macroeconomic instability and the absence of privatization mean that Turkey departs from neoliberal recipes for success. Neoliberals, however, claim Turkey as a success story.[43] If Turkey can be considered as vindication of neoliberal prescriptions despite its reform failures, then it can also be used to question the sufficiency of those prescriptions.

Incremental Reform in Syria

Syrian elites evinced significant ambivalence in their approach to economic reform. On the one hand, they consistently implemented liberalizing policies, prompting one scholar to conclude that by 1990 Syria had fulfilled an economic stabilization program of the type prescribed by the International Monetary Fund without entering into a formal agreement with it.[44] On the other hand, the regime deployed sufficient antibusiness measures to lead other scholars to conclude that Syria retained its socialist and statist orientation.[45]

We can partially reconcile these two interpretations by focusing on the interplay of economic calculations and coalition strategies. Deteriorating economic circumstances and the unreliability of future capital inflows forced the regime to give greater concern to improving economic performance. But Syria's leaders' reliance on broad social support during the Islamist revolt convinced them of the need to secure their incumbency by maintaining a broad-based coalition. The regime confronted these conflicting imperatives by incrementally liberalizing without fundamentally dislodging the state from its commanding role in the economy or eradicating constituency clientelism. The goal of liberalization was to open space for expanded private-sector activity that would provide resources for renewed economic growth. But by 1980, it was clear to the Syrian leadership that the side-payments made to coalition members had vastly overextended the fiscal and administrative capacity of the state. The en-

---

[43] See footnote 5 for Anne Kruger's assessment of Turkish economic performance in the 1980s.
[44] Heydeman, "Political Logic of Economic Rationality," 17.
[45] Patrick Clawson, *Unaffordable Ambitions: Syria's Military Build-Up and Economic Crisis* (Washington, D.C.: The Washington Institute for Near East Policy, 1989).

suing economic crisis was severe enough to threaten the political stability of the regime. Their immediate objective was to prune side-payments far enough to inject elements of rational practices into the economy, but not so far as to result in the disintegration of the regime. Syria's leaders, in other words, sought to retain their broad coalitional base while minimizing side-payments.

Elites minimize side-payments in three ways: First, the elite can reduce membership in the coalition either by dropping one class of members or by shedding membership from each class. Second, the elite can trim the size of side-payments by cutting subsidies or allowing wages to lag behind inflation. Finding the minimal level of side-payments that will reconcile political stability and economic performance is tricky; uncertainty over how deeply subsidies could safely be cut perhaps best explains the hesitant nature of Syrian economic reforms.[46] Finally, efforts to link privilege to performance allow the regime to maintain its coalitional base while discouraging suboptimal economic behavior and encouraging efficient economic practices.

Beginning in 1981, Syrian political leaders and economic managers responded to the growing crisis of the Syrian economy with pragmatic measures recasting the character of state economic intervention.[47] Before mid-decade, these measures included inflation-taming austerity budgets and a partial floating of the Syrian pound, designed to encourage exports and worker remittances. These measures were motivated by the need to economize on scarce foreign exchange, not by ideological commitments to liberalization. Liberalizing measures were thus adopted slowly and were accompanied by distinctly illiberal measures that economized scarce foreign exchange by increasing state regulation of private-sector foreign trade.

Both the pace and the tenor of reform changed in early 1985. At the Eighth Regional Congress of the ruling Ba'th Party, convened in January 1985, the regime and party congress engaged in raucous debate over the course of economic reform, pitting partisans of the public sector who urged the party to "stay the course" of the transformation from a capitalist to a socialist society, against advocates of recharged reform, who called for an acceleration of change toward a capitalist society.[48] Although the pro-

---

[46] There is no precise metric for calculating the critical balance between payoffs and austerity; the problem is exacerbated as the requisite amount surely changes, perhaps drastically, over time. The uncertainty over what level of withdrawal from prior commitments is politically acceptable explains why the regime adopted an incrementalist approach to reform, and why it countered cutbacks in subsidy levels with wages hikes. As William Riker, *The Theory of Political Coalitions* (New Haven: Yale University Press, 1962), 77–78, writes, "The uncertainty of the real world and the bargaining situation forces coalition members to aim at a subjectively estimated minimum winning coalition rather than an actual minimum."

[47] For assessments that Syria's approach was pragmatic, see *Middle East Economic Digest (MEED)*, May 22, 1981, 38; and *MEED*, May 7, 1982, 20–22.

[48] Yahya Sadowski, "Cadres, Guns, and Money: The Eighth Regional Congress of the Syrian Ba'th," *MERIP Reports* 15 (July/August 1985), 6.

public-sector lobby pushed for the revitalization of state control, the majority of delegates voiced approval of the regime's efforts to cultivate private-sector investment to compensate for the failure of the public sector to rally the country's productive forces. By obtaining the support of local party cadres for the acceleration of economic reforms begun in the period 1981 to 1985, the Asad regime was able to state publicly what had been regime policy for the first half of the decade: a decision to encourage the private sector to enhance and extend its productive role in the economy. The final communiqué of the congress recommended encouraging the private sector to invest in productive sectors, as defined in the budget and five-year plan. But while the communiqué criticized the poor performance of the public sector, it stopped well short of advocating privatization.[49]

The post-1985 strategy of economic reform assigned continued control over large-scale industrial activity to the public sector.[50] The regime also renegotiated its relationship with private capitalists, encouraging them to supplement investments in traditional areas of importing, real estate, and tourism with industrial investments. Subsequent measures granted the private sector greater latitude to import goods and easier access to foreign exchange. At the same time, the regime encouraged exports by devaluing the currency and allowing exporters to retain the majority of their hard currency to finance future imports. Further reforms created new joint-stock companies in agriculture and tourism, in which the state owned 25 percent of equity. Among the privileges granted to these companies were exemptions from trade restrictions and several taxes as well as greater access to and control over foreign exchange.[51] In late 1989, mixed companies were permitted to convert hard currency at the higher, parallel market rate instead of at the official incentive rate.[52] Although these liberalizing measures benefited the private sector, they provided few incentives for private industrialization.

The regime made it clear that it would continue its commitment to precocious Keynesianism, but fiscal constraints curtailed the state's generosity. Budgetary allocations for consumer subsidies were reduced, while prices of subsidized commodities rose throughout the 1980s.[53] Employ-

---

[49] *MEED*, February 1, 1985, 37. Subsequent statements and actions made it clear, however, that the private sector was not being given carte blanche to enrich itself at the expense of the state. Numerous public condemnations of the "parasitic" bourgeoisie, coupled with harsh crackdowns on illegal money changers, indicated that the regime expected the private sector to play a truly productive role in the economy and to do so by following the parameters set by the state.

[50] Volker Perthes, citing the Minister of Industry, Antun Jibran, in "The Syrian Economy in the 1980s," 49.

[51] *MEED*, November 16, 1985.

[52] *MEED*, September 29, 1989.

[53] In one standard ploy, a new "higher quality" bread whose price was not subsidized was introduced; over the next six months, the lower quality, subsidized bread was made less

ment in the public industrial sector was reduced from 141,000 workers in 1985 to 139,000 in 1989, and employment in public-sector construction fell from 155,000 to 138,000 workers.[54] A moratorium was placed on hiring recent college graduates by the civil service, and salaries and wages of public employees were allowed to lag well behind inflation. Furthermore, the regime experimented with disciplining its constituencies by linking payoffs to performance. In public-sector industries, a merit-based wage system was introduced that relied on production incentives.[55] Agricultural spending was dedicated toward increasing rural productivity, not redistributing income from urban to rural constituents. Prices for selected agricultural products were raised in an effort to induce peasants to increase production of goods needed in the industrial sector.[56] Finally, the Syrians linked payoffs to performance by encouraging exports. Reforms of the foreign exchange regime encouraged private businessmen to export, while public-sector firms were given the incentive to "dump" their products on foreign markets, that is, sell them at below cost, with the government subsidizing these losses in local currency.[57] These measures reveal the obsession of state managers with the foreign currency crisis.

By 1990, however, Syria's strategy of incremental reform had yielded only marginal economic benefits. Private economic activity expanded but made relatively insignificant contributions to economic development or to solving the state's fiscal crisis. Indeed, the chambers of commerce admitted that a substantial portion of expanded private exports were dumped in foreign markets solely for the purpose of gaining access to foreign currency, which could then be used to finance imports of luxury goods. Furthermore, there is no evidence of increased private investments in the industrial sector through the end of the decade. Indeed, it appears that Syria's foreign exchange crisis was alleviated only by increased oil exploration, production, and exports, resulting in balance-of-trade surpluses after 1988. Despite this mini-boom, real GDP at the end of the 1980s was barely above its level of 1980; given a population growth

---

available. See American Embassy, Damascus, "Foreign Economic Trends and Their Implications for the United States," October 1989, 7. Official discourse continues to proclaim the regime's ongoing commitment to the material well-being of Syrians, as expressed, for example, in an editorial in the March 24, 1993, issue of *al-Ba'th*, the party newspaper, titled "The Protection of the Consumer is the Role of the Public Sector."

[54] Figures from Perthes, "The Syrian Economy in the 1980s," 44. This absolute reduction might seem minimal, but given Syria's stupendous rate of population growth, even a slowdown in the rate of growth of public-sector employment would have significant repercussions for the labor force.

[55] Ibid., 45.

[56] The price paid for cotton, which had lagged during the 1970s, was raised in an effort to increase production of an increasingly important export crop that substituted for oil as a major export item in the mid-1980s. Prices paid for sugar beets were also increased.

[57] Perthes, "The Syrian Economy in the 1980s," 46.

rate of 3.7 percent annually, per capita income must have dramatically fallen over the decade.[58]

The Syrian economy did expand rapidly in the early 1990s, for the most part due to traditional means: massive capital inflows. As a reward for participating in the American-led coalition against Iraq, Syria received an estimated $2 billion in the immediate postwar period.[59] Added to the increase in oil exports, this windfall guaranteed that Syria's current account was well into the black, and with foreign exchange reserves at an all-time high, the regime even began to pay back its international debt that had been in arrears.[60] But this relaxation of the foreign exchange crisis did not dull the regime's appetite for reform. Not only were earlier reforms not reversed, but also the scope of new reforms went well beyond earlier measures.

The most important new measure designed to coax the private sector into boosting its manufacturing operations was Law 10 of May 1991, which contained a series of incentives for private industrialists/exporters: on approval of their projects, they were exempt from customs duties on imports of machinery, equipment, and vehicles; they received seven-year tax exemptions and permission to hold foreign currency accounts with the Commercial Bank; and they were permitted to repatriate foreign capital after five years. The regime also created a higher council for investment, headed by the prime minister, to oversee investments and streamline operations.[61] In return for these incentives, the regime expected eligible projects to develop national production, provide jobs, increase exports while reducing imports, and use modern technology.[62] Furthermore, determined not to squander its new-found wealth, the regime tied capital inflows to specific, mostly infrastructural, projects, such as new telephone lines, electricity-generating plants, new wastewater systems for major cities, extension of oil and gas exploration, and a number of heavy industry projects expanding production of steel, fertilizers, and cement.[63] In short, the regime determined to use capital inflows to complement and support private investment, not displace it.

The continuation of reform after 1990 raises a question: If it is correct that the opening to private capital was a response to shortages of foreign

[58] According to one estimate, the price index increased by 579 percent between 1980 and 1989, while GDP in current prices increased only by 392 percent. *MEED*, February 1, 1991, 22.

[59] *MEED*, August 30, 1991, 29.

[60] By 1991, daily production was 480,000 barrels, three times the 1984 level.

[61] In contrast to earlier laws concerning mixed-sector companies, Law 10 of 1991 did not stipulate partial state ownership of new enterprises. In addition, the new law specifically called on private investors to move out of the fields of agriculture and tourism and into industry.

[62] *MEED*, May 17, 1991, 22. The full text of Law 10 is available in *al-Hayat*, May 13, 1991.

[63] For a full list, see *MEED*, June 4, 1993.

exchange, why didn't the regime retreat from this policy as the economic crisis eased? Although the regime could reverse the economic liberalization of the 1980s, it has no reason to do so. Reversal of liberalization would only mean returning to the clearly unsustainable pattern of the 1970s, whereas continuation of the reforms promises to foster economic development while not substantially altering the regime's monopoly of political power. As I have argued, positions on pragmatic issues relating to efficiency often reflect intellectual constructs that are highly amenable to empirical confirmation, not deeply held value commitments. Insofar as pragmatic issues do not undermine political stability, political elites should adhere to measures promising to improve economic performance.

Slouching toward the Millennium

Syria and Turkey made concerted efforts to break with their precocious Keynesian paths and to forge new political-economic orders that would promote rather than deter development. Neither country has successfully done so; rather, they have crafted hybrid systems, combining elements of precocious Keynesianism with measures designed to tame its most deleterious consequences. Turkey's political leaders have maintained their commitment to further liberalization and structural adjustment; successive governments throughout the 1990s have issued ambitious agendas of privatization, rapid growth, and further integration with the global economy. Unfortunately, Turkey's weak coalition governments rapidly succeed one another, and no government has enjoyed the political mandate and secure incumbency needed to push through painful reforms. Privatization has yet to diminish the size of the public sector, whose continued deficits and borrowing requirements still produce budget deficits, fuel inflation, and drive down the value of the currency, while Turkey's foreign debt, which amounted to just under $80 billion in 1996, has led international agencies to downgrade its credit rating. Exports have continued to grow, reaching over $23 billion in 1996, without, however, surpassing imports, which reached just under $42 billion in 1996.[64] On the bright side, Turkish firms have taken advantage of the state's incapacity to resolve Kaldorian collective dilemmas: automobile-sector exports of spare parts for discontinued European models like the Renault 12 and the Fiat Tempra, which are now produced only in Turkey, amounted to over $400

[64] Turkey's partial return to precocious Keynesianism was consistent with ELG because side-payments were reduced so drastically between 1980 and 1988, because of increased capital intensity, because of export subsidies, and because floating the local currency partially decoupled domestic inflation from world-market prices. In addition, by the late 1980s, light industrial sectors played a diminished role in overall industrial output.

million in the first half of 1995.[65] Overall, annual GDP growth has fluctuated wildly, from negative or no growth in some years to almost 10
percent growth rates in others. There is little reason to expect vastly improved macroeconomic performance, let alone microeconomic performance, until a future Turkish government establishes a stable coalitional
base for economic reform.

While Turkish governments lack the political capacity to realize their
economic visions, the Syrian regime has ceased experimenting with economic reform, although without returning to pre-1980 arrangements.[66]
Since 1991, one of the few new reform measures was a 1995 decree authorizing Syrians to use credit cards. More recently, the regime came to
an agreement with the World Bank to make a large payment on its debt
arrears accumulated since 1990. Meanwhile, inflows of foreign capital by
the mid-1990s were extremely low, many private investment projects approved under Law 10 of 1991 were in the service sector, and fewer than
50 percent of approved projects had been completed by late 1997. The
regime appears reluctant to pursue the ancillary measures needed to further boost private investment, such as reform of the financial sector. Economic growth in the 1990s has been fueled by oil exports, which also allow Syria to cover its import bill, but production has peaked at 600,000
barrels a day and is projected to decline steadily. Consequently, after six
years of steady growth averaging 5 percent annually, the 1997 rate is projected to be 1 percent.[67]

[65] *MEED*, July 14, 1995, 13.

[66] There is insufficient evidence to assess whether the slowdown of reforms is a result of
ideological intransigence, fears of political instability, or because President Asad devotes his
time to the also-stalled peace process with Israel.

[67] *MEED*, September 5, 1997, 4–5.

CHAPTER TEN

Theory and Method Reconsidered

Economic development outcomes are best explained by tracing the extended causal chain linking levels of elite conflict to the formation of states with differential capacities to resolve the collective dilemmas inherent in development. Given the existence of numerous rival hypotheses accounting for economic outcomes, how much confidence can we have in this argument, and on what grounds? In Chapter 1, I used John Stuart Mill's comparative methods to provide a provisional defense of my hypothesis. For reasons discussed below, Mill's methods provide insufficient warrant for accepting my argument. Many scholars recommend scrapping Mill's methods and replacing them with causal process tracing. But process tracing is also insufficient to confirm most arguments. Instead, I explore below some ways in which these two methods complement one another to provide more compelling arguments.

The research design presented in Chapter 1 listed the variables with clear theoretical relevance that, because they took on different values in the cases of Syria and Turkey, were provisionally eliminated as candidates for inclusion in an adequate explanation of similar economic outcomes: regime type, property regime, elite ideologies, level of external military threat, share of military spending in gross national product (GNP), absolute value of foreign direct investment, source of technology, politicization of ethnic cleavages, access to oil rents, history of colonial rule, and popular-sector mobilization before state transformation. Moreover, including Korea and Taiwan in the research design demonstrates that none of these variables covary systematically with the dependent variable: for each variable, either Syria or Turkey represented the same value as either Korea or Taiwan, or both. Finally, in subsequent chapters, I demonstrated that levels of elite conflict covaried with the dependent variable. To what extent does this research design provide confirmation for my argument?

Unfortunately, there are excellent reasons for considering the methods first presented by John Stuart Mill inappropriate for use in the social sciences to either discover or test and confirm hypotheses.[1] First, Mill's methods either discover or confirm hypotheses only if all potential variables have been incorporated into the research design. But because the content of the set of all candidate hypotheses can never be ascertained with any certainty, this condition must be violated, rendering the methods fallacious for discovery or confirmation. Mill's methods might retain value, however, as a means to *eliminate* rival hypotheses, on the grounds that, with reference to the Method of Agreement, "*Nothing can be the cause of a phenomenon which is not a common circumstance in all the instances of the phenomenon.*" Alternatively, with reference to the Method of Difference, "*Nothing can be the cause of a phenomenon if the phenomenon does not take place when the supposed cause does.*"[2] Given that philosophers of science provide strong grounds for believing that strict confirmation is logically impossible, a central element of our explanatory strategy must be to disconfirm or falsify rival hypotheses.[3] Testing hypotheses against the most powerful rivals increases confidence in their credibility, though without actually confirming them.[4]

But even this limited, eliminationist function of Mill's methods is subject to powerful critiques. Rival hypotheses can be rejected only if their causal effect is nonprobabilistic, if there are no interaction effects, and if there are no multiple causes of phenomena.[5] Given that they are designed to demonstrate perfect covariation between one and only one cause and its effect, valid use of Mill's methods assumes monocausal, de-

---

[1] Indeed, even John Stuart Mill rejected the application of his methods to the study of politics and history. See his, *A System of Logic, Ratiocinative and Inductive,* 8th ed. (New York: Harper & Brothers, 1884), 324. See also Morris R. Cohen and Ernest Nagel, *An Introduction to Logic and Scientific Method* (New York: Harcourt, Brace & World, 1934), 251–61; and Stanley Lieberson, "Small N's and Big Conclusions: An Examination of the Reasoning in Comparative Studies Based on a Small Number of Cases," in *What Is a Case? Exploring the Foundations of Social Inquiry,* ed. Charles C. Ragin and Howard S. Becker (Cambridge: Cambridge University Press, 1992), 105–18.

[2] Cohen and Nagel, *Introduction to Logic and Scientific Method,* 255, 259, italics in original. For a similar interpretation of the value of Mill's methods, see Jukka Savolainen, "The Rationality of Drawing Big Conclusions Based on Small Methods: In Defense of Mill's Methods," *Social Forces* 72 (June 1994), 1218–19.

[3] The falsificationist position is stated most forcefully in Karl Popper, *The Logic of Scientific Discovery* (London: Hutchinson, 1959). For a concise introduction to the issues, see Russell Keat and John Urry, *Social Theory as Science* (London: Routledge & Kegan Paul, 1975), 15–16.

[4] Arthur L. Stinchcombe, *Constructing Social Theories* (Chicago: University of Chicago Press, 1968), 17–28.

[5] Lieberson, "Small N's and Big Conclusions," and idem., "More on the Uneasy Case of Using Mill-Type Methods in Small-N Comparative Studies," *Social Forces* 72 (June 1994): 1225–37. Note that although arguments about selection bias impeach the credibility of Mill's Methods of Agreement while endorsing his Method of Difference, arguments about the nature of causal effects force us to consider discarding *both* methods.

terministic arguments, allowing us to reject as a cause any variable that did not correlate perfectly with the outcome. But this assumption is arguably indefensible; it is, after all, quite easy to construct scenarios in which this assumption yields absurd conclusions. More strongly, many authors insist that we live in a probabilistic world and so reject even the possibility of deterministic causes, meaning that rival hypotheses cannot be eliminated through Mill's methods, nor would a deterministic hypothesis be warranted in even an ideal research design.[6] Moreover, both observed phenomena and constructed examples amply demonstrate the role of interaction effects, whereby the value of one variable influences the causal effect of another, and of multiple causes of similar effects in different contexts. By assuming without warrant the existence of singular deterministic causes and by denying the existence of interaction effects, Mill's methods may yield inconclusive or even fallacious results.[7] Finally, Mill's methods provide no grounds for discriminating between multiple variables that perfectly covary with the dependent variable. In my four cases, in addition to levels of elite conflict, religion covaries with the dependent variable: the majority of the inhabitants of Syria and Turkey are Muslims, whereas large numbers of Koreans and Taiwanese continue to be influenced by Confucian cultural values. Insofar as we accept Max Weber's contention that, given certain material conditions, Protestantism played a central psychological role in the development of capitalism, as well as some version of the argument that Confucianism acts as a functional substitute for Protestantism, we have a competing explanation.[8] Although there are good reasons to reject this hypothesis, the research design itself can neither eliminate nor sustain it.[9] Similarly, while a Japanese colonial

[6] For various statements of this position, see Paul Humphreys, *The Chances of Explanation: Causal Explanation in the Social, Medical, and Physical Sciences* (Princeton: Princeton University Press, 1989); John H. Goldthorpe, "Current Issues in Comparative Macrosociology: A Debate on Methodological Issues," *Comparative Social Research,* 16 (1997): 1–26; and Gary King, Robert O. Keohane, and Sidney Verba, *Designing Social Inquiry: Scientific Inference in Qualitative Research* (Princeton: Princeton University Press, 1994), 55.

[7] Lieberson, "Small N's and Big Conclusions," 109–14.

[8] Max Weber, *The Protestant Ethic and the Spirit of Capitalism* (New York: Charles Scribner's Sons, 1958). For a sensible discussion of the Confucianism thesis, see Winston Davis, "Religion and Development: Weber and the East Asian Experience," in *Understanding Political Development,* ed. Myron Weiner and Samuel P. Huntington (Prospect Heights, Ill.: Waveland Press, 1987), 221–280.

[9] Ernest Gellner, *Muslim Society* (Cambridge: Cambridge University Press, 1981), 6–7, for example, argues that "Muslim burghers too should have felt impelled to accumulate in an endless effort to persuade themselves that they were the Elect of God." Gellner's contention thus supports an institutionalist perspective. Alternatively, we could note the frequency with which an earlier generation of scholars explained the absence of Korean development in the 1950s with references to the otherworldly influence of Confucianism, again concluding that it is institutions and not culture that explain economic outcomes. For example, "The traditional ideal of Korean Confucianism did not have much respect for technical and physical or manual labor but rather despised this.... Therefore, industrial techniques could never be developed." Cited in David Morawetz, *Why the Emperor's New Clothes Are Not Made in*

background was present in Korea and Taiwan, it was absent in Syria and Turkey. I suggested in Chapter 6 why this argument is insufficient, but again, its presence is enough to demonstrate why Mill's methods are inappropriate as either a canon of discovery or of proof. Finally, trade strategy—import-substituting industrialization (ISI) or export-led growth (ELG)—also covaries with the dependent variable across all four cases.

Are there any alternatives to Mill's methods that validate the use of comparative case studies? Mill's methods are inductive and empiricist; they seek simple correlations, so that if one and only one variable correlates with the dependent variable, it can be considered the cause. Mill himself rejected reasoning about human affairs solely from experience, as do contemporary defenders of comparative case studies.[10] In their methodological briefs, analysis must start from primarily deductive hypotheses about causal relationships that posit necessary and/or sufficient conditions. Confidence in these hypotheses is supplied through the provisions of detailed evidence that these causal sequences actually connect the independent and dependent variables by way of the hypothesized causal chain.[11] Explanation, then, entails an adequate account of the causal relationships underlying observed correlations, and not simply the subsumption of an event under a covering law and statement of initial conditions.[12]

My argument rests on a deductive framework at four key points. First, levels of elite conflict were not simply correlated with coalition strategies;

Colombia: A Case Study in Latin American and East Asian Manufactured Exports (New York: Oxford University Press, 1981), 141. Finally, we could simply reject the logic of the thesis or impeach its evidentiary base. For an exhaustive critical account, see Richard F. Hamilton, *The Social Misconstruction of Reality: Validity and Verification in the Scholarly Community* (New Haven: Yale University Press, 1996), 32–106.

[10] See the discussion in Charles Tilly, "Means and Ends of Comparison in Macrosociology," *Comparative Social Research* 16 (June 1997), 43–45.

[11] In their *Capitalist Development and Democracy* (Chicago: University of Chicago Press, 1992), 36, Dietrich Rueschemeyer, Evelyne Huber Stephens, and John D. Stephens recommend a method they call "analytic induction," which begins with carefully selected analytic arguments and then moves "from the understanding of one or a few cases to potentially theoretical insights capable of explaining the problematic features of each case." For a variant of this method, see Jack A. Goldstone, "Methodological Issues in Comparative Macrosociology," *Comparative Social Research* 16 (1997), 113. A complementary method is proposed by Robert H. Bates et al., *Analytic Narratives* (Princeton: Princeton University Press, 1998). These prescriptions closely mirror earlier statements defending "process-tracing" as an adequate method for establishing plausible causal explanations, although they place greater emphasis on the initial specification of causal arguments. See Alexander L. George, "Case Studies and Theory Development: The Method of Structured, Focused Comparison," in *Diplomacy: New Approaches in History, Theory, and Policy*, ed. Paul Gordon Lauren (New York: Free Press, 1979), 43–68; and Alexander L. George and Timothy J. McKeown, "Case Studies and Theories of Organizational Decision Making," *Advances in Information Processing in Organizations*, 2 (1985): 21–58.

[12] For the classic statement of the deductive-nomological model of explanations, see Carl G. Hempel, "The Function of General Laws in History," *Journal of Philosophy* 39 (1942): 33–48. For an introduction to causal mechanisms, see Jon Elster, *Nuts and Bolts for the Social Sciences* (Cambridge: Cambridge University Press, 1989), Chap. 1.

rather, coalition strategies were explained through a microanalysis of elite preferences. Only under conditions of intense elite conflict did elites subordinate their basic preference for exclusionary politics and incorporate a mass base. Second, high levels of side-payments necessarily produced a particular institutional profile. This argument was not inductively derived, but rather hinged on logical derivation of the necessary effects of side-payments. Third, use of a theoretical framework based on the widely accepted concept of collective dilemmas revealed systemic and inherent obstacles to economic development. Finally, a simple bargaining model explained why precocious Keynesian states were less capable of resolving collective dilemmas than developmental states were; different types of states produced distinctive economic outcomes. In short, cases of high levels of elite conflict set into motion an extended causal chain, resulting in outcomes different from those following from low levels of elite conflict. Case studies then presented historical narratives that not only demonstrated the hypothesized values of the independent, intervening, and dependent variables, but also that the specified causal mechanisms linked them together.

Although I am committed to this articulation of comparative methods, it is not immune from critique. Most obviously, insofar as it seeks to confirm theoretical statements through case studies, any form of analytic induction or process tracing suffers many of the same defects plaguing all efforts to confirm hypotheses. Recent efforts to outline a logic of confirmation, rooted in a scientific realist ontology, still stress the fundamental role of disconfirming rival hypotheses.[13] Because arguments against confirmation were first articulated as critiques of logical-empiricist methods, especially Carl Hempel's model of deductive-nomological explanations which explicitly omits causal relationships, the specification of deductive causal statements mitigates this weakness to some extent.[14] But the fact remains that most complex phenomena of interest to social scientists generate an evidentiary base that can be harnessed to more than one causal account of historical sequences.[15] Our goal, then, must be to combine our causal accounts with efforts to eliminate rival hypotheses inspired by, but not overly indebted to, Mill's methods. Once we have made central the role of causal claims in explanatory accounts, new avenues for rejecting rival hypotheses emerge: we can discredit rival hypotheses not simply on strict inductive-empirical grounds, but also by demonstrating

---

[13] Richard W. Miller, *Fact and Method: Explanation, Confirmation and Reality in the Natural and the Social Sciences* (Princeton: Princeton University Press, 1987).

[14] For discussion, see Jerrold L. Aronson, *A Realist Philosophy of Science* (New York: St. Martin's Press, 1984).

[15] Compare, for example, Dankwart Rustow's causal account of the Turkish transition to democracy in 1950 to my account advanced in Chapter 3. See his "Transitions to Democracy: Toward a Dynamic Model," *Comparative Politics* 2 (April 1970): 337–63.

either that their causal logic cannot account for observed causal sequences or that our hypothesized causal chain contains their contending causal claims within a more comprehensive set of causal relationships. Process-tracing, in other words, can eliminate contending hypotheses by demonstrating that their causal mechanisms probably did not operate.[16] Indeed, in at least some cases, we can employ Mill's methods not just to assess the covariation of a hypothesized cause and its effect, but for comparing extended causal chains.

To posit the inherent probabilistic nature of the world is not sufficient to resuscitate previously abandoned hypotheses that specify nonprobabilistic causal mechanisms: we can use Mill's methods to eliminate these hypotheses not simply because they do not covary perfectly with the dependent variable, but because their causal logic predicts that they *should* covary with the dependent variable. Broadening the scope of Mill's methods to encompass causal mechanisms permits us to eliminate hypotheses rooted in singular, deterministic causal relationships. Consider the hypothesis of regime type. There are nonprobabilistic and certainly plausible if not compelling accounts of how democratic regimes necessarily produce suboptimal outcomes.[17] These theoretical statements plausibly explain and derive support from the dynamics of Turkish development. According to this argument, however, Turkey and Syria should have reached different economic outcomes, and it is thus appropriate to use Mill's empirical methods to eliminate it from further consideration. We do not need a lengthy literature review to recognize that most of the variables held constant across my cases are typically presented as monocausal and deterministic, usually though not exclusively in the monographic literature.

To be sure, these rejected hypotheses could be salvaged by recasting them as probabilistic, as interactive, or as one of multiple possible causes. But this possibility is perfectly consistent with current methodological canons that commit us to vindicate a hypothesis in comparison to actual and not hypothetical challengers. In contrast to the positivist belief that adherence to logical rules yields absolute confirmation to which all reasonable people must agree, we seek tentative commitment to hypotheses for which the reasons for belief outweigh reasons for disbelief, relative to existing rival hypotheses and open to revision in the face of future challenges.[18]

---

[16] For an excellent example, see Timothy J. McKeown, "Hegemonic Stability Theory and 19th Century Tariff Levels in Europe," *International Organization* 37 (Winter 1983): 73–91.

[17] For early and influential statements that democratic regimes cannot foster development, see Richard Lowenthal, "Government in the Developing Countries: Its Functions and Its Forms," in *Democracy in a Changing Society*, ed. Henry W. Ehrmann (New York: Praeger, 1964), 177–210; and Karl de Schweinitz Jr., *Industrialization and Democracy: Economic Necessities and Political Possibilities* (London: Free Press of Glencoe, 1964).

[18] The contrast between relative and absolute commitment to a hypothesis is one of the themes of Miller, *Fact and Method.*

Still, it is worth noting that a scholar enamored of arguments from regime types could respond that although democratic regimes are sufficient conditions for derailing development, authoritarian regimes are a necessary but not sufficient condition for rapid development and industrial transformation. Presumably, the rentier state thesis, which does not covary with the dependent variable in Syria and Turkey and so would be rejected according to Mill's methods, could be advanced as the sufficient condition for suboptimal Syrian development: external rents interact with authoritarian regimes to render them developmentally inefficacious.

Mill's inductive methods offer no grounds for rejecting this claim, but closer scrutiny of its causal logic attenuates its persuasiveness. In Chapter 5, for example, I observed that no analyst considers Syria to have become a rentier state until the mid–1970s, and even then to have only temporarily qualified for status as a rentier state. But the outcomes explained by the rentier-state thesis emerged in Syria before the mid-1970s. In addition, I argued that the causal logic underlying the rentier state thesis is insufficient, because it does not distinguish between permissive and constraining causes. Moreover, the logic of side-payments incorporates the same causal mechanisms used in arguments linking democratic regimes to suboptimal economic outcomes, while also specifying the conditions under which the same logic applies to authoritarian regimes. Finally, an argument based on side-payments encompasses a greater number of relationships, accounting for state-society relations, the nature of the bureaucracy, fiscal structures, and specific patterns of state intervention in a range of markets. The argument I presented in this book, then, is more compelling because it accounts for the same outcomes as arguments based on regime type, demonstrates that its causal logic holds across regime types, and implies a greater number of causal sequences and relationships. Our initial rejection of both the argument from regime type and the rentier state thesis, then, is sustained by closer scrutiny of their causal mechanisms.

Alternatively, we can reject hypotheses that covary perfectly with the dependent variable—religion and trade strategy, for example—by demonstrating that their causal mechanisms are insufficiently stated or cannot account for the sequence of observed causal relationships leading from the independent variable to the dependent variable. The argument from trade strategy, for example, identifies ISI with extensive state intervention and ELG with limited state intervention. Because market determination of prices and allocation of resources is more efficient, and because state intervention provokes directly unproductive rent-seeking behavior, neoliberals argue, trade strategy explains difference in outcomes. As the discussion in Chapter 8 demonstrated, however, the Korean and Taiwanese states also intervened extensively in their economies: at this link in the causal chain, the association between trade strategy and economic outcomes is less compellingly demonstrated. Finally, I showed how the superior economic performance of Korean and Taiwanese firms was in large part a function of state intervention to resolve Gerschenkronian and Kaldorian collective dilemmas. In making this argument, I explored how trade strategy interacted with state institutions to produce distinct outcomes. This link of the causal chain, well supported by evidence, is simply missing from the neoliberal causal chain, and cannot be added to it without negating prior steps in the causal chain. Thus, the neoliberal causal argument, as opposed to its correlational argument, does not square well with the evidence.[19]

In summary, the research design elaborated in Chapter 1 eliminates alternative monocausal and deterministic hypotheses. Moreover, by employing this research design in tandem with a deductive framework and causal process tracing to confirm my hypothesis while disconfirming its rivals, I can reject alternative hypotheses not simply because they fail to vary systematically with outcomes, but because their causal mechanisms are logically insufficient, ignore evidence of other causal processes, are unsupported by evidence, or are causally subordinated to the causal mechanisms of my argument. What, then, are the grounds for disconfirming my argument? Disconfirming my argument requires impeaching its causal adequacy by demonstrating that the causal mechanisms I have presented do not imply observed outcomes, that evidence does not support my causal chain, or that other, more fundamental causal mechanisms with greater scope can be advanced and defended. Successful counterarguments could demonstrate, for example,

- that in the absence of intense elite conflict, elites who were secure in their incumbency voluntarily incorporated lower classes through high levels of side-payments;
- that high levels of side-payments created institutional structures distinct from those constituting precocious Keynesian states;
- that other states with institutional profiles analogous to precocious Keynesian states produced substantially different economic outcomes, especially by resolving Kaldorian collective dilemmas; and
- that other cases of cross-class coalitions divided between authoritarian and democratic regimes with demonstrably different capacities for resolving Gerschenkronian and Kaldorian collective dilemmas.

Can my argument linking high levels of elite conflict to suboptimal development outcomes be rejected on the grounds that it is both monocausal and deterministic? Arguing that structural conditions are deter-

---

[19] Robert Wade criticizes neoliberal economists for ignoring evidence of state intervention in East Asia in his "East Asia's Economic Success: Conflicting Perspectives, Partial Insights, Shaky Evidence," *World Politics* 44 (January 1992), 270–85.

ministic under some specified conditions does not imply that they are always so constraining. In East Asia, it will be recalled, low levels of elite conflict were necessary but not sufficient conditions for the construction of developmental states. The level of structural constraint and the validity of deterministic arguments, then, are a function of specific initial conditions. As much as we might wish to treat questions of structure and agency as purely philosophical, social scientists can only benefit from a dialogue between a priori reasoning and empirics, for my analysis suggested that structure and agency are not ontological constants but, to some extent at least, variables.

Consider the analogy of a chess game. In principle, the staggeringly large number of legal chess moves assigns an overwhelming role to agency and precludes prediction. When a valued piece is threatened, however, the menu of moves is sharply constrained, although players still have the choice of saving the piece or sacrificing it on behalf of a longer-term strategy. But under a small set of circumstances, moves are so highly constrained that to prevent disaster—checkmate—only one move is possible, a "forced move." As Daniel Dennett explains, "Such a move is not forced by the rules of chess, and certainly not by the laws of physics (you can always kick over the table and run away), but by what Hume might call a 'dictate of reason.' It is simply dead obvious that there is one and only one solution, as anybody with an ounce of wit can plainly see. Any alternatives are immediately suicidal."[20]

Can we identify analogues of forced moves in human interactions? I argued that situations of intense inter-elite conflict are reasonable analogues of forced moves. To repeat, I consider conflict to be intense when not only the short-term material interests of elites are threatened, but their capacity to reproduce their elite status as well. I have also identified, in Chapter 6, the conditions under which conflict is likely to be sufficiently intense. To be sure, the analogy is not perfect; the causes and implications of intense elite conflict are not rule-governed the way checkmate is. Perceptions of threat matter, and I cannot rule out the possibility that an "enlightened leadership" can resolve conflict, though this seems as much a resort to a *deus ex machina* as a warrant for asserting agency. But note that, as Goldstone has argued, macro-level determinism does not reduce to micro-level determinism.[21] We do not have to argue that all elites must recognize the threat as equally intense, and that all of them made the determination that incorporation was necessary. For circumstances to resemble a forced move, it must only be argued that a subset of elites in a

---

[20] See his *Darwin's Dangerous Idea: Evolution and the Meanings of Life* (New York: Simon & Schuster, 1995), 128.

[21] Goldstone, "Methodological Issues in Comparative Macrosociology," 116–19.

position to resolve elite conflict through popular-sector incorporation made these two calculations and acted accordingly. So long as an analyst can specify the reasons why conditions resemble a forced move, monocausal and deterministic arguments cannot be rejected simply because they are monocausal and deterministic; indeed, under these conditions, singular and deterministic causes may be necessary for adequate explanations.

The argument presented in this book should be applicable to other cases of late development. The temporal applicability of the argument, however, remains limited. The changing structure of the global economy creates new opportunities, but also imposes new constraints. The obstacles to development studied in this book, then, may be historically specific. The state-building processes that I argued account for the origins of institutional profiles are not recursive. As Chapter 9 demonstrated, institutional configurations can persist, even in the face of determined efforts to transform them. But major instances of institutional change subsequent to the transformation to direct rule are certainly possible; those that occur require reformulated explanatory hypotheses.

More generally, the obstacles to economic development and the repertoire of tools for overcoming them change over time. The challenges Syria and Turkey face in the coming years are different in many ways from those of the past; both countries must further adapt themselves to the global economy, but that economy has itself undergone fundamental changes. Over the past two decades, transnational flows of capital, labor, and goods have created a new global economy, while multinational corporations have created global production networks of component sourcing by farming out production of lower value-added inputs to developing countries.[22] Strategic location in these networks is an important resource for developing countries, as they act as conduits for the transfer of new product and production technologies and new management and marketing strategies, while providing access to overseas markets: commodity chains, in other words, are the institutionalized expression of past solutions to collective dilemmas. In this sense, state intervention to resolve collective dilemmas is less critical, and for many developing countries, becoming integrated into global production networks offers the best opportunity for achieving future international competitiveness. On the other hand, integration into global commodity chains may condemn low-cost producers of finished goods or components to occupy the bottom end of the product cycle indefinitely; global production networks may simply be

---

[22] For a good set of case studies of how these networks operate in various industrial sectors, see Gary Gereffi and Miguel Korzeniewicz, eds., *Commodity Chains and Global Capitalism* (Westport, Conn.: Praeger, 1994).

a new form of dependency.[23] Finally, there is limited space in these commodity chains: not all countries can become producers of competitive industrial products. Both Syria and Turkey, for example, have largely been excluded from these networks. Increasingly, then, peripheral countries may be in direct competition with each other for access to multinational investment oriented not toward the domestic markets of host states, but toward a single global market. Thus, whereas before 1980, states sought to break the bonds of dependency, today, for most developing countries the only alternative to dependency increasingly appears to be complete marginalization in the global economy.[24] Whether states can simultaneously create opportunities for local firms to join global commodity chains and secure long-term development remains to be seen. When asked by his biographer how he wished his story to conclude, President Asad stated: "Say simply that the struggle continues."[25] The same can be said for the efforts of Syria and Turkey to transcend the legacies of precocious Keynesianism and to produce viable economic development.

[23] For this perspective, see the essays in Martin Carnoy et al., *The New Global Economy in the Information Age: Reflections on Our Changing World* (University Park: Pennsylvania State University Press, 1993).

[24] Fernando Henrique Cardoso, former radical sociologist and current president of Brazil, described the new global division of labor in these terms: "Therefore, we are no longer talking about the South that was on the periphery of the capitalist core and was tied to it in a classical relationship of dependence. Nor are we speaking of the phenomenon, described some twenty-five years ago by Enzo Faletto and myself in our book *Dependency and Development in Latin America*, whereby multinational companies transfer parts of the productive system and the local producers are tied to foreign capital. . . . We are dealing, in truth, with a crueler phenomenon: either the South (or a portion of it) enters the democratic-technological-scientific race, invests heavily in R&D, and endures the 'information economy' metamorphosis, or it becomes unimportant, unexploited, and unexploitable." See his "North-South Relations in the Present Context: A New Dependency?" in *The New Global Economy in the Information Age*, 156.

[25] Patrick Seale, *Asad: The Struggle for the Middle East* (Berkeley: University of California Press, 1988), 495.

Index

agricultural policies:
 in Korea, 134–136, 140–141
 and side-payments, 36, 47, 58, 61–64,
  78–79, 83–85, 97, 102–103, 109–110,
  117–119, 126, 129–132, 134–136,
  138–141, 197–198, 204, 214
 in Syria, 83–85, 87, 117–119, 226
 in Taiwan, 139–140
 in Turkey, 58, 61–64, 102–103, 109–110,
  214
Allocation State Thesis. *See* Rentier State
 Thesis
Amsden, Alice, 155–156, 199
Ansal, Hacer K., 183
Ardant, Gabriel, 45–46
Asad, Hafiz al-, 1, 88, 91, 92, 101, 121, 240
Asali, Sabri al-, 80
Asfour, Edward, 49
Ataturk, Mustafa Kemal, 11, 54, 71
Azm, Khalid al-, 79

Barkey, Henri, 116–117, 182
Bates, Robert, 5, 10, 46–47
Ba`th Party, Syria:
 early reform efforts, 79–81
 elections of 1954, 80
 role in policy making, 101, 224–225
 United Arab Republic, relations with,
  81–82
Baumol, William J., 168
Bayar, Celal, 57
Bendix, Reinhard, 25
Bhagwati, Jagdish N., 157
Bitar, Salah al-Din al-, 87
Boratav, Korkut, 62
bureaucracies:
 and development, 41–42

 in Korea, 131, 143–144
 politicization of, 41–45, 98–102
 and precocious keynesianism, 73,
  91–92, 98–102, 143, 205, 216
 and side-payments, 44–45
 in Syria, 91–92, 100–102
 in Taiwan, 130, 143–144
 in Turkey, 71–73, 98–100, 216–217

causal mechanisms, 9, 11, 16, 233–234,
 236
Chandler, Alfred, 161
Chang, Myon, 133
Choi, Byung-Sun, 198
class-power model, 126–127
coalitions:
 definition of, 34
 elite conflict and formation of, 47, 233
coalition theory, 4, 8
collective dilemmas (*see also* Gerschenkronian collective dilemmas and Kaldorian collective dilemmas):
 as causal mechanisms, 7–9
 definition of, 153, 164
 economic development, impact on,
  164–167, 234
 side-payments, effect on, 202–203
colonial legacy in Korea and Taiwan,
 126–127
comparative methods, 11, 15–17, 230–237
conservative coalitions, 137–141
constituency clientelism:
 definition of, 39, 96
 origins of, 40–41
 popular sector incorporation, form of,
  39–40
 in Syria and Turkey, 95–98